SISTERHOOD OF THE NIGHT

A TRUE STORY

SISTERHOOD OF THE NIGHT

BECKY USRY

Requests for permission should be addressed to:
New Horizon Press
P.O. Box 669
Far Hills, NJ 07931

Usry, Becky
        Sisterhood of the Night: A True Story

Library of Congress Catalog Card Number: Pending

ISBN: 0-88282-134-2

New Horizon Press

Manufactured in the U.S.A.

1999 1998 1997 1996 1995 / 5 4 3 2 1

This book is dedicated to
all the people who want to get out of prostitution,
in the hope that you reach your goal.

CONTENTS

ACKNOWLEDGMENTS

I would like to thank God and the following people:

—My children, whom I appreciate and respect. I am very proud of all of them, for, without their support and participation, there would have been no Project New Life.

—My husband, a most remarkable man. He not only loves us, but he loves all people in need.

—My mother, who has been my example.

—My stepfather, who has endured.

—My husband's family, who have been so tolerant.

—The many churches and individuals who lent their support.

—The many volunteers who made Project New Life an island of refuge.

—The many people whose stories appear on these pages, and the many more who are not mentioned. They shared their lives with us, and their superhuman efforts to achieve their goals are acknowledged, admired, and applauded.

—Mary Alice, a very special friend, without whom this book could not have been written. She has encouraged and corrected.

—Claudia and Lily, who both said, "I want more." Their enthusiasm provided the reassurance I needed for my writing.

—My cousins Linda and Gary, who made me laugh.

—My dog Misty, an able secretary. She provided a warm soft body to pat when I needed understanding but not conversation.

AUTHOR'S NOTE

This story is based on my actual experiences. The personalities, events, actions, and conversations portrayed within the story have been reconstructed from my memory, interviews and research, utilizing letters, personal papers, and the memories of participants. In an effort to safeguard the privacy of most individuals except myself and my husband, I have changed their names and, in some cases, altered otherwise identifying characteristics, chronology and minor events.

INTRODUCTION

When I began my odyssey to the streets of my city, I hoped that I could help a few women change their lives. I did not know then that my journey would take me to the heart of darkness, where I would find espionage, sex slavery, blackmail, murder, incest, child molestation, pornography, sadism, masochism, weapons sales, gambling, drug-dealing, nationwide prostitution rings, government involvement, and cover-ups.

Johns and pimps can be police officers, politicians, pastors, professors, business executives, and factory workers. Prostitutes can be housewives, nurses, teachers, divorcees, students, runaway teenagers, drug addicts, young mothers and fathers, even quiet heroines or heroes. There are victim prostitutes whose families' abuse forces them into the life; criminal prostitutes who sell their souls for drugs; homosexual youths who use prostitution as a sexual outlet; career prostitutes whose adult choice to enter the life is made freely. Profits from prostitution buy political influence, pay for protection, put crooked officials into office, purchase government and industrial secrets, and provide financial support for thousands upon thousands of people worldwide.

Despite the evil that surrounds prostitutes, I grew to deeply care for the people with whom I worked each day, and I continue to support them in their efforts to leave the life. Until now, I haven't told anyone the dark secrets that I have learned. Keeping silent allowed me to work in safety until the time came that the sinister forces opposing changing prostitutes' lives caused my family and me to flee. Since then I have continued to fight these forces but in a different way. I am now involved in proposing to Congress new legislation which will change the lives of prostitutes nationwide and, eventually, I hope, worldwide.

I'm no one special. I learned business management in my parents' department store in Anchorage, Alaska, where I was born. As a teenager, I worked for my folks until my father died and Mom sold the business. I had enough work experience by then to land a job as Collection Manager of a major department store chain. During that time I married and had three children. At twenty-three, I got a position as Administrative Director of a social service agency where I did rewarding work, helping drug addicts and runaways. When my marriage dissolved two years later, I resigned from the agency and moved to California, where my mother and her new husband lived.

Money from my father's estate enabled me to be a full-time mother for several years. It was a role I accepted wholeheartedly, but then I had to: I couldn't keep baby-sitters for more than a few weeks. My older son David was hyperactive, and, during his grade school years, I was constantly called to the principal's office for parent-teacher conferences. Toward the end of this period, David became interested in taking things apart and putting them back together, when he could, in some fashion he considered an improvement. I never knew *if* my appliances would work, or *how*.

It was during this time that I first became involved with the people I've written about in this book.

I consider myself fortunate to have had the opportunity to work with people who may not have otherwise been able to change their lives, but I still believe my most important job is that of wife and mother. My real name is Becky Usry, but almost every other name herein has been changed. The people and events in this book are real. They will sometimes make you laugh and may even bring tears to your eyes, but, like me, I believe you will never forget the sisterhood of the night.

PROLOGUE

One of the sheds on our property had been ransacked. Immediately we called the Sheriff who took down a report. Then we phoned private detective Lindsey Baxter and police detective Lou Silverman who both warned us to be careful.

Several evenings later, my teenage son David was working on his copper wire sculptures in another outbuilding when he thought he heard voices in the woods.

"I'm going to sleep in the camper tonight," he announced. "I want to keep an eye on the sheds."

Our neighbors had cautioned us not to venture into the forest after dark because of wolves, coyotes, and mountain lions, so I wasn't happy to let my young son spend the night outside, but my husband, Lee, reminded me that David wasn't a little boy anymore. I elicited a promise from David that if he saw trespassers he would do nothing but get a good description, and I admonished him to lock the camper against wild animals. Then I gave him a thermos filled with hot chocolate and bade him good night.

When Lee and I went to sleep, the darkness of the forest was complete; not a thing could be seen outside on this cloudy night. At three o'clock we were awakened, startled by a strong light coming from the window. I got up and peered outside.

"My God, Lee, it's a fire!"

Grabbing our robes and a fire extinguisher, we rushed outside only to see the sky darkening again. We were running toward the camper when suddenly a smoke-blackened apparition staggered toward us. David's head, arms, and torso were covered with soot. Only two blue eyes peered out at us. He coughed and gasped.

"David!" Lee cried. I was still half asleep and only now realized it was indeed my son who stood before me.

"What happened? Are you okay?" I yelled.

"Just bring the fire extinguisher," David exclaimed.

"If the fire starts to spread, the whole forest can go up in flames. Let' s go," Lee said and followed him. I was right behind him. "Stay there," Lee called back. Now he was at the back door of the camper. As he opened it, red flames shot out. Lee sprayed orange foam through the back door, then clambered inside and sprayed some more.

About fifteen long minutes later they were back. "We put it out," David said.

"What happened?" I asked David again, as Lee climbed down from the camper.

"I was sleeping, Mom. I don't think it was an accident; I think someone set it on fire," our still-shaking son answered.

Suddenly, we became aware of the chill in the air. It wasn't just that we were in our nightclothes: the cold seemed to emanate from a grave—ours, perhaps, I could not help thinking. Not long afterward the clouds passed, and stars twinkled brightly overhead. The glowing silver moon lit the ground around us. I couldn't take much comfort from the lovely scene: it would have been easy, too easy, for an arsonist to set fire to the house by that bright moonlight.

"Let' s go inside," Lee said. "We'd better get some sleep."

After a quick shower David went right to bed, and soon we heard him snoring. I turned to Lee and asked, without much hope, "Do you think the fire could have started by itself?"

"There was no electricity hooked up in the camper tonight. David had been asleep for hours—how could a fire start by itself?" he muttered angrily. "I've been trying to think of every possible way it could be an accident, but all I can come up with is that someone set that fire."

I responded then with the question that neither of us wanted to consider. "Do you think they knew David was in the camper?"

Lee put his arm around me. "Shhhh. Let's go to sleep," he wearily whispered.

But I couldn't sleep. I kept thinking that it was my involvement with Project New Life and prostitution which had brought fear and now peril to my family.

1

TIME FOR A CHANGE

It was the kind of California Sunday morning for which public relations people yearn: glittering golden sunshine and azure blue skies. During our mammoth pancake breakfast my children talked non stop of spending their afternoon alternately baking on lounge chairs and swimming in the pool. At ten o'clock we headed for church in my trusty old station wagon.

Now, in the cool serene sanctuary, we were singing my favorite hymn, "Amazing Grace." Suddenly my son David dropped the handful of coins he'd been holding for the collection. They clattered noisily to the floor, and David dove after them. As the startled congregation turned to stare at us, David tried to stand up. His sister Claire, who was next to him, was wearing a red and blue peasant skirt, and David accidentally caught his head in the fabric as he rose. Dismayed, he ducked and tried again, only to be netted by the gauzy material once more. This proved too much for Claire, who was certain he was doing it on purpose, and she began batting her brother over the head with the prayer book. Red-faced, I turned my attention to the minister's announcements. It was the first time that I really heard them. "The ladies' tea . . . the pastor's birthday party . . . pray for the missionaries."

As if I was seeing the scene for the first time, I looked around at my fellow parishoners. Here we were, a congregation of hundreds of good people, and we were nothing but a "bless me" club. No one was doing anything to help people in real need. This was my moment of truth. I completely forgot David's mishap and began to search my conscience. Yes, I was taking care of my family and friends. But I was doing nothing for anyone else.

As we walked out of the church a young man behind us muttered, "Damn. Look at the sky." Others took up his complaint.

I looked up. The perfect horizon of the early morning had become a mass of dark clouds.

"Thank God. Some rain. It will wash away the musty odor around here," I said, turning slightly to see my none too happy children staring at me quizzically.

"What was that about?" Claire asked as we hastened down the remaining steps and into our wagon.

"Call it the call to arms for a spiritual housecleaning. At least I'm going to begin one," I said and pressed one finger to my lips.

Aware that I wasn't going to explain further, the children for once were utterly silent on the trip home.

My resolve held. Early the next morning, I called a counselor at the women's jail, where I knew there was a program which matched ex-offenders with people from the community to provide a friend who would help them go straight. By that afternoon I had completed the program's paperwork. During the next couple of weeks, I attended training classes. Finally, Norene, the administrator, said I was ready.

"Would you like to sponsor a street prostitute?" she asked.

Looking at her appraisingly, I wondered for a moment if I

really would like working with prostitutes, then in a moment frozen for all time in my memory, I quickly said, "Of course I will."

Two days later, I went to Norene's office to meet Samantha Rice, the woman I would sponsor. I watched in amazement as Samantha walked up the hall: she was obviously very pregnant. In fact, I'd never seen so huge an abdomen.

After our introduction in the counselor's office, Samantha told me that she had been a heroin addict as well as a streetwalker for the past thirteen years. Now that she was going to have a baby, she wanted to change her life. Her sister Debbie, she said, had room for her, and she hoped to be released from jail before she gave birth.

As she spoke, I felt an immediate empathy. We liked the same music, clothes, and movies. She was so sadly real. In other circumstances I felt I could have been her once. The thought horrified me but made me even more determined to help her.

Within the week a sensible judge ordered Sam's release, and I drove her to her sister's house. Debbie and their mother lived in a three-bedroom home, and they had made room for Samantha. We had to arrange for Aid for Dependent Children and get medical coupons for Sam, because the jail doctor had told her she needed to see an obstetrician immediately. I drove Samantha to the welfare office and helped her complete the paperwork. Then I saw the caseworker with her.

"We need the father's name so we can collect child support," the social worker told her.

Embarrassed, Sam replied, "I'm a prostitute, I don't know who the father is."

"Next time, honey," the caseworker said with a jaded smile, "make your customers use a credit card. Then you'll have a list to choose from for a paternity suit."

I threw the caseworker a scorching look but from that moment on, I knew I had to set aside my middle class values and face the reality of life on the street.

A week later, Samantha phoned me after her first visit to the obstetrician.

"I'm going to have twins!" she exclaimed.

"Wonderful!" I responded a little less enthusiastically than she would have wished. Realizing she was waiting for me to reply, I went on. "When are they due?"

"The doctor says any day now. I think that's about right, because I got pregnant just before I went to jail, and I was there about eight and a half months."

Samantha sounded happy and positive. Yet, during the weeks that followed, I got my first experience with long-term, hard core drug use in pregnant women. I worried each day that the twins would have birth defects. But they weighed more than seven pounds each and were healthy, although they were born a month late.

When they were a month old, Sam informed her sister and me that she planned to move into an apartment with Vickie Chase, another "former" streetwalker and heroin addict who had a seven-week-old baby. Debbie and I were unhappy with her choice, but Samantha was determined to run her own life.

The rent on the small apartment that Sam and Vickie moved into ate up most of their welfare checks. Instead of budgeting their remaining cash for necessities, the two women bought expensive clothes. I learned later that this is part of the victim syndrome: it made them feel good about themselves. With their money spent, Sam and Vickie decided they would use the apartment to turn a few tricks to earn some cash.

They knew that tenants of rundown hotels frequented by hookers tend to ignore their neighbors' stream of visitors. They were surprised to learn that residents of well-kept apartment buildings do not ignore signs of prostitution. Soon the ladies were back in jail. Their children went to foster homes.

This time, Samantha spent a month in jail. When I picked her up the day of her release, she wanted to visit her babies immediately. As she clutched her children tightly to her, I could see she loved them, and my heart ached when we had to leave them. Next, I drove her to her sister's house. Here Sam only wanted to get some clothes and go to a hotel. In order to regain custody of her children Sam would need to show the authorities that she had a permanent home. In this situation, I couldn't understand her reluctance to live with her sister, but there seemed nothing I could say or do to change her mind. I was at a loss as to what to do with this stubborn young woman.

However, twelve years as David's mother had taught me perseverance, so I dug my heels in and told Sam I'd help her do whatever she thought necessary to get back on her feet. For a while this consisted of taking her to see the twins and visiting her at her hotel where she began, bit by bit, to reveal her personal history. Soon, her behavior started to make sense to me.

Her mother had deserted the family when Sam was five. Her father had then molested her teenage sisters until eventually one of them called the police. Sam didn't know for years why her beloved daddy had been taken away in handcuffs nor why their lives were torn apart. She lived in a series of foster homes for the next ten years.

"Most of the foster parents were in it for the money, but there was one family who really loved me," she said one day. "The social worker wouldn't let me stay anywhere too long, though, because they didn't want people to try to adopt me, since my mother hadn't given me up."

At thirteen she ran away. A pimp found her and convinced her he loved her. Soon she was prostituting herself for him, and she learned to anesthetize her emotional pain with drugs while she worked the streets.

Now that I understood her better, I began to look for a program to help her. While I was searching, I continued to visit her.

Often, there were streetwalkers in Sam's room when I arrived. She proudly introduced me as her friend.

One of those I met was Ginger Pettit, a pretty woman in her mid twenties with long black hair and blue eyes rimmed with thick dark lashes. When she laughed she covered her mouth with her hand to conceal her teeth which had rotted away from years of heroin use. She wanted to change her life, she said, but after ten years of prostitution she had no job skills. "My stepfather began molesting me when I was nine years old, but when my mother discovered it a few years later, she accused me of seducing him. So at thirteen I ran away." Like Sam and so many other women I was to meet, she was given food and shelter by a pimp who told her he loved her, but soon put her to work on the street.

My daughter Claire was thirteen years old, and the thought of Ginger at her age turning tricks made me weep.

Another of Sam's occasional visitors was Carrie Hope, a striking green-eyed redhead. She always seemed to carry a pad of paper on which she created lovely pen and ink drawings. While in jail, she had endeared herself to the other inmates by illustrating poems and stories which they wrote for their families. Her deft, adroit, artistic hands, however, were swollen with fresh needle marks. At age twenty-six, after twelve years as a heroin addict, Carrie had run out of veins in her arms and was injecting the drug into her hands. I knew that if she missed a vein and injected into a muscle she might develop an abscess and never sketch again.

The quiet desperation of Ginger, Carrie, and the others I met in Sam's hotel room haunted me. I began to search our city for an organization which helped prostitutes.

I made a list of local social agencies and charities, certain that one of them would champion the cause of prostitutes once they understood the need.

First, I approached the group which had introduced me to Sam. I met their representatives in the bare and austere library of the women's jail. The only books in this house of knowledge were confined to one wall. The tables were placed far apart for security. Alice Chesterton, a local socialite, conducted the meeting.

I made my proposal. When I finished, the "ladies who lunch" applauded resoundingly, and Mrs. Chesterton stood to thank me.

"We all know how dedicated you are to helping Samantha Rice, Becky, but perhaps you should consider sponsoring someone who won't present so many problems for you. Prostitutes are hard to help," she said. "While we want you to know that we appreciate your efforts, you must understand that we're busy with our own lives."

She gave me her perfectly manicured hand in dismissal. For a moment, in my mind I saw in its place Carrie Hope's swollen hand, with her ever present pencil, and I wondered what she would think about these comfortable women who dismissed her needs so easily.

I couldn't give up. Next, I spoke to several boards of directors for large social service organizations. They all explained that they were overburdened with projects and could not take on any thing new, but they offered to help when I got my program started. I came away from these meetings feeling disappointed in them and confused about myself, because I had neither considered nor mentioned starting a project myself.

More prostitutes continued to arrive. The agencies I'd contacted to help me sent me their hooker clients! I couldn't bring myself to send them away. Although I had no experience and no funding, I did have hope. I began arranging for the women to stay with friends while I continued to present my plan to organizations.

The low point came when I conferred with Paul Lantz, the director of a live-in program for ex-offenders. In the last week of November he greeted me magnanimously in his plush downtown office and proffered a red leather easy chair on which to sit.

Certain that his organization would be sympathetic to the problems of prostitutes because of its work with ex-offenders, I launched into a carefully-worded plea that they establish a shelter for these women.

Paul flashed a disarming smile and then made a devastating statement. "There are plenty of drug rehabilitation programs for prostitutes, if they want to take advantage of them," he said, "but most of these women like what they're doing!"

I jumped up, angry at his patronizing, chauvinistic remark. "You refuse to recognize the real desperation of street-walkers," I cried out. "Obviously you think that whores are less than human." I left abruptly. There seemed to be no one but me who was interested in establishing a program to help prostitutes. My commitment made on that Sunday in church was stronger than even I had suspected.

Angry and determined, I made a list of reasons to open a shelter on my own versus reasons not to attempt such a major undertaking. On the positive side, I had prostitutes already working on changing their lives whom I'd agreed to help. I couldn't let down Sam, Ginger, Carrie, and their friends: they needed a break. Also, I knew something about grassroots programs from my social work experience in Alaska.

On the negative side, I had three children to consider. I switched back to the positive: they didn't consume all my time. Claire was busy studying afternoons and evenings because she had decided to take her high school exams at the end of tenth grade, and she was employed during the summers. David was going to be thirteen that spring, and I knew I had to find some summer occupation for him—he was hyperactive and needed scheduled activities. Since David was mechanically inclined, I asked my friend Ted Hawkins, who owned an appliance sales and service center a few blocks from our house, if he would train my son in his repair department. Ted agreed to give him a chance. Darroll presented the only real obstacle, but he would be seven in a few months, he was in school most of the year, and he was old enough so that I didn't have to be at his side constantly when he was at home.

Finally, I decided that despite my family's needs I wanted to work on the project. Then I had to decide how to do it effectively. My knowledge of prostitution was based on brief meetings with some thirty streetwalkers and the minuscule amount of research I had been able to accumulate. Books on the subject were hardly helpful. They were either written by people who knew someone who knew a prostitute or they were of the rose colored "Happy Hooker" variety. The hookers I had met were not happy, and material gleaned third hand seemed useless. My clients needed shelter, employment training, jobs, professional counseling, and clothes that didn't scream, "Buy me!"

Naming my organization "Project New Life," I contacted every public shelter in the city to introduce myself and it, and requested bed space. Every space granted was filled continuously from the very first day. I agreed to provide case management. I developed a list of people who could help my clients: admissions counselors at local colleges and business schools assisted the women in educational grant and loan applications; medical and psychological counseling organizations provided low cost or free services to "my girls;" church groups donated clothing and household items; Alcoholics Anonymous and Narcotics Anonymous experienced a sudden increase in attendance at meetings. For the price of gasoline and a telephone, I was suddenly helping women who had previously been considered incorrigible.

While I was patting myself on the back for these small successes, certain that I'd found a solution to an age-old problem, two women came into my life who gave me an entirely different perspective on prostitution.

The first was Pamela McLeod. An escort service prostitute in Atlantic City for eight years, she had expected the most difficult part of her transition to straight life to be her escape from her pimp. It wasn't. The hardest part was finding legitimate work, even though she had a college degree.

Our first meeting was at her mother's home in an older middle class neighborhood. Tea was laid out on the coffee table, complete with pink linen napkins, a sugar bowl, and milk. Pamela was a gracious hostess and a striking beauty. Delicate ivory skin framed pale blue eyes, and golden hair cascaded down her back. Every movement she made was graceful, every gesture refined. She was a sharp contrast to the unsophisticated street-walkers whom I had met.

By now, I had evolved a standard interview to assess the needs of new clients, and I asked Pamela my usual questions. Her answers were different. I was surprised to learn that her background did not include abuse, neglect, or molestation, which I'd found to be almost universal springboards for entry into streetwalking.

"I became a prostitute when I was eighteen," she told me. "It began when I was in kind of a teenage rebellion and met Casey Sullivan. He was a handsome, polished young black man who masqueraded as a student. In reality, I was to find out, he was a pimp who recruited his whores from college campuses.

"Anyway, we had a whirlwind romance. He told me he loved me but he had to return to Atlantic City to help his father. Thoroughly mesmerized, I dropped out of college to go with him. However, after a month in New Jersey, Casey told me that he had no money left for the rent and that he'd been unable to find a job.

"'I have a few friends who would pay you if you would sleep with them,' Casey went on. 'I hate to ask you to do this, honey, but we need the money. If you don't want to, I'll under-stand.'"

Pam grimaced. "I must have been the most gullible fool he'd ever met."

"No," I interjected, "I'm sure you weren't," I said sincerely. "In fact, streetwalkers often tell me that their pimps use the same line."

After Pam had given me her history, she turned to the problems she'd encountered trying to leave the life. "I've already applied for several positions, but can't get past the personnel managers," she said disgustedly.

"What specific part of the job interviews gives you trouble?" I prodded.

"It's the part where they ask me what I've been doing for the last eight years. How am I supposed to answer that," she exploded. "I'd like to say it's none of your damn business but that would hardly work."

I tried to calm her. "They have no idea you worked as a prostitute, Pam," I interrupted. "The question is asked to find out if you've been doing work that's similar to what they need. A lot of the women I work with just say they've been housewives."

Pamela relaxed visibly and managed to laugh at herself. "I guess I'm just too sensitive." She lit a cigarette, then continued. "I still use an alias, Starr Light, when I'm talking with a legit guy. I keep asking myself why, if I'm going straight, am I afraid to tell people my real name?"

"Starr Light is a confident, intelligent, witty, charming person," I explained. "You are comfortable with her, you feel self-assured. Pamela McLeod was a rebellious college student the last time you knew her. Now you have to go back eight years and develop the person you want to be."

I came away from that interview with a new knowledge that prostitution was not the simple problem I had earlier thought it to be. Pamela was unlike the streetwalkers I'd met in background, type of prostitution, class of customer, level of education, social skills, and health. She was like them in resultant problems. She was experiencing identity crisis, fear of ostracism because of her past, an inability to relate to men in a non-sexual way, as well as the fear of fleeing from a violent pimp—Casey had promised to break her knees if she left him. I wondered if this was the flip side of prostitution, or only one of its many facets, and it wasn't long before I found out more.

Only a week later, Christine Mayer came into my life. A nude dancer/prostitute, she was concerned that her work would be a bad influence on her six month old son.

Christine's father had been a voyeur who punished his four daughters by lining them up nude and spanking all of them for the transgressions of one. At fifteen she ran away from home. Unable to support herself by any other means, she used false ID to obtain work as a nude dancer. Her employer soon introduced her to johns who paid high prices for the "professional" services.

During her eight years as a dancer/prostitute, she got her General Education Diploma, took college classes, and joined an amateur theatrical group. Christine was tall and graceful with an hourglass figure and the lithe body of a dancer. She was also intelligent, articulate, and a free spirit.

Like each prostitute I met, Christine badly needed one-to-one personal contact. They all had to have a person to love and encourage them if they were to succeed after prostitution, or they would return to their pimp for emotional security. Since my family still needed my love and comfort, I began to reach out for other sponsors to help me. But because Christine and I formed a bond of friendship almost immediately, I sponsored her myself.

Often, during our early relationship, she phoned to challenge me.

"I'm going to a party!" she declared testily one time.

"Have fun," I said.

"Well, there's going to be marijuana there," Christine added.

"Oh," I responded noncommittally.

"I feel like you don't want me to go," she offered, as if she were one of my children.

"Why should I tell you where you can go?" I asked gently.

The testing went on and on. Sometimes, Christine would say that since she had a beautiful body, perhaps she should be a nude dancer, and sometimes she would state that prostitution was a good way to demonstrate her love and concern for a man's well-being. I understood that these challenges were her way of defying the authority which I now represented, so I didn't argue. Every authority figure she'd known until now had abused her, and I had to let her know that I accepted her as she was. As we continued talking, her confidence built up and soon she was talking herself out of things that she suspected were inappropriate.

After meeting Christine and Pamela, I realized that there were no stereotypes which fit all prostitutes. I would have to design individual programs for each woman, since, although they shared many traits, they were all unique persons. Some needed elementary education in reading, writing, and arithmetic, while others held college degrees. Some were mothers; others were children themselves. Some used drugs; others ate only natural foods and didn't even use aspirin.

I kept searching for established methods to help prostitutes go straight, but I found no guidebooks or textbooks, nothing but mystery, prejudice, and hatred. The more I learned through experience, the more determined I became to give these women a choice—something they obviously didn't have.

Almost all the real information I came across was provided by those I met—the good and the bad.

2

PROSTITUTES, PIMPS, AND JOHNS

I had heard about Robert Kvale almost from the first day I met Samantha. First Sam and then several other women told me how wonderful Mr. Kvale was to "the girls" on the street. He would pick them up from jail, buy them dinner, pay for clothes if necessary, and sometimes give them a place to stay. They could call "Big Bob" anytime, night or day, and he would help them if he could. With such an endorsement, I was not suspicious. And then one day Sam showed up at my door with Bob himself.

Robert Kvale was about five feet nine, with blue eyes and sandy blond hair with a touch of gray. I had learned from Sam's friend, Carrie, who had stayed with Bob for several months, that he had a daughter who was a streetwalker, and that he had begun helping prostitutes in our city when he failed to get his daughter to leave the life. He sounded like a concerned father who wanted to apply the lessons of his own tragedy to help others.

Claire and I had been working on a quilt, and my guests had to step around the almost completed product onto which we'd been pinning a border. As they sat down on the sofa, Bob looked over our work.

"That's a lovely wedding ring pattern," he said, indicating the patchwork side. "What's the significance of the blue and gold?"

"This is a gift for my aunt and uncle's fiftieth wedding anniversary," I explained. "The blue and gold are the colors of Alaska's flag, in honor of their years there." Intrigued, I asked, "How do you know so much about quilts?"

"Oh, I have an extensive art collection," Bob replied, "which includes several quilts. I've made a point to learn as much as possible about art, and especially the things I collect."

Claire went to get refreshments and now she returned with a carafe and cups on a tray. I watched as she poured the coffee and took a seat with us. My children were present and interested in my clients, and I was glad to have Claire participate. I wanted my children to understand that even though people become involved in unsavory activities they are still human beings who deserve our empathy. I also wanted them to learn to respect those who come forward to offer their help.

Robert Kvale was truly knowledgeable about many subjects, but he didn't monopolize the conversation. However, when it turned inevitably to prostitution, Bob offered some fatherly advice.

"I used to do everything I could for the women, bought them clothes, let them stay with me, picked them up from jail when they got out, but I've learned that letting them completely lean on someone isn't the way to help them. It only makes them think they still have to depend on another person just as they depended on their pimp. I still buy them necessities when they have no money, and I give them a place to stay when they're in a bind, but they know they have to contribute what they can and ultimately they have to depend on themselves. Don't let these women take advantage, Becky," he offered amiably.

All too soon, Sam said they had to leave, so Claire and I walked them to Bob's car. As they drove away, we squinted to read Bob's bumper sticker: "Gas, grass, or ass—Nobody rides for free."

"Gee, Mom," Claire remarked sarcastically, "it's good to

find out you're not the only person interested in helping prostitutes. You'd never have time for anything else if you were trying
to do this on your own."

I didn't know whether to laugh or cry.

A few weeks afterward, Robert Kvale phoned to tell me
about a woman he thought would do well in the Project New Life
program. Carol Bradley was twenty-six years old, a victim prostitute who wanted to leave the life. I conducted a preliminary interview with her over the phone and decided that Bob's estimation
of her was correct. I arranged for her to stay at a public shelter
while she participated in the program, then drove to Bob's apartment to pick her up.

Did I say "apartment?" "Bawdroom" would be a more apt
description of the place I walked into: dozens of erotic pictures,
statues, and paintings were arranged on the walls and tables.
Some art collection! Needless to say, I didn't see any quilt. As I
looked around, I thought it was the largest efficiency apartment
I'd ever seen. Kitchen, bathroom, closet, and living area were
about twenty-five by forty feet. There was an expensive wall system composed of a television with a huge movie-sized screen,
VCR, and stereo at one end of the living space, and a custom
styled bed larger than king-size at the other end. Except for four
black leather stools at the breakfast bar, there was no other furniture in the place. Leafy plants, which provided the apartment's
only wholesome touch, were arranged tastefully around the
room. In the car, Carol confirmed that Bob's home was his own
personal brothel, where he consorted with whatever hooker he
considered himself to be "helping" at the time.

After this experience with Robert Kvale, I began to cate-
gorize the johns by nicknames. Those who didn't always pay for
sex because they tried to help the women became "Harold the
Helper." Ironically, like Robert Kvale, these men often considered themselves to be my colleagues and sometimes even
referred prostitutes to me for assistance.

"Billy Blue Collar" is the most common john for street-walkers. He works construction, shipyards, and in factories. There is nothing romantic about sex between Billy and a ho: for him, it's an erotically powerful feeling to have a woman on her knees, subservient, performing the basest of labors. For her, it's twenty dollars. Billy works for "the man" all day or night. By hiring a prostitute he becomes "the man." Sometimes, as I drove the women to downtown shelters, they pointed out regular customers. I had always thought of johns as dirty old men, but they looked as regular as any other man on the street.

As Carol and I talked on the way to the shelter, we got to know each other better. Several days later, driving downtown, she told me about "Weird Wendell," a vicious type of john. I was wondering aloud why streetwalkers lean in car windows and commented, "It makes what they're doing so obvious. No wonder they get arrested."

"You have to be careful," Carol explained. "Johns can turn on you before you know it. When the hoes lean in the window, they're making sure that the windows roll down and the doors open from inside.

"When I first started, I was raped with a Coke bottle at knife point by a "Wendell" who had removed the door and window handles from the passenger side of his pickup truck. Fortunately, we were in a factory parking lot, and the security guard heard me screaming. If he hadn't rescued me, the trick might have killed me."

Carol's explanation made me understand something that had bothered me about Sam, who watched every move of my hands, when I scratched, when I gestured, when I opened my purse. Through Carol I came to realize that Samantha had probably been assaulted by Wendells so often that she habitually watched everyone for signs of danger.

While I tried to provide Carol, Sam, and the others with the support they so badly needed, I continued to forge ahead on my plans to launch Project New Life. I became acquainted with "Beauregard the Good Ole Boy" when I phoned the Welcome Committee, an organization of black community leaders, to ask for support for the program. Lloyd McVittie was president, and I thought he would be interested in what I had to say when I called him one sunny June morning.

"I'm forming an organization to help women leave prostitution," I said. "I've been researching prostitution arrest statistics: nearly half of all arrests involve black women, yet the city has only an 8 percent black population. Would someone from the Welcome Committee," I asked, "be interested in sitting on our Board of Directors?"

McVittie, a minister, responded in a condescending tone. "Well, you know, we've tried to get some of those ladies to come to church, but they like what they're doing. I don't think we can help you."

My heels stiffened. I was angered by his tone, but I was also baffled—I hadn't said anything about religion. When I mentioned the conversation to Samantha, who was by now used to my naivete, she shed light on the subject.

"Becky," she explained patiently, "do you remember the pimp Ginger Pettit used to have, Lucky Christopher? His father is a member of the Welcome Committee. I've been with some of those men myself. That's why he won't help you."

"Beauregards"—men like McVittie—are always members of a good ole boy network who wield power in their communities and share a belief that a woman's place is on her knees.

As the turndowns continued, I felt disappointed but not defeated. More and more I learned to depend on myself. I knew I had to plan for the future of the program. As I put together a budget for Project New Life, I realized that I would need all the facts and figures if, as I hoped, some existing community organization were to some day take over the project. I began pricing the merchandise I would need to open a house for my clients.

Going to furniture, appliance, department, and discount stores, I compiled a list. My days got longer and longer. Once, driving home at six-thirty, I remembered that I had intended to visit Brahn's Department Store that day. I felt I couldn't walk another step, but I had a nagging urge to go to Brahn's. Reenergized as I had so often been during all these months, I turned the car around, parked, and went into the large, warehouse-type store. Once there I became engrossed in pricing the items on my list.

"Can I help you find anything?"

The voice startled me. I turned to see a muscular man with thick brown hair and blue eyes. He wore a badge that said: Jerry Hudson, Manager.

I explained that I had a long list of items to be priced. He took notes and led me from aisle to aisle until I completed my list.

"May I ask what all this is for?" he inquired politely as I wrote the last prices in my notebook.

"I'm trying to start a program to help women get out of prostitution," I replied wearily. "And I need to determine our budget."

This statement had been met with snickers, wisecracks, and lewd remarks for so long that Jerry Hudson's reply took me by surprise.

"I want to help! I'll do anything I can to help! When I was stationed in South Carolina I had a girlfriend who I found out was a prostitute. I tried to get her out of the life. We even went to the police for protection, but her pimp killed her, and the police wouldn't do anything!" he said, a look of grim determination on his face. "Let me give you my phone number."

Jerry Hudson was the genuine article. He was the first person besides me to be committed to my project to help people get out of prostitution. In the next few weeks he joined in helping me put the project together. Soon I found that I could trust him to do any job efficiently. He was a whiz with public relations, wonderfully empathetic with the prostitutes, and he could be counted on for good advice in all areas.

His management talent was a shot in the arm to the organizational side of Project New Life. Matters of policy, public image, even the forms we used, were determined by the two of us putting—or butting!—our heads together.

We were quite different: me divorced, him single; me a parent, him childless. Our greatest diversity was that Jerry was an atheist while I am a practicing Christian, which made our approaches to some things very different. For instance, if we parked my car in a bad area of town, I would pray that God would keep it safe until we got back. If we took Jerry's car he would put on a lock device which sounded an alarm if anyone came near.

Jerry was able to relate to women in the same way as he related to men. There was not a chauvinistic or moralistic bone in him, and I found myself on equal footing with him, in his eyes as well as mine. This attitude soon caused me to entrust him with my clients' welfare. It was trust that was well based.

One day Jerry came with me to the County Hospital, where I tried to convince Gail Barkley, a social worker, that one of our clients needed medical detoxification. Liza Carlyle, a streetwalker, had been using medication from which one had to withdraw slowly. To withdraw from it suddenly might mean convulsions and possible death, and Liza was already dangerously ill. However, Gail Barkley had seen too many drug addicts in her career and wasn't sympathetic.

"Your client can detoxify herself on the street, by taking fewer pills each day," Barkley advised us.

Jerry sat up straight in his chair, leaned forward, and pounded his fist on the social worker's desk.

"And what do you think are her chances of withdrawing on the street? How is she going to monitor her vital signs? Will she have the willpower to refuse the extra stuff her pusher will try to sell her?" he demanded.

"I doubt she'll do that anyway," the social worker retorted.

"Well, dammit, she definitely won't if you don't give her the chance," Jerry insisted.

"All right," Barkley finally said with resignation. "But she'd better not leave this facility before her treatment is complete."

She pulled forms from a desk drawer, inserted one in her typewriter, and asked, "What's your client's full name?"

I looked at Jerry with increased admiration after that. Until then, I had carried all the responsibilities myself. I had driven the women to appointments, advocated for them, designed their individual programs, and matched them with sponsors. But I could no longer do it all. The overwhelming numbers of people needing help were more than one person, especially one with a family, could manage. Now I had another effective advocate. Things were looking up.

And they got better. Evie Evans was the new wife of my longtime friend, Frank Evans. Frank was a school administrator and Evie was an interior designer. She didn't drive, and I teased her that she had only married Frank because he lived close to her shop. She was active in the community, and she had a heart of gold. When she expressed interest in my clients, I was delighted.

God, it seems, has a sense of humor. Evie Evans was a wonderful person, and my clients and I badly needed her generous help. Her only negative quality was a tendency to promise more than she could deliver.

In September, my phone rang as I was doing the breakfast dishes. I wiped my soapy hands on a dish towel and grabbed the receiver.

"Becky?" a masculine voice demanded.

"Who is this?" I asked.

"Paul Williams, Concetta's husband. She's in labor,

Becky, and I don't have no car. You take her to the hospital."

Paul Williams was a heroin addict as well as a pimp. He ran a stable of prostitutes, and he had recruited Concetta during a trip to Mexico. I presumed that he had married her to bring her to the United States. Marriage also qualified them for welfare, food stamps, and medical benefits.

I had met Concetta six months earlier when she had applied to a battered women's shelter for help. A Spanish-speaking counselor had phoned me after discovering her client was a streetwalker trying to escape from her pimp. She wanted to return with their baby son, Paul Junior, to her family in Mexico. I agreed to take her case, and the shelter promised to provide housing. Evie had come with me to drive Mrs. Williams and her baby to the welfare office where we arranged to have her monthly checks mailed to the shelter.

No sooner had we left the building that day when Paul appeared.

"Concetta! I missed you, Baby! Where you been?" the little pimp enthused. He was sporting a black leather jacket and an expensive haircut. His brown eyes were anything but warm. Evie and I recognized at once that he was an addict pimp.

Concetta was visibly shaken, but she managed to introduce us. "These are my friends Becky and Evie who gave me a ride." We smiled politely. But Paul said nothing.

"Concetta," Evie said, thinking quickly, "you're late for your appointment. We have to leave."

But our client, unnerved by her husband's sudden appearance, shook her head and went with him submissively.

Now Paul Williams wanted my help. I agreed to take Concetta to the hospital and phoned Evie as soon as he hung up. It made me nervous talking to him, but most of his power seemed to be in intimidation. And I wasn't about to let him frighten me. Evie wasn't scared of Paul, either.

"You bet I want to go!" Evie said. "He actually had the

nerve to ask you for help, huh?" She was laughing.

"Ask is not exactly accurate. Demand is more like it."

I shook my head. "We have to get Concetta away from him." I knew she was as eager as I was.

In fifteen minutes I was at Evie's door. The sun beat mercilessly on us as we trudged back to my car. We were thankful for the air conditioning's flow of arctic air through the station wagon.

When we arrived at the East End hotel where the Williams stayed, they were waiting in the lobby. I turned to Paul. "How close are her contractions?"

He shrugged. "I don't have no knowledge about such things."

Exasperated by his lack of concern, I turned to Evie who was helping Concetta to the car.

To Paul, I said, "Do you want us to watch Paul Junior while Concetta's in the hospital?"

"Nah, I can handle him okay," the baby's father assured me. He waved to his wife, who was wiggling her fingers goodbye at her husband and son.

"Okay. Do you want to go to the hospital with us?" I asked him grimly.

"I got some business I gotta take care of. I call her later," he answered. He fidgeted with his collar as he spoke.

He was wearing his leather jacket in the heat of the day, so I presumed his "business" consisted of getting his next fix. I hated to leave Paul Junior with him, but there was nothing I could do. Concetta needed me more at this moment.

We waited at the hospital until Concetta was settled. I wrote my telephone number on a piece of paper and handed it to her. I said, "Call us anytime."

As we turned to leave, our client said, "Mister Richie— you call?" She wrote a number on the bottom of the paper I had given her, tore it off, and handed it to Evie.

"Okay, honey. I'll call him. Do you want me to tell him you're in the hospital?"

"Si!" Concetta smiled her appreciation.

I left Evie at her house and drove home, a place that was beginning to look like it belonged to someone else. My Schnauzer, Misty, barked when I opened the door and, when she recognized me, danced around excitedly. As I went to my bedroom to find out if there were any calls, the dog jumped on my bed to listen. The calls were recorded aloud on my machine, and Misty monitored every one.

"Becky, this is Evie. Call me when you get home. It's important." There was an air of urgency in her voice.

Quickly I kicked off my shoes and sat on the bed to dial Evie's number. Behind me, Misty rolled on my pillow so I pushed her off the bed, laid back, and relaxed for a few seconds while the number connected.

"Hello," Evie answered on the first ring, her voice agitated as if she had been waiting by the phone for me to call.

"What's up?"

"I just phoned that Mister Richie. He says Paul and Concetta are really living in the back of an old van in the parking lot on Second and Grand, behind a building he owns. They don't have a room at that hotel where we picked them up, Becky. That was just for show. What are we going to do? It's bad enough that they have Paul Junior in that old van, but they just can't take a newborn baby there!" She sounded indignant, angry, frustrated, and determined, all at the same time.

There was something very wrong here. The victim streetwalkers who had children usually tried to take good care of them, although criminal prostitutes made poor mothers. Concetta was neither an addict nor a criminal. Why would she live in an old van with her babies? Unless . . .

"Maybe Paul's heroin habit is taking all their money, and that's why Concetta asked us to call Mister Richie, so he could tell us. We'd better notify Child Protective Services. I'll phone my friend Booth Martin, one of the social workers there, and call you later," I told Evie.

Hanging up, I gazed out the sliding glass door for a moment. The temperature gage read ninety-one degrees. I hated this heat, and I hated Paul Williams. What kind of creep would make his wife and babies live in a van? I got up to find my address book.

Luckily Booth was in his office. He promised to investigate the problem immediately and said he would call me later.

It was after four p.m. when Booth called back. My kids were home and splashing each other in the pool. I had finally gotten the breakfast dishes done and straightened the house a bit. I was ready to concentrate on Paul and Concetta again.

"I talked to a social worker in the East End district," Booth told me. "She said there have been complaints about the Williams family and that the police have given them three days to move. That was two days ago. That means they have to be out of the van tomorrow."

I thanked my friend and phoned St. Joseph's Hospital maternity ward. The nurse who answered told me that Concetta was in the delivery room. I called Evie and filled her in. "We'll visit her first thing in the morning," I said.

The following day, however, Evie's secretary at her interior decorating shop phoned in sick, and Evie could not leave work. I drove to the hospital alone. I stopped by the nursery on the way to see Concetta, but I couldn't find the Williams baby. Hoping the baby was with its mother, I hurried to her room. There I ran into Paul.

"Hey, Becky! What do you think of my new daughter, Gracie?" Paul grinned proudly at the little bundle which lay on Concetta's bed.

I stared at him. Not "our" new daughter, but "my" new daughter, I noted with disgust.

"She's beautiful," I said as I leaned over to get a better look. Wrapped in hospital flannel blankets, a tiny red face peeked up at me. Dark fuzz covered her head, and her fists searched for her mouth. A warm tingling feeling filled me, and, for a moment, I forgot Paul Williams. Babies, I thought remembering an old saying, are God's way of indicating the world should go on.

"Can you give us a ride back to the hotel?" Paul asked, interrupting my reverie.

"Shouldn't Concetta stay in the hospital another day or two?" I protested.

"Nah, Paul Junior don't do too good without his Mama. She'll be okay at home," the little jerk assured me.

Concetta got dressed in the same clothes she had worn the day before, apparently ready to leave. Paul Junior, four months away from being two years old, toddled around the room. "How were you going to get there before I came?" I asked.

He shrugged. "By bus."

At least I could make Concetta's life a little easier today. "I'll take you," I said. Then, wondering what he would say, "Where do you want to go?"

"Just drop us off at the hotel where you picked Concetta up yesterday," he replied.

"Thank goodness he's found a place for them," I murmured, trying to believe him.

An aide appeared with a wheelchair for Concetta. Tiny Gracie was placed in her mother's arms. I carried Paul Junior since his father seemed to expect it. The nurse hung Concetta's purse on the back of the wheelchair, and Paul burdened himself with a small diaper bag. At the entrance to the hospital, I remanded Paul Junior to his father's care while I brought the station wagon from the parking lot.

The aide helped Concetta into the back seat with the baby and Paul Junior, and I made a mental note to buy a child car seat. Paul made himself comfortable in the front while his wife tended both children in the back.

About two blocks from the hotel, Paul said, "You can just let us off here. I wanna get something to eat."

My heart seemed to stop beating for a few seconds. How could I have been so stupid as to believe he had secured a hotel room for his family? He must be planning to deposit them in the old van where they had been living. It was just four blocks away. I had to do something.

"I'm hungry, too," I said. "I'll buy!"

Before he could protest, I pulled into a parking lot and got out of the car. I held Paul Junior's hand as we walked across the street to a greasy spoon diner. Since I was buying, Paul ordered a complete dinner. Concetta had toast and juice which she shared with her son. I ordered a sandwich for myself and one to go for Concetta and her son. Mine seemed to stick in my throat as I ate it. I watched the new mother turning pale as the minutes ticked by. Finally, I turned to her husband. "Concetta needs to get to the hotel to rest," I said, looking him directly in the eyes.

"I spent the night at a friend's house," he lied. "And they ain't got our room ready yet."

"Maybe we should go check, Paul," I insisted. "Concetta badly needs rest. Having a baby is a big strain."

"Everybody worries about Concetta! What about me? I need rest, too, but nobody cares about me!"

I was speechless at his outburst. Was he setting up a straw man to distract me from the subject of the hotel room, or was he serious?

"I'm sorry, Paul," I said, trying a new tack. "I didn't know you'd been ill. C'mon. I'll help you both to your room." I rose to leave, but the little pimp remained where he was.

"Nah, we'll be okay. Our room will be ready at three. We'll wait here till then."

Outside, the sun beat down mercilessly on the city. I walked slowly to my car trying to plot a course. I decided to do some spying. I drove to the street where Mr. Richie's building was. It was easy to locate the old vehicle the Williams family had been living in. It was an abandoned 1940's furniture van. I double parked and peered inside. There was no ventilation except the double doors in the back. I wondered how they survived in the heat. Clothes were hung on hangers on a rope along the inside wall, and a large mattress filled the floor. I got back into my car, drove to a side street where I could see the van, rolled down my windows, turned off the engine, and waited.

Twenty minutes later the Williams family walked up the street from the direction of the diner. Concetta, looking exhausted and her purse slipping off her shoulder, carried the baby and held Paul Junior's hand. Her husband carried the diaper bag. They didn't notice my car. I watched while Paul opened the doors of the van. He held his son while Concetta climbed inside. He handed the toddler to her. Then he turned and walked away. Concetta pulled one of the doors closed and disappeared. I could hear the baby's thin wail coming from the van.

I started my car and drove home. I intended to phone Booth Martin as soon as I got inside.

My son Darroll had begun third grade and was happily doing what third graders do. He loved swimming, badminton, and comic books. He loved to read and to be read to. He played soccer and joined the Cub Scouts. I did everything I could to make sure he had a happy childhood. When my work with prostitutes began, I could not help comparing my children's experiences with the horror stories I was hearing every day.

Sarah Flowers was first sexually molested by her stepfather when she was in the third grade, as Darroll was now. Her brothers sometimes watched from a balcony. No one told her mother. When Sarah confided in her aunt, she was told, "Well, just don't let him."

Sarah tried to go to bed early to avoid her stepfather's

advances, but he dragged her from her bed. Her grades fell. Then she stayed up late to study and raised her grades to A's and B's.

"I thought," Sarah told me, "if I'm a good girl and do well in school he'll leave me alone."

He didn't.

She ran away from home at twelve. "Ringer Michael," so called because of the rings he wore, found her alone and scared at a bus station. He told Sarah that she was beautiful and that he loved her—words she longed to hear—and took her home to his stable of prostitutes. Soon she was working the streets. She had to share him with the other whores and that bothered her, so she confronted him.

"I have to tell them that I love them, Baby, because we need the money. As soon as I can afford to buy you a house, I'll send them away," he promised, and she believed him. It was years before she realized he told all his whores the same thing.

"All I ever wanted was someone to love me," Sarah confided. "And I thought that if I had his baby, maybe he'd love me more than the others."

Poor Sarah. It took her seven years on the streets to come to the realization that it's all a game, and the pimps make the rules.

Like Christine Mayer and Samantha Rice before her, Sarah Flowers wanted to give her baby a better life. Sam had fallen back into her pattern of drug abuse and prostitution, but Christine had made remarkable progress and wanted to sponsor one of my clients.

It was my duty to assess my clients' needs, design their personal programs, and obtain services for them, but mentorship, I had decided, would be the responsibility of caring volunteers who agreed to befriend the women. However, as the former prostitutes progressed, they often wanted to help others, and I couldn't think of a better therapy, so I assigned Christine to help Sarah.

3

I LEARN MORE

Jerry, Evie, and I had formed a very close friendship. By now we all realized that we had to get as much information on prostitution as we could and that the only way to get it was to explore the downtown areas. I was delighted when they said they would go with me. That way we would all be able to view the interaction between streetwalkers, their pimps, and prospective customers for ourselves, and compare notes.

Our first forays into the streets proved to be an education. The women I had met in Sam's room had been sober and well-behaved; those same women outside on the street were often high on drugs, foul-mouthed, and obstreperous.

The first time we saw Ginger Pettit at work her black hair was windblown and her clothing disheveled. She was hanging drunkenly on a lamppost, trying to attract customers. As an old Chevy, badly in need of a paint job and with one taillight missing, cruised slowly by her corner, Ginger puckered her lips and blew the driver a kiss. The car pulled to the curb, and my friend leaned in the window for a few seconds, before she opened the door and got in.

I wished I could rush over and grab her away, but of course I couldn't—not then.

In November we began visiting the downtown area in the guise of evening Christmas shoppers. One of the first things we noticed was that many of the prostitutes we saw were just kids. On Sixth and Seventh Avenues, from G to I Streets, girls about fourteen to sixteen years old waited by telephone booths. When a phone rang, one of the girls would pick it up and hold a short conversation. In five or ten minutes, a car would pull up and the girl would get in. This was very different from the approach used by Sam's friends: when a car stopped, either specifically for them, or for a traffic signal, they leaned in the window and made a deal. The older streetwalkers dressed casually, in shorts and a halter top in the summer, in jeans and a short coat in the winter. The young girls wore heavy makeup, miniskirts, and ankle boots. When the weather was cold, they added short jackets.

One evening, as we walked down I Street, we noticed several girls who appeared to be only twelve or thirteen at a busy bus stop. As parents, Evie and I were appalled.

"I can't imagine letting kids ride the bus alone no less hangout on street corners at this time of night," Evie fumed.

"I can't either," I agreed. "It's sad."

Just then, as Evie and I watched, a car pulled up to the bus stop. One of the girls leaned in the window for a few seconds, talked to the driver, and then looked nervously in each direction and got in.

"There's nothing to worry about," Jerry grimaced and quipped. "Their pimp is keeping an eye on them."

My mother always says, You can either laugh, or cry. The three of us realized then that we'd better learn to laugh, or we would never have the stomach for this work.

That Friday night, Jerry, Evie and I went to a bus station. Many of the streetwalkers had mentioned that pimps had recruited them there. We wanted to watch the process.

The bus terminal obviously was built in the 1960s. Video games had replaced pinball machines, and some of the torn red plastic chairs in the waiting room now had pay TVs, but the greasy spoon cafe, the seedy bar, the newsstand stocked with girlie magazines, the barbershop, and the scratched parquet floor which were part of the original design still remained.

Pretending to be waiting for a bus, we took our time looking around. At 7:00 P.M., a man dressed in cowboy boots and hat and wearing several gold chains got off a bus with two girls with long blonde hair who couldn't have been more than fifteen years old. The girls wore sweaters and miniskirts without jackets despite the cool night air. The man carried three bags, and the girls, purses over their shoulders, went outside where they began signaling passersby that they wanted a ride. Within a few minutes, both girls had sped off in cars.

Evie and I looked at each other and then at Jerry, who was staring as the second car pulled away with its young passenger. We hadn't imagined there would be such blatant prostitution in this public place.

"Let's separate to get a better look at the entire scene," I said. Evie positioned herself near the arriving passenger entrance, Jerry stood by the front door, and I watched, sitting on a bench inside the waiting area.

The man in cowboy attire sat alone in the cafe drinking a Coke. Seedy characters, smelling of wine and sweat, dozed or watched television in some of the chairs around me. Teenage skinheads played video games, and a young woman in an ankle-length dress carried her crying baby into the women's rest room. Denim-clad men and women, some wearing leather jackets, carried overstuffed baggage as they waited in line at the departure gates. Swaying with a limp, an elderly cleaning woman pushed her mop and bucket across the floor, spraying soap suds in all directions. A man in a flamboyant striped suit with red lining and red cowboy boots approached a girl of about fourteen as she walked toward the front door alone, carrying a backpack. Evie was strolling casually behind her. The man neared his prey and, smiling, began speaking to her. In a few moments, the two of them went into the cafe. If she fell for his spiel, she would spend the rest of her life in places like this, I thought.

Just as Evie took a seat next to me, Jerry returned from his post near the front door.

"I just saw a punk rocker prostitute!" he said incredulously. "She had orange hair cut in a flattop, and she was wearing a leather miniskirt and high heels!"

A pair in the restaurant were eating sandwiches. The man seemed to be doing all the talking. We tried to blend into the scene as we observed the action around us. Several more buses arrived. One of the girls who had arrived with the cowboy returned while we watched, went into the cafe, and sat down near him. We saw her give him a small wad of bills, which he pocketed. Then she went out into the night again. A few minutes later, the fourteen year old and the flamboyant man came out of the cafe. His arm was wound around her. They left the bus station together.

Another bus brought a dismal bonanza of information. Three boys, a bit ragged, carrying sports bags, got off. No one met these kids, all of whom appeared to be young teenagers, and they left the building alone.

"Runaways, I'll bet! Let's see where they go," I whispered.

We followed about half a block behind them. This was no easy feat, because these youngsters were fast walkers, with the easy stride of adolescence. At the corner of Kennewick Street and Fourth Avenue, they slowed and began to watch the traffic. Five minutes and two blocks later, a silver Lincoln pulled up next to them. We stared as the driver leaned toward the trio and spoke a few words. Without hesitation, the boys got in, and the elegant auto disappeared around a dark corner with its young passengers.

"Did you see that?" Jerry exclaimed in astonishment.

"Huh? Oh yeah. Yeah!" I was in a daze. Male prostitution was something new to consider.

We walked back to our cars in silence. We were parked close to the bus station, so we could have continued our observations, but we didn't have the heart for it. It wasn't that we were more upset by the prospect of boys prostituting themselves than we were by girls doing it: it was the idea that prostitution was so much more blatant and extensive than we had suspected.

I began to watch for boys as well as girls on the street when I went downtown. When I visited Sam in jail, I asked her about boys.

She shrugged. "There's some transvestites who work between Kennewick and Lacey, from Fifth to Seventh. Sometimes we girls talk to them. They're just out there to earn money for a sex change operation. Most of their customers never even know they're guys." She seemed to consider them peers, but none of them were her friends.

"The boys that I saw weren't cross-dressers," I said. "They definitely looked masculine." During the next week or so, I observed eight men who seemed to regularly work the area Sam had mentioned. Just one block south of that district, almost all of the prostitutes were males in masculine garb, except for the corner of Fourteenth and Nantucket, where a trio of male hookers in very theatrical female garb plied their trade. Evie quickly term them "jiggle-o's."

We were struck by the modus operandi of the "boys": most were identifiable by their styles of clothing. Young gentlemen wearing tweed business suits leaned casually against the First National Bank building, one foot on the sidewalk, the other against the wall. As a well-dressed man passed, one of the youths would make a seemingly innocent comment, which to the indoctrinated was a suggestion of sexual favors. Some of the male prostitutes looked very masculine in leather jackets and carried gym bags. Others dressed casually in jeans and warm coats. The one signal common to most was the ever present bandanna, known as a "fag tag," worn around either knee, hung from a back pocket, tied around an upper arm or the neck, or stuffed into a shirt pocket. Each placement represented a different type of sexual service being offered. I wondered if in light of the AIDS threat they used condoms. I doubted it.

While female streetwalkers phoned me frequently at that point, the men and boys who asked for help were few and far between. I wanted to reach everyone who worked the street, male and female, to tell them they didn't have to be there, but the sheer numbers were overwhelming, and I wondered how I could possibly help all of them even if somehow I could get my message across.

However, as word about my work spread and I began to work with more male prostitutes, I learned that they don't experience the prejudice that females encounter. Many male hookers are homosexual and are accepted in the gay community. In time, I found that men who want to get out of the trade generally make their transition in less than half the time it takes women, because they aren't ostracized.

Ginger Pettit supported her boyfriend Tim who was not only a heroin addict, but also a cancer patient. Although I usually extended the designation of "pimp" or "Frank" to everyone except children who profits from a prostitute's earnings, I felt sorry for Tim, and always thought of him as Ginger's "project."

Tim had a gastrostomy feeding tube to his stomach that he used to inject himself with heroin. Supporting two habits kept Ginger busy working the street, but she occasionally took time out to walk with me for an hour or two. One evening, she pointed out a stairwell behind a dilapidated building.

"That's where I take a lot of my dates who don't have cars. I don't do 'flatbacking' (frontal sexual intercourse) there, though!" she said.

"Do you do a lot of flatbacking?" I asked.

"No. It's too hard. I get sore, and I have to douche between dates and worry about the ones who don't use protection," she explained.

I remembered the dozens of pairs of lacy bikini panties Sam owned.

"Is there any type of man you prefer to date—like a businessman, or a soldier?" I prodded.

"The foreign guys are pretty cool. They're away from home, and they miss their wives, so they're real nice to me. They treat me like a lady. Most of the Americans call me 'Baby' and just want a BJ and maybe a feel, but the foreigners want to talk to me a little, like I'm somebody important," Ginger confided, her voice soft, as if in pleasant memory.

"Are there some men you try to avoid?" This was fascinating, and I wanted her to tell me everything she would.

"Well, there's the guys who want to maim us whores, of course." She thought for a moment, then continued. "I guess the ones who really give me the creeps are the men who want to call me by their daughter's name and want me to call them 'Daddy.' It always makes me wonder what the guy is doing or wants to do to his daughter."

Many of the women expressed the same sentiments about johns who wanted them to pretend to be their daughters. I came to realize how deeply some moral values are ingrained in human beings and how some others can be discarded. These prostitutes were people who were selling their bodies, but they were as offended as anyone else by the thought of incest. Although many of them had been sexually assaulted as children by stepfathers or other relatives, relatively few prostitutes I met had incestuous relationships with their natural parents. One of the few I got to know whose birth father had violated the incest taboo was Renee Davis.

Renee was thirty-five years old when Sam introduced us.

At first, she seemed a good candidate for Project New Life because she had begun the life as a victim prostitute. Slender and as lovely as a model, she carried herself gracefully despite twenty years on the street, and she still wore makeup, which was rare among older streetwalkers.

When she began to tell me her story, I winced. The youngest of five children, Renee became her father's sex slave when she was only seven years old.

"My daddy said, 'Girl, your mother won't give it to me any more, so it's up to you.'" For a few moments Renee stared at some invisible spot on the wall, then she went on. "I put up with it for eight years, to protect my brothers and sisters until they left home and went to college. Daddy used to say if I'd do it for him, he'd leave them alone, and I guess he did.

"I ran away when I was fifteen, after my sister Virginia went off to school. I knew he couldn't hurt them, then. One of my brothers is a doctor, and one is a professor of history at Carolina State. One of my sisters is a high school teacher, and Virginia is a psychologist. But I'm nothing but a damned whore."

Renee's attitude toward herself, her job, and her life were similar to revelations of other prostitutes we met who were victims of parental incest. They revealed a major schism in the viability of victim prostitute rehabilitation. In general, I found that victim prostitutes were optimistic about the possibilities for their futures only if they had been molested, or otherwise maltreated, by people other than their parents. Those for whom the incest taboo had been violated suffered from such a negative self-image that psychological counseling was necessary before they could address the issue of prostitution.

Unhappily, we were not able to help Renee. Jerry and I had made a hard and fast rule that no one would enter our program if they refused to take care of their arrest warrants. This was partly for their protection, so that they wouldn't be arrested at some time in the future when they were doing well. It was also for our own security. If a person refused, she might have serious charges against her somewhere, and we didn't want to be inadvertently involved with a dangerous criminal. Renee Davis refused to turn herself in. We later learned that she had been involved in a murder in another state.

As Christmas approached, I spent more time in the stores downtown, both shopping and observing. I didn't have time to explore the streets for several weeks before the holidays, but that didn't halt my education. I was developing radar: any prostitutes in the vicinity immediately attracted my attention. One evening, however, my radar seemed to beep at an incorrect signal. A pair of well-groomed ladies, one with sleek black hair and ivory skin and the other a honey blonde, both of them clad in silk dresses and high heeled shoes, walked briskly past me in the upscale downtown mall. My senses flashed the word hookers, but my conscious mind rejected that. They were too high class. Even so, I followed them at a distance. They wore no coats, but many shoppers didn't—the mall was warm, and most people parked in the enclosed parking garage below the building. As the women walked past a brightly lit window display, the light highlighted their lack of undergarments. I felt then that my intuition had probably been correct, but I was certain of it when they approached a sailor who was window shopping. As he stood before a clothing shop display, the women walked to either side of him, and one of them spoke to him quietly. He turned to her with a smile, and then to her companion. A few words were exchanged, and then the sailor walked toward an exit, a woman on each arm.

Prostitutes and their problems were getting all my time and attention. My mother offered to treat the kids and me to Hawaii for Christmas. How could I refuse?

My mother, my children, and I flew to Waikiki, where we

visited shops, toured the battleship Arizona, which greatly impressed seven-year-old Darroll, ate fresh hot Famous Amos cookies, swam in the warm water, saw the ocean floor from a glass-bottomed boat, paid our respects to war correspondent Ernie Pyle at his volcanic grave site, and got a thorough indoctrination into South Pacific life at the wonderful Polynesian Cultural Center. Our week passed all too quickly in a delightful jumble of colorful people, places, and events.

The day before we were to leave Hawaii, we took one last tour, around the island of Oahu. The handsome young driver of the sixteen-passenger bus expounded knowledgeably about local superstitions, surfing events, history, geology, flora and fauna. I had passing thoughts about a career as a tour bus driver for David, who never stopped talking. When we got back to Honolulu, we received a final commentary on the city. In Chinatown, our driver pointed out the streetwalkers.

"See those pretty hookers on the street corners?" he asked as he nodded at them. "They're *not* girls!"

At this, I sat up and peered out the window.

"Mom!" Claire said in a tone of warning.

"Sorry," I apologized. "I forgot we're on vacation."

Not long after I returned home, Bob Kvale phoned me. "Carrie Hope is in the hospital. She injected heroin into her forearm, hit a muscle, and developed an abscess. Would you go to see her?" he asked.

"Of course," I replied, glad he didn't suggest joining me.

When I arrived at County Hospital, they directed me to the ward where Carrie was. She lay in the starched white sheets of the hospital bed. Her face was the color of the sheets. A picture flashed through my mind of the tanned redhead I'd seen the autumn before. The person before me seemed someone else. A nurse bent over her to hear Carrie's whispered words. Seeing me, the nurse stood up.

"Are you a family member?" the nurse inquired.

"No, just a friend," I said softly.

With a look that asked if I were an addict too, the nurse turned back to her work.

On the day Carrie was finally released, I went to the hospital to drive her to the downtown hotel where she had a room. A nurse was talking to her as I entered her room, and I was able to hear her discharge instructions.

"You're going to need physical therapy for that arm if you're going to regain full use of it. Here's the address of a therapy center," she said as she handed Carrie a slip of paper. "Call us if you develop a fever, or if the pain gets worse."

Carrie would be feeling no pain in an hour or two, I was sure: her bottle of codeine would be ingested or traded for heroin. In addition, I knew she would have to go to work today, to pay her hotel bill. Therapy was out of the question: there was no time for such extravagance because she worked fourteen-hour days. If only she would ask me for help, I thought, looking at her sadly, but it had to be her own decision and in her own time. I counseled myself to be patient and to keep my offer of help open.

If Carrie would soon be feeling no pain, Sarah Flowers was suffering enough for both of them. Sarah had moved in with her mother, who was divorced. For the first few months, things went well. Christine Mayer had proven an able and caring mentor, and Sarah blossomed under her tutelage. Their babies were being well cared for, and both young women were meeting the goals we had set together. I was proud of them both, and happy that they were making such terrific progress. It was when Sarah began to explore her feelings with her family members that she experienced her first rebuff. Her brothers had sometimes witnessed their stepfather's sexual molestation of her, and she decided to confront them about it.

"I don't know what your problem is," Sarah's oldest brother retorted. "*I* have a good relationship with Mom's ex-husband."

Sarah was devastated. For a time I thought she would drop out of the program but I kept calling and visiting her and somehow she weathered the storm.

In the autumn, Barbara Wanamaker, Presiding Judge of the Juvenile Court, invited me to her chambers to discuss an exciting idea she had. She asked about Project New Life.

"We want to help these teenagers, but their special needs, coupled with legalities, have made that next to impossible," I told her.

"As you may know, we have had very little success with juvenile prostitutes," the Judge answered. "Kids are seldom charged with solicitation, but a great number of street kids who come through our courts are prostituting themselves. They run away from foster homes, and when we send them back to their parents, they run away from them, too. I've been thinking about what to do about it, and I'd like to send juvenile prostitutes through your program."

"Your Honor," I replied, "I'd dearly love to reach juvenile prostitutes, but because they are kids they need the same loving guidance other teenagers do. My program is designed for adults. What I would like to do for kids in prostitution is to train foster parents to work with them."

"Let's try that, then. I'll authorize eight hundred and forty dollars a month for foster care and I'll license any home you recommend," Judge Wanamaker responded.

In my mind's eye were the twelve-year-olds working the bus stop, the pretty fourteen-year-olds at the phone booths, and the fifteen-year-old boys hopping into the Lincoln Towncar.

"Thank you!" I replied joyfully. "I'll get to work on this right away."

Project New Life's responsibilities were growing by leaps and bounds. I would have liked to limit the new clients, who took the most time, to a number our small program could adequately handle; but how could I? Sometimes there was call after call. I couldn't put anyone on a waiting list, because the prostitute population, at street level, is extremely transient. So I made it a policy to give help whenever I was asked. The expanding program and the expense put a strain on my budget and my time. Setting up a whole new program for juveniles would be a difficult task but it needed to be done, and I knew I had to try.

Jerry and Evie were overburdened, as I was, working with streetwalkers. They had no time for a new endeavor, so I approached various volunteers about recruiting and training foster parents, but—as had happened so often in establishing our program—to no avail.

We tried to do the best we could for them within our project, but I had to put the idea of a separate program devoted to teenage prostitutes on the back burner until I could find others who felt it was as important as I did.

4

LITTLE FISH
AND
BIG FISH

As any fisherman knows, if you keep your line in the water long enough something you don't want is as sure to nibble as something you do. What you catch depends on where you are fishing. In my case, the throwbacks were piranha or barracuda, and a few killer sharks. All these predators were pimps.

I don't know why we met so few pimps during those early days of helping hookers—beginners' luck maybe. However, our good fortune didn't last. As our organization grew we began to run into the big boys. Some, like Paul Williams, were minnows in the sea of sex slavery. A few others looked friendly but were piranhas. Sill others, like Pete Masterson, were killer sharks.

I first heard of Masterson when Leslie, one of the prostitutes who worked for him, called me to say he and his other call girls had been arrested. Upper class prostitutes didn't get arrested often, so I knew that for these women handling the humiliation of an arrest would be extremely difficult, and I thought I could help her.

When I met the prostitute, Leslie Van Ryann, a tall sophisticated young woman whose blonde hair was expertly cut to make her look like Sharon Stone, I was impressed by her beauty and manners. I soon learned to my surprise that she was only seventeen. She had been groomed to service wealthy clients and was schooled in poise, dress, conversation, the social graces, and something more.

During that first conversation, I asked Leslie, "What are your goals for the future?"

Her answer would give me a better insight into our chances of succeeding with her. She replied, "I'd like to finish high school, attend college, and become a Russian translator at the United Nations. My sophomore English teacher insisted that all of her students learn a foreign alphabet and a few words and phrases of that alphabet. I chose Russian and then got so interested I went on studying. I still remember a little."

"Vi govereet Parusky?" I asked, meaning, "Do you speak Russian?"

Leslie was delighted at my being able to respond in the language and answered, "Da!" then rattled off several more sentences in Russian.

"Wait!" I laughed. "I only know a few phrases! I don't understand!"

"I just asked where you had learned to speak Russian," she explained.

I told her. I didn't want to press her, but I definitely intended to learn more about this unusual ability of Leslie's. Not many seventeen-year-old Americans, no less a prostitute long since out of school, are so interested in studying a language that they learn to speak it fluently. I decided to talk more about it with her another time. Right now there were other vital things I needed to know.

"Do your parents know where you are?" I queried. Because she wasn't a streetwalker, it was unlikely that Leslie was in the life because of abuse, neglect, or molestation—somewhere, a mom and dad were probably very worried about her.

"I've called them to say I'm okay, but I've been living away from home since I was fourteen and Peter began training me," the teenager confessed. "I was adopted but I just never felt close to my adoptive parents. A psychiatrist who I was with told me I hadn't bonded properly, because I was abandoned at birth."

A psychiatrist she'd been with! I suppose it wasn't exactly a breech of the doctor-patient relationship since he was the one who had paid her for professional services, but his free advice certainly didn't heighten my respect for johns. I thought of him as a piranha because he had joined so many others in nibbling away at my client.

Leslie was not in need of money or shelter so I promised to contact her regularly. At first, I thought this might be a negative because I couldn't get Leslie out of her environment immediately. I worried that this might mean she would face more temptations than most of the other women in the program, but I hadn't taken into account Leslie's determination.

Leslie entered high school and went to work part time as a kennel assistant. To hold a minimum wage job after making fifty dollars an hour took courage. I couldn't help but admire this young person, yet I still had trouble accepting her explanation that she had learned to speak Russian so fluently all by herself.

One Saturday morning in April, I decided to ask my young client more about it.

"Leslie, tell me about your learning to speak Russian so well."

Leslie avoided my eyes for a minute, then murmured, "My friend, Sergai, taught me."

"Was Sergai one of your customers?" I was pushing, but I really wanted to know.

"Yes," she sighed, then added forcefully, "Look, Becky, I don't want any trouble about my past. Peter Masterson is in jail, but I don't ever want him to know I told anyone who my dates were."

"Leslie, I always pretend I don't know anything about anything. I could get into a lot of trouble, too, if I told anyone what I know. In the case of Peter Masterson and his escort service, though, what I learn could someday help other people get out of prostitution. I don't blow anyone's cover. If you don't want to answer, I'll understand, but I'd like to ask you some questions."

Leslie nodded. She took an apple from the bowl of fruit which was on her dining room table and sliced it while she spoke.

"Peter and I met through a friend. One Saturday he drove me to the mall and encouraged me to try on some expensive clothes I admired in a store window. Then he bought them for me, saying I could pay him back sometime and offered me a modeling job. Of course they weren't real modeling assignments as I soon found out, but by then I was in too deep and owed him a lot of money."

"Were all his call girls teenagers?"

"At the beginning," she laughed, "but we all grew up fast."

"Why teenagers?" I asked. I thought I knew, but her answer surprised me.

"Well, one reason was older men like young women—it makes them look good to have a babe on their arm," she answered as I'd expected, then astounded me by continuing, "but Peter had another reason. He trained us to get information. Grown women might be infiltrators."

"Were you part of a spy network?" I asked, both fascinated and fearful.

I watched Leslie take her apple core into the kitchen where she deposited it in the trash compactor. Her every move was graceful, even elegant. Peter had obviously taken time with the superficialities. I wondered if he had even taken more time with another more ominous kind of education.

It was then that Leslie confided her darkest secret—one which sent chills up my spine.

"Becky, I'd like to confide in you, but I don't want you ever to tell anyone, okay?" Leslie murmured.

She seemed unable to meet my gaze, and studied her shoes.

"Agreed." I had many secret "files" locked in my head. I would add hers.

"Sergai, the friend who taught me to speak Russian, was a fairly high up official at the Soviet embassy, and Peter paid me to get information from him." Her foot tapped nervously as she spoke. "It wasn't like I was giving the Soviets secrets about our country, at least not with Sergai. But of course there were others." She stole a momentary glance at my face, appeared about to go on, and then stopped.

"I know you wouldn't do that, Leslie," I assured her. I would have put my arms around any other girl who divulged a forbidden secret, something that terrified her, haunted, her, made her ashamed, but I never hugged Leslie. She was too aloof, independent, proud, and fiercely determined to make it on her own. Accepting a hug would have meant relinquishing some of her control to me. Nevertheless, she was only seventeen years old, and this skeleton in her closet clearly weighed heavily upon her. For the moment, I kept quiet. My first job was to get Leslie out of the life. The rest would come later.

I was developing a network of professionals, from speech therapists to educators to social workers to private investigators, upon whom I relied for assistance. I met many of them when I phoned to ask them for advice, but sometimes they called me to offer help after they learned about Project New Life through the media.

I was invited to attend a meeting of the National Organization for Women one evening when an outspoken proponent of prostitution was the guest speaker. The chairwoman introduced me as the Director of Project New Life, and I fielded questions for a portion of the evening. The following morning, I got a call from one of the people I had met at the conference.

"Hi," said my caller. "I'm Melody Gavers. I was at the NOW assembly last night. Do you help all kinds of prostitutes, or just streetwalkers?"

"I've worked mostly with streetwalkers," I answered, "but I help people in all types of prostitution."

I thought perhaps my caller was a professional who would offer her assistance to the project, but she turned out to be a pro of another kind.

"I work as a prostitute in a massage parlor," Melody confessed. "And I want to quit, but I don't know how to go about it. Can you help me?"

When we met, I learned that Melody had worked at Sweet Barb's Massage Parlor for seven of her thirty-eight years. A petite woman of Euro-Asian ancestry, her five-foot-two-inch frame didn't appear conducive to executing vigorous massages, but she somehow managed to do five per day.

"Why do you want to leave the life?" I asked as we sipped coffee at a booth in Lanie's, a nearby restaurant. I needed to understand her motives so that I could use them to help her make the break.

"It seems that every time I get into a relationship with a man, I break it off before he gets too serious. I'm always afraid that the guy will find out what I do for a living, and that he'll hate me for it, so I never give him the chance, but I want to get married again some day. I certainly don't want to be a prostitute forever.

"I've been taking classes at the university for three years. I only go part time, but I've completed two years toward my degree. I have to earn enough money to make the payments on my house and my insurance, and put my sons through college, so I have to get a good job when I quit prostitution."

"For your safety and for mine," I said gently, "I need to know whom your employer works for."

"Barb is the sole owner," Melody insisted. "She doesn't work for anyone."

I doubted that greatly, but I chalked it up to ignorance on Melody's part. Since pimps generally tended to let their whores leave when they got as old as Melody Gavers—so long as they weren't planning to work as prostitutes elsewhere—I figured Barb wouldn't give us much trouble.

I helped Melody set goals, but I felt she needed professional counseling to deal with her ambivalence, so I referred her to Prescott Morrisett, Ph.D., a psychologist who had recently volunteered to work with my clients.

Dr. Morrisett had phoned me after a television news story. He assured me that he had often worked with women who were prostitutes and offered to see my clients for a nominal fee. Most of the streetwalkers would not have felt comfortable in his plush office, but Melody was more sophisticated, and I thought she would do well with him.

I attended, by invitation, their first session, and I was delighted to leave my client in what I believed to be the good doctor's capable hands.

A streetwalker of twenty-three is "middle-aged." Unless she's remarkably attractive and unaddicted (both rare qualities after ten years on the street), she's sold to an addict-pimp who doesn't travel from one city to another, because he needs to stay close to his supplier. Another three years of prostitution finds most street hoes on their own. Most of them cohabit, often with a drug addict or a john known as a "Clinging Clem," but some of them get lucky and find a "Sugar Daddy," a man who can afford to take care of a drug-addicted whore.

In March, Sam's boyfriend Keith phoned to tell me that she was in the hospital after a particularly close call with a narcotics overdose. I went to see her immediately.

Sam was the only patient in a two-bed room. She was

hooked up to various tubes and monitors. She was pale and sweaty. Keith sat in a chair beside her bed, his arms covered by long sleeves to hide the track marks. When I entered the room, he stood and walked to the door.

"I'll get a cup of coffee in the cafeteria so you two can visit," he said.

After Keith left the room, Sam said, "I asked him to leave when you got here, because I want to talk to you alone, Becky. I don't want him to hear this."

"Sure, honey," I replied as I sat in the chair Keith had occupied.

"Remember last year when I lived with 'the Shark,' my Sugar Daddy?" she asked.

I nodded.

"I never told you, but he's a major drug dealer," Sam confided. "He keeps at least seven apartments around town, full of dope. He has an arsenal of guns and ammunition there, too, in case somebody tries to rob him. He sells to dealers, never at street level, except for me, because I lived with him. I want to turn him in, Becky, because the 'shit' he gave me last night almost killed me."

"That's a good idea, but why don't you want Keith to know?" I asked.

"Because he'd probably go tell the Shark just to get free dope for turning me in," she replied in disgust.

That was what I suspected, but I wanted her to speak the words: it was much more effective for my prostitutes to come to a conclusion like that themselves than for me to preach to them. Although he didn't actually pander, Keith was a pimp of sorts, because he lived on Sam's prostitution earnings. I think of men like him as "Franks," because any attempt to discuss their cohabitation arrangement begins with, "Frankly . . ." and ends with an excuse.

When she was released from the hospital, Sam showed me one of the Shark's drug warehouses. Ironically, it was located downtown, directly above a drugstore. Addicts milled about on the street corner around the building, and drug deals were made openly. Glassy-eyed men and women leaned against the wall or wandered, zombie-like, down the pavement. I wondered why the police hadn't done something about the scene before this.

After several weeks of procrastination, Sam decided she was too afraid the Shark would learn that she had snitched on him, so she asked me to do it. I was happy to: the Shark had ruined enough lives.

I phoned the Drug Enforcement Agency narcotics reporting hotline and went to see the local vice squad, but each of them told me that unless I had personally bought drugs from the Shark, they couldn't do a thing. I was angry and frustrated until I thought of trying to get the media interested. One evening a few days later I took Roger Jenkins, a reporter, downtown for a "prostitution tour." We stopped for a red light at the corner where Sam had shown me one of the Shark's drug warehouses.

"On the second floor of the building next to us," I told Roger, "is an illegal-drug store. The guy who runs it sells only to dealers, and he has six other places like it around the city."

Just then the door of the stairwell which led to the Shark's quarters opened, and a man stepped out. He was small with silver-gray hair. He left the building and entered an elegant silver Rolls Royce which was parked one half block from us. The light turned green and cars behind us began honking. As I pulled away, we watched the Rolls from the corners of our eyes.

"That was Thanh Duc Nguyen, godfather of the Asian gangs around here," Roger said.

"Now I know where the Shark gets his drugs, from Thanh Duc Nguyen," he continued. "If you're successful in busting the Shark, his boss may come after you. He has the resources and the wherewithal to discover who dares to expose one of his lieutenants."

I took a deep breath. "I guess I'll have to take that chance," I said, "if I get the opportunity to expose him."

Though I didn't know it, I was to tangle with him again soon.

For a while things were quiet. Dr. Morrisett phoned a few weeks later to relate Melody Gavers' excellent progress.

"You know," said the psychologist, "Melody is afraid she won't be able to support herself without prostitution. I have a suggestion that may help her leave the business sooner. How do you think she'd feel about striking out on her own as a masseuse? I know lots of executives who would pay a hundred dollars an hour for private massage. I could refer her."

Oh no! "Well, that's a wonderful idea, Dr. Morrisett," I lied. "I'll mention it to Melody right away."

When he hung up, I phoned a private investigator, Lindsey Baxter, and related the conversation to him. Lindsey promised to run a background check on Morrisett. I explained the doctor's offer to Melody and asked her not to give him an answer until she had thought it through.

I was in the living room folding clothes when the doorbell chimed. I peered through the peephole and saw Lindsey Baxter and his assistant Greg Landers on my doorstep. I opened the door wide to let them in, but when I moved backward, I stepped on Misty's paw as she rushed to greet our guests.

"Yipe!" screamed the dog.

I tried to shoo Misty and greet Lindsey at the same time.

"Hello, Misty," Lindsey said.

Misty lifted her paw for Lindsey to shake, then jumped on the pile of clean clothes I'd been folding for an illicit roll while I was distracted.

I knew that only important news would bring the detective and his partner to my door. Greg, a slim man of about twenty-eight, wore wire rim glasses and had sandy brown hair. He affected a homely air by wearing long-sleeve cotton shirts and sweater vests, like your friend's older brother. Lindsey was heavyset and grizzled and walked with a cane. Neither man gave a hint of their purposeful, forceful natures, and both men garnered tremendous sympathy with their humble manners, which made them very good detectives.

I made coffee and served it. I sipped from my cup while I waited for Lindsey to begin. His left hand scratched Misty's ear absently, and his right hand held the coffee mug. He looked over at me.

Finally, Lindsey said, "We looked into Dr. Morrisett's background, Becky." He turned to Greg. "Tell her what we found."

Greg spoke haltingly. "Well, Dr. Morrisett has been here three years. He came from Richmond, Virginia, where he had, as you've probably guessed, connections with organized crime figures."

Lindsey interrupted. "I know you're not going to like this, Becky, but I think he was setting you up to supply him with whores for a prostitution ring." He smiled an embarrassed look. "This isn't a guy you or your clients want any help from."

"Oh, no," I said. "Melody's already his patient. I have to get her way from him."

Another shark!

"Have you given any thought to Dr. Morrisett's offer?" I asked Melody the next day, affecting a casual voice.

"Yes," she replied and added, to my delight, "I've decided not to do it. It might be like jumping out of the frying pan into the fire."

I wondered if she sensed Morrisett's subterfuge, but I didn't ask. I cautioned myself to be patient.

Later in the month, a magazine writer requested an interview with some of my clients. Melody Gavers was one of the women who agreed to meet him.

"Can you arrange for me to speak with your madam?" the writer asked Melody after the interview.

She hedged. "I don't want her to know I'm planning on quitting," she said. "She might fire me."

"I won't mention that," he promised. "I'll make up something about how I met you, but I'd love to get an interview with a madam!"

"Look," Melody pleaded earnestly, "she might get in trouble with her bosses."

When we were alone, I confronted her.

"You told me Barbara Maddox was sole owner of Sweet Barb's," I accused her.

"Becky, I didn't want to tell you because I thought you might not help me if you knew the massage parlor I work for is owned by organized crime."

"Melody," I replied, "if you don't level with me, I can't help you."

Despite my words Melody wasn't ready to make any further disclosures. I told myself it might be safer for me that way but I began to realize that eventually in helping my prostitutes I might have to confront their bosses. However, for the moment, I should concentrate on my main objective, changing my clients' futures.

Despite my many clients and their problems, I devoted a good portion of my time and efforts to my family. That May my son David's hyperactivity had improved but was still a problem. David, who had just turned fifteen, suddenly began complaining of insomnia. He often knocked on my door in the middle of the night and asked if he could have something to help him sleep. I was a bit concerned about this, but a cup of hot chocolate seemed to help, although he sometimes missed a few hours of school when he overslept on the mornings after he had lain awake.

One night at ten thirty, about three weeks after the insomnia episodes began, Claire came into my room to report that David wasn't in his room. We searched the house calling for him, but he was gone. His bicycle was missing from the garage. I was not only worried by then, I was angry. In my nightgown and bathrobe, I drove through the neighborhood to look for him. The search was futile, so I returned home. Claire was still awake. I told her to go to bed and not to worry and climbed beneath my own covers. An eternity seemed to tick away before I heard the garage door being closed and David's furtive footfalls in the hallway. I listened as he went into his bedroom—he must be changing into his pajamas. Now he was walking up the hallway, but not as quietly as when he came in. I glanced at the clock: midnight. My bedroom door opened, and David called softly, "Mom?" I pretended to be asleep.

He came closer, leaned over me, and repeated, "Mom?"

"What's the matter, honey?" I asked.

"I can't sleep," my son said innocently. "Do you think I should make some hot cocoa?"

I reached up, grabbed his pajama top at the collar, and threw David onto my lap as I sat up at the same instant.

"Where have you been?" I thundered. I was inches from his face as I bent over him.

He looked up at me nonplussed.

"Don't you ever leave this house in the middle of the night again! Do you understand me?"

"Yes, Ma'am. I was just riding my bike." His voice quavered.

I had to be strict: there was no one to back me up, and David's hyperactivity had to be controlled. I knew that if I were the least bit soft on misbehavior, the battle could be lost forever. But I also wanted to be understanding so he would continue to communicate with me. I gave myself some time to think about what I should do and to calm down. "Go to bed. It's very late and we'll talk about it in the morning."

In the morning, David appeared at the table at six thirty. He was too scared to dare to be late getting up. We ate breakfast in silence, then I took him aside while his sister and brother got ready for school. After the few hours of sleep, I had decided serious punishment was needed.

"You're grounded for three months, young man. You can go to school and to work, but nowhere else, unless I take you. Is that clear?"

"Yes, Ma'am."

"And I want to know where you were last night, and where you've been going when you told me you couldn't sleep." I took a deep breath and went on, softening my tone. "David, I hope you'll be truthful with me because this kind of behavior can lead to some really dangerous things."

"I was just riding my bike, Ma'am." He was being much too polite.

"Were you seeing Sherrie?" I asked.

"Oh no. Her mother wouldn't let her go out so late," he assured me.

I wondered how old he'd been when he had quit thinking I was the smartest person in the world and had started believing I was the dumbest. I said to him, "David, I'm going to be waiting for you to tell me the whole truth."

Occasionally, some of "my girls" told me that they'd had a religious conversion while they were working the street. Some had become believers after watching a TV evangelist, and others had accepted Christ through a street ministry. This was not the blessing it might seem. The other side of the story was that they then began to pray that God would send them a trick so they could have a place to sleep that night, or they'd pray for drug money, so they could go home and have a fix in the morning. These were very sincere individuals, and I grieved for them, because what they needed was help to get out of the life—not a quick fix.

A few weeks after my encounter with David, I had to drop off Violet Morgan, another one of my clients, at the County

Hospital. Sitting there with her, I realized I was going to be late picking up my daughter Claire. When I arrived at her school, I saw her foot tapping angrily, and I felt a knot form in my stomach.

"I'm sorry," I apologized to my daughter as she slammed the door. "I had to drop off Violet Morgan. She's coughing up some blood, and I took her to the hospital and had to check her in before I came here."

"Geez, Mom," Claire fumed. "Don't you ever get tired of helping these people? They only go back to the street!"

Suddenly it struck me that my children only saw the crises in my work. It was time they saw some victories.

"Claire, I'm sorry. You and David and Darroll have only seen the worst parts of my work. I haven't shared the successes I see every day," I said. "How would you like to see for yourself what it's like to sponsor someone who really does leave prostitution?"

"Whom?" she asked bluntly.

I knew she was interested, or she would have declined my offer, so I told her about a new client for whom I'd been seeking a sponsor. It may seem that a streetwalker is an unfit companion for one's children, but Libby Walters was an exceptional young woman. I'd been impressed by her quick mind, her determination, and her courage.

"Libby's eighteen years old," I told Claire. "She was working the street one evening when she was approached by a street evangelist. When the young man shared his beliefs with her, Libby confronted him. 'Will you give me a place to live and get me a job if I leave the street?' she demanded.

"Thankfully," I continued, "the young man promised to do as she asked, and she agreed to meet him at a restaurant called Danny's in an hour. Then he ran to the phone and called his pastor, who referred him to me.

"Well, an hour later, I met Libby. She was what we call a 'victim prostitute.' She wanted very much to leave the life and become an attorney. She's only a few years older than you, and

I've been helping her get ready to take her GED so she'll be able to begin college in the fall. You're so very good in school, Claire. Would you take over tutoring, Libby?"

Claire nodded.

The match was perfect. The girls got along well. Claire came to me several weeks later. "Mom, I was wrong. I've learned that there is hope for 'our girls.' I know Libby is going to make it."

And she did. With Claire's help she passed the exam. And then she found her birth father living in another state. The next fall she moved in with him and began college.

Not all my cases went so smoothly.

I met Margaret Holman late that September. She was a pathetic figure: her mother had died when she was very young. She'd finished only the second grade and had been a streetwalker since she was twelve years old. At twenty-three she was an alcoholic.

Though Margaret clearly seemed in rough shape, she too wanted to go back to school, and I realized it was my only hope of helping her. We ordered her birth certificate immediately to get identification, because she couldn't start school without it, and she would also need it for a social security card to get a job. Even before the birth certificate arrived, I insisted Maggie go to job interviews.

One afternoon I picked her up at McDonald's, where she had put in an application. To my utter astonishment, she had fuzzy red bedroom slippers on her feet!

"You need to wear shoes to interviews, Maggie," I chided gently as she got into the car.

"They don't look at your feet," she rejoined.

Poor Maggie! It was true that men who hired her as a prostitute probably didn't care what she wore on her feet, but, as I tried to explain, in a straight job people care how you look. I sighed looking at her.

In addition to her sloppy appearance, Margaret's health was poor from years of drinking. Between job interviews, I asked Jerry Hudson to take her to a doctor's appointment. Maggie was frustrated with several weeks of disappointments and worried because her birth certificate hadn't yet arrived. As Jerry waited for a traffic light to change, she pointed to a neighborhood bar.

"Let's forget the whole thing and go have a drink," Margaret suggested hopefully.

Jerry refused politely and took her to the doctor. That evening, he phoned me. "I've never turned a girl down for a drink before!"

Unfortunately, Maggie gave up several days later and disappeared. Two days after she left, her birth certificate arrived and, within a week, three prospective employers called with job offers for her. I was disappointed and hoped she would get in touch with me again.

I didn't have time to dwell on such thoughts. More and more prostitutes were calling me. Emerald Harbison read about Project New Life in the newspaper. Like other upper income prostitutes who called me, she wondered if we helped only streetwalkers. "I began by trying to help streetwalkers, but I want to work with all prostitutes who want to change their lives," I answered honestly.

The next day we met. Emerald got her name from her eyes, which were deep, clear green. Her black hair was shoulder length, and her beauty was striking. She had the same kind of grace that Christine Mayer did, and I couldn't help thinking about my friend when I saw her, but the resemblance was only superficial. Whereas Christine was affable, artistic, and caring, Emerald was businesslike and analytical.

She was one of the 5 percent of prostitutes—the very top call girls and gigolos—who don't have pimps. It was a relief to know I wouldn't have to deal with another one of those barracudas this time, but there were other kinds of predators in the vast sea of prostitution. Pimps and johns weren't the only vicious species these young women encountered.

Emerald was forthright and not shy. "What do you do?" she asked.

"That depends. What do you do?" I shot back with humor in my voice.

"I'm a call girl. I don't have a pimp. I'm thirty-two."

"What are your reasons for wanting to leave the life? I need to understand your motives so we can work together on goals." I began with my usual opening.

As though her thoughts had been welling up inside her for a long time, Emerald began to quickly speak. "I've been planning this for a long time," she replied. "I've been taking classes at the University, and I'm getting my degree in Business Administration next spring. One of the things I've been thinking about is what do I tell a prospective employer about the last thirteen years of my life?"

She didn't wait for me to answer.

"Also, I've been seeing a guy I really like, and he doesn't know I'm a call girl. Should I tell him before we get too serious about each other? I don't want to lose him."

With only a slight pause to catch her breath, she rushed on. "Sometimes I worry about getting arrested. What would I do? I couldn't stand to have a record. I've never even gotten a traffic ticket, and what about my chances to have a business career? That would finish them."

"Emerald," I broke in gently, "I've run across these problems before. If you really want to pursue a future career and to get out of the life, it's possible, believe me."

"I don't want anyone to know I'm a prostitute," she said. She was polite but obviously worried. "What if people see me with you?"

I had to laugh. "I'm not that well known! The press doesn't

follow me around," I assured her. "I'll tell you what—there are several businesses which have volunteered office space to my project. I'll contact one of them and ask for a meeting room instead. That way we'll just be two women who happen to enter an office at the same time."

Emerald agreed to this, and we met a week later in a conference room across town.

Whenever I met with her, I felt as if I could have been meeting with a chairperson of the board. She would present ideas, listen to my comments, then weigh and decide what she would do. I was a listening post and a sounding board, and I was fascinated.

Developing our relationship took time and while it progressed I was meeting and attending to other prostitutes who also wanted to change their lives.

Sarah Flowers, like her sponsor Christine Mayer, came from a religious background, and they had begun attending church together recently. One day Sarah announced happily, "I'm going to have my baby, Dustin, baptized. I'm going to talk to the pastor at my mother's church this afternoon," Sarah went on. "Will you come to the ceremony?"

"I'll do so gladly," I said smiling. She and Christine left my house a little while later with their babies and promised to call when the christening date had been set.

Sarah phoned later that afternoon, but her voice sounded lost and drained.

"What's the matter?" I asked, concerned.

Her voice broke as she told me. "The pastor said it wouldn't be right to baptize a whore's bastard."

A "chickenhawk" is a pimp who victimizes young boys. These men are like moray eels, which suddenly pop out of their hiding places with gaping jaws to inflict deadly wounds.

Chickenhawks recruit young teenage males who spend a

great deal of time alone at parks, arcades, shopping malls, and movie theaters. They befriend youngsters, invite them home, and eventually introduce them to liquor, drugs, and sex.

I received a phone call from one of Jack Keats' boys, Tim Campbell, in July. While he professed to be sick of working as a bathhouse prostitute, he also admitted to being too afraid of his pimp to leave.

"Jack has had some of the 'boys' killed when they've tried to leave him—even when they moved to other cities," Tim told me. "He owns gay whorehouses around the country. I was hoping you could help me."

"I'm not sure I can help you, Tim," I apologized. "I need to know if you understand the ramifications of what you're asking. You would have to leave everyone and everything you know, assume a new identity, and have absolutely no communication with any friends or relatives. Are you willing to start a new life?"

Crossing a chickenhawk as dangerous as Jack Keats could be fatal, but I didn't want to refuse to help Tim, either.

"I don't know," he replied nervously.

"Your only alternative is to go to the police, tell them everything, and place yourself under their protection," I said. "I'll go with you if it will help," I added.

"I can't," Tim sobbed miserably. "Some of my clients are cops."

Because he wasn't certain he was emotionally strong enough to assume a new identity, I couldn't risk hiding Tim with the underground railroad we had established: there were too many lives at stake. I never heard from him again.

My daughter Claire came home the day after I met Tim with a happy announcement. "My essay on Harriet Tubman's role in the Civil War won first place in the student writing contest." With a great deal of pride, I accompanied her to a local television station, where she appeared on a talk show to receive her prize.

One of the segments on that morning's show featured Denny Altmann, a former hit man, who was promoting his auto-biography. I watched in fascination from the audience as he told of his life, his training in assassination, of his former life as president of the Iron Eagles, and his new mission to divert kids from gangs. At the end of the broadcast when we were introduced I invited Denny to make a return visit to our city.

During the summer, he called and said he planned to be in Southern California later that year and asked me to arrange conferences and radio and television appearances for him.

"Becky," Denny added seriously, "there's something else I have to tell you. I have a price on my head. The Iron Eagles want me dead, because I know too much."

"Your message is too important to me to let a contract stop me, Denny," I assured him.

My courage sprang from naivete. Later I was to learn just how dangerous criminal brotherhoods could be.

Success for Sam continued to mean two steps forward and one step back. While she served her jail sentences, she took classes for high school credit. However, her academic progress was a kind of compromise: although she wasn't able to leave prostitution, she did get an education. Upon her release from jail, however, her scholastic endeavors left her hungry for a better life.

After her nearly disastrous overdose of heroin in March, Sam faithfully participated in a methadone program. One day in April, Ginger Pettit spoke excitedly about a new drug, less expensive than heroin and not as addicting. Sam had nothing against getting high—in fact, she was all for it—but she couldn't risk it while she used methadone, because of the weekly urine analyses. Ginger had a couple of doses of the new drug combination, called "loads," which was made up of two prescription drugs, codeine and doriden, a schedule three controlled substance sleeping pill, and she shared them willingly with Sam.

Loads proved the undoing of many of the heroin-addicted prostitutes in our community. It was an extremely potent combination which enabled the user to function in a zombie-like state for eight to twelve hours. Addicts who had been promised a cheap, harmless substitute for heroin now found themselves in a constant state of somnambulation, with little or no appetite and declining health. They were completely unaware of their surroundings. Seizures plagued those who waited too long for their doses, or who tried to withdraw from loads.

The police often arrested streetwalkers for jaywalking violations or blocking the sidewalk, held them three days, and then released them without pressing charges, which was entirely legal under a law that a person had to be charged within seventy-two hours or released. In this way, officials hoping to persuade prostitutes to leave the city could harass them at a reduced cost to the overburdened judicial system. With the advent of loads, however, this became a dangerous policy, because of the severe withdrawals experienced by addicts. A few women died, and some suffered permanent brain damage from seizures while in detention.

In July, Samantha called to ask me to accompany her to court where she was to be tried on a prostitution charge. I was very anxious that she be acquitted, partly because I knew the futility of jailing streetwalkers, but mostly because I was worried about her abrupt withdrawal from loads. There was nothing I could do to help her legally, and she had a court-appointed attorney, but I prayed for her and went to court to show my support.

The eight men and four women on the jury listened carefully and sat poker-faced throughout the proceedings. I was uncomfortable hearing the officer who had arrested Sam describe the sexual activities he had witnessed because Samantha had never discussed her on-the-job sex with me. I had no clue what the jury was thinking while they listened to the testimony.

Sam's attorney, a handsome, slender, silver-haired, silver-tongued man in his early thirties, eloquently closed his arguments with, "Ladies and gentlemen of the jury, it is not up to you to judge Samantha Rice's morals: there is a Higher Judge Who will someday do that. Your job today is to decide whether she is guilty of prostitution, according to the laws of man. Did money change hands between Samantha and her lover, or was their passion, as she has testified, merely an afternoon tryst?"

The jury left the courtroom after the closing arguments. Twenty minutes later, they returned. Sam and I held our breath as the foreman, a portly man in a sports coat and wide necktie, rose to read the verdict. When he didn't even glance at Sam, my heart thundered so loudly I could hardly hear his words.

"Not guilty."

As we left the courtroom, I whispered to her, "Thank God!"

"I don't know if it was God, Becky," Sam said thoughtfully. "The foreman of the jury is one of my regular customers."

The men at David's after school job called me "The Warden."

"Ah, c'mon, Becky," Ted, the boss, pleaded. "I sneaked out at night, too, when I was a kid. It's not so terrible. Let up on David."

Ted and his manager Lee had been taking turns telling me they desperately needed David's help after work, but I knew very well the two, who were really good guys, were just trying to give David a break from his over protective mother who had imposed three months' restriction on him. I pretended to believe they needed David because I knew my son needed male models, but I couldn't actually relent. David's lack of internal controls made my external prohibitions necessary. I was accustomed to people thinking I was too hard on him, but I knew they wouldn't feel that way if they had a hyperactive child.

David and Lee adored each other. Lee was the father David missed, and David was the son the thirty-two-year-old bachelor never had. I approved of their friendship, but when Claire and I returned home one evening from picking Darroll up at summer camp in the mountains, I was angry to find that my older son had gone to Lee's house without permission.

I immediately drove the twenty-five miles to Lee's house in the country, confronted David and sent him to the car, then told the man who had become his friend that I'd like to have a serious discussion with him. We went into the kitchen because his house mates were watching television, and I wanted to bawl him out. He obviously realized this, as he sat ramrod straight on his chair across the table from me.

"Lee, David didn't ask me if he could come here tonight. I expected him to be at home when we returned, and he knew very well he was still under restriction," I began.

"He only has a week to go," Lee offered in a conciliatory tone.

I reached across the table and laid my hand on his.

"Look, Lee," I pleaded earnestly. "I really like you, and my son likes you, but he's playing us against each other, and I need your cooperation. We've got to be partners in this, because David expects you to get me to let him do what he wants. I'm not being mean to him. I've raised him all by myself, and I don't have anybody to back up my authority, so I have to be strict. Please help me." Lee placed his other hand over mine gently. Suddenly, a tangible warmth permeated the air around us, as if we were alone on a tropical island.

I knew he felt it, too, but, looking into my eyes, he said only, "I will, Becky." Then getting up, he walked me to the car where David was waiting.

A week later, Lee called to ask me to have dinner with him.

5

A VERY IMPORTANT DATE

On the appointed day, I looked at my watch: one o'clock. The heat of the Southern California afternoon danced in little ripples off the cement around the pool outside the sliding glass door. This evening I had a date with Lee, but there would be time for a swim first.

Rrrring.

The phone disturbed my afternoon reverie. Outside my window, the pool beckoned, cool and blue in the hot August sun.

Rrrring.

Swimming would have to wait.

"Hello."

"I hear you help prostitutes." The voice was young, female, husky. The slight timidity of her tone told me she was probably a streetwalker. The huskiness indicated she might be a heroin user. I put on a vocal smile: she needed a friendly response.

"Yes, I do. Tell me a little about yourself."

"I'm a prostitute. I'm twenty-five. I use heroin. I'm pregnant." Almost as an afterthought, she added, "My name's Melissa."

Another drug-addicted baby on the way. It was the third time this month that a pregnant prostitute had called me. I hoped she'd be a good candidate for my program, but I had to know more about Melissa first.

Quickly, I found out that her baby was due in three weeks, that she had last shot up a gram of heroin a few hours before, and that she had only been using hard drugs since her two older children had been taken away by Child Protective Services, in February. Well, at least I knew why she had chosen to telephone me now. CPS was probably initiating an action to remove the children permanently so they could be adopted. This was the usual procedure after six months of little or no progress by the parents.

"Why were your kids taken away, Melissa?" I asked. Although it was probably too late to help the older children, I needed to determine whether she could care for a newborn.

She choked on tears as she told me. "When I rented an old house last February, a social worker came before I could even unpack. The place was filthy, and she said my children couldn't live in that mess. I cleaned the house, but I had to wait thirty days to go to court for the kids, and welfare had cut off my money by then. The judge said I had to get a job before I could have my babies back. I couldn't pay the rent without welfare. I've never had a job."

That was plausible. I'd certainly heard enough versions of that story before, but someone had to have filed a complaint for CPS to have visited the family. The question was why.

"Where are you living now?" I asked her.

"With Gary. He's sort of my boyfriend. I lived with him for a while before CPS took my children away, but he sells drugs, and he wants me to work the street. That's why I rented a house, because I didn't want my kids to be around drugs. I'm only living with him now because I don't have any place else to stay."

I was willing to bet that Gary had called CPS himself. He didn't want to lose Melissa's prostitution income. He had probably given her heroin to "ease the pain" of losing her kids, igniting the fires of addiction to keep her from taking steps to get the kids back.

"Couldn't you live with your family until the baby comes?" I asked, wanting to find out more. If she were a criminal prostitute, a streetwalker who used prostitution only to support her drug habit, her family probably wouldn't let her near them, and if she were a victim prostitute, she would likely be better off without them.

"My dad died three years ago," the husky voice replied. "My brother hates junkies, and I don't want to stay with my mom, because her husband molested my sisters and me when we were little."

There was that elusive clue. Melissa had been molested as a child: she was probably a victim prostitute. Eighty percent of all streetwalkers begin their careers between ages twelve and fifteen when they run away from molestation, abuse, or neglect at home.

"How can I help you, Melissa?" I felt sympathetically toward her and hoped she would say exactly what she did.

Her voice grew soft and childlike. "I want to quit using drugs and get my kids back. I don't want to work the street any more."

Listening to her earnest voice, I wanted to shout, Yes! Now I knew Melissa had the desire to change. The first problem would be to find her a place to stay. I reviewed my files looking for a volunteer. My primary concern would have to be for Melissa's baby. There was no one available that day.

"Melissa, I'm going to call the head social worker at the County Hospital. Stay on the phone, and I'll three-way the call so we can all talk. She can get you help withdrawing from drugs before the baby comes," I told her. The baby would be born addicted even if the mother gave up heroin at this late date, but maybe the withdrawal trauma wouldn't be so severe.

"I'm using a business phone, and I have to hang up," Melissa said. "Could I come to your office?"

She didn't know it but my "office" was my kitchen table and a desk in the den off the living room where my files were stored. If I had to bring clients to my home, I greatly preferred to have worked with them for a month or two so I could get to know them, but that wasn't possible in this case. Oh well. "I'll pick you up. Where are you?" My children and I were growing used to emergencies by now. With any luck, I would have this woman settled in a hospital bed before they got home from school.

When I returned home with my pregnant client, I got her settled on the couch while I phoned Kaylee Mills at the County Hospital. When we discovered that Melissa had recently gotten medical coupons, Kaylee was immediately able to procure a bed for her. There she could detox in relative safety.

Melissa wanted me to stay at the hospital with her while she was being admitted and, afterwards, while the various medical equipment was being hooked up. So I waited while my client donned a hospital gown and then watched as a nurse attached a fetal monitor to her huge belly. A tiny hand or foot hit at the belt, and, with a smile, the nurse adjusted the straps.

An hour passed as we talked about her goals, and I made notes. Melissa seemed relaxed. When the nurse returned to read the printout from the monitor, she turned to Melissa in astonishment.

"Don't you know you're in labor?" the nurse demanded.

"I am?" Melissa seemed quite surprised.

It was the heroin. Narcotics users never knew they were in labor until they were close to delivery.

I glanced at the clock on the wall—five o'clock. I had my date for dinner with Lee at six. My prostitutes always had their own schedule, and it usually preempted mine, but tonight was different. Ironically, considering the work I was doing, I myself didn't get many chances to date nowadays, and tonight was an exception I'd been looking forward to. I didn't want to have to telephone the guy and say, "Sorry, but I picked up a prostitute this afternoon, and she had to make a delivery . . ."

Once Melissa had been taken care of, I hurried home in the afternoon traffic. The August heat wafted up among the cars in waves. I turned the air conditioner up and tried to slow my racing mind. I knew Melissa would give birth to a heroin-addicted baby, and I would have to find a place for them to stay. It was too late to do that tonight, I told myself. I tried to concentrate on my upcoming date with Lee. I wouldn't have much fun, or be good company, if I kept thinking about my client. I pulled into the driveway. My daughter Claire was sitting in the window seat in the second floor bedroom. Her hair, of the darkest brown, hung in curls over her shoulders. She was playing the guitar. I could hear classical music from behind the closed window, and I strained to listen. Was it Bach, Mendelssohn, Beethoven?

As I walked in the front door, I realized Lee hadn't mentioned where he was taking me for dinner, so I decided to ask Claire for fashion advice.

"You don't even know where he's taking you?" My daughter acted exasperated.

"That's why I need your help," I confessed.

She dropped her teenage arrogance and became enthusiastic about choosing my attire. "How about your black silk dress—the one with the pink flowers? You can wear your pearl earrings and . . . "

"Okay. The black dress is fine. Would you just pick out the accessories? I still have to shower and do my makeup, and," I glanced at my watch, "I only have about fifteen minutes."

Quickly, I undressed and jumped into the shower. By the time I got out of the bathroom, Claire had everything laid on my bed, and I finished dressing with two minutes to spare.

Soon Lee arrived in white dress jeans and a blue shirt. His wavy brown hair was still damp from his shower, and a faint fragrance conjured up a mixture of woods, leather and horses. I hadn't realized until then how handsome he was.

During the evening that followed, I tried to put Melissa— in labor at the hospital—out of my mind and to concentrate on how lucky I was to have such an attractive escort. But the thought of the heroin-addicted baby she would bear kept returning. Despite Lee's company that night, my heart ached for the tiny person who would soon be going through the pain of withdrawal.

In the middle of dinner I could stand it no longer. I excused myself and called the hospital. Melissa had given birth to a girl. Somehow I felt relieved just knowing the baby was no longer actively ingesting the drug. I returned to the table determined to get to know Lee better.

The following afternoon, Melissa phoned to tell me she had named her baby Laura. "Please come to the hospital," she begged. I set aside my work and went to visit her.

Before going to Melissa's room, I stopped at the nursery and found the bassinet with little Laura. She was trembling and screaming. A nurse picked her up and rocked her in a vain attempt to comfort her tiny pain-wracked body. Distressed, I turned away and quickly walked to my client's room.

"I just saw your baby, Melissa," I said, unable to keep my voice calm.

"Becky! The baby's so sick." I stopped. Melissa didn't look very well herself. Her golden hair was disheveled, her skin was pale, and dark circles had formed beneath her eyes.

I pulled the single chair closer to her bed. "Melissa, are you still determined to get off drugs and get your children back?" I asked. It was hard to smile when I had just seen what Melissa's drug use had done to her baby, so I didn't even try.

She stared out the window for several minutes while I waited silently. When she turned back, her eyes brimmed with tears.

"I didn't know it would be so bad for her, Becky. I wish I could make it up to Laura. I'm ready to do anything to get out," Melissa offered.

"I'm glad," I said softly. "I'll help you do it." My words were upbeat, but I wished it were that simple. I didn't even know if I could find a place for them to live.

On the way home from the hospital, I stopped at the neighborhood market for steaks and salad makings. Lee and I had arranged another date at my house that evening, so he could meet Claire and Darroll.

I had been a single parent for nearly ten years. The men I had gone out with in the first years after my divorce had been disappointing. During the past three years, I had seldom dated at all.

The kids hadn't gotten home yet when I arrived at the house, so I put away my paperwork and started vacuuming. A few minutes later, the phone rang.

"Becky, is that you?" a raspy voice hiccuped when I answered.

"Who is this?" I replied cautiously, realizing the sound of drunkenness.

"It's me, Margaret. How you doin'?"

Margaret Holman! She had left the program six weeks earlier, and I hadn't heard from her since. I had wondered what had happened to her.

"I'm okay, Maggie. What's up?" I was noncommittal.

"Becky, will you come and get me? I've been drinkin' ever since I last saw you, and I need help."

I didn't usually rescue people from problems they had made for themselves, but Margaret sounded sick.

"All right," I sighed. "Where are you?"

"I'm at the Red Rock Motel in Eagle Crest. Room 216."

All the way across town! I looked at my watch—four o'clock. I'd be fighting the evening traffic, but I had to go. "I'll be there in half an hour. Get ready," I told her without enthusiasm.

It wasn't that I didn't want to help, but why couldn't she have called earlier?

I found the motel below a neon sign which advertised, "ADULT MOVIES" and "ROOMS BY THE HOUR" beneath "Red Rock Motel." It was in a rundown section of town amid sleazy adults-only theaters and topless booze joints.

Maggie opened the door of 216 as I raised my hand to knock. Apparently she'd been watching for me. I walked into the shabby room with its tattered drapes and filthy carpet. A bottle of scotch sat, unopened, next to the TV. More distressing to me was the moon-faced woman with bloated body who stood before me. She looked fifteen years older than when I had last seen her six weeks earlier. She gave me the scotch and a twenty-dollar bill for safekeeping. Once outside, I helped her into my car and began the crosstown drive through heavy traffic. I debated whether to take her to "Detox" (a non-medical detoxification facility) or to a hospital. At last, I decided to call an alcoholism counselor for advice, and we headed to my home.

As I pulled into the driveway, I was chagrined to see Lee's car already parked in front. In the midst of Margaret Holman's crisis, I'd forgotten all about our date. All he knew about my work was the little we had discussed the night before. I certainly didn't want to introduce him to it so soon but I had no choice.

I took Maggie into the house, where my children were visiting with Lee. He was obviously surprised by my choice of a companion but rebounded quickly.

"I was a paramedic for several years, Becky, and, in my professional judgment, your friend needs a hospital. Why don't we go in my car?" Lee offered gallantly.

I nodded, grateful for the help.

When Claire saw the shape Maggie was in, she ushered Darroll and David into their rooms, aware that I was uncomfortable having her younger brothers being exposed to this sort of thing. In a moment, she returned to the living room and suggested that she take the boys out for hamburgers and a movie while I dealt with this latest problem. I quickly handed her my keys and some money, then helped Lee maneuver Maggie to his car.

At the hospital, the emergency staff insisted that I remain until Margaret had been examined. Lee and I walked outside to the garden area, where we watched visitors bring in magazines and flowers, and saw the flashing lights of ambulances arriving. My family doctor waved as he walked by, en route to making his evening rounds. As we waited, the sky grew purple, and stars began to twinkle. Twilight crept slowly up the eastern horizon. Lee and I talked about everything and nothing at all. Just as the velvet blackness of evening began to enfold us, a nurse signaled us in to talk with the doctor. A middle-aged man with a receding hairline, he looked officious in a white jacket.

Are you Margaret Holman's family?" he asked.

"She's my mother," Maggie grunted before I could answer. Streetwalkers often claimed such invalid relationships. It seemed to comfort them in difficult situations. Sometimes the words elicited snide remarks or angry glares, especially when I was the same age, or a different race, but this doctor only raised an amused eyebrow in response to her comment.

"I'm sending Ms. Holman home tonight. I've called the County Hospital, and they'll admit her to their detox tomorrow morning. Can you take her there?"

I knew this game. Small hospitals always sent charity cases to the overburdened facility and if there was intervening time tried to palm off the patients on whoever was available.

"Doctor, I wouldn't know what to do in an emergency," I said. "Can't you keep her here overnight?" My protest probably wouldn't do any good but I had to try. Meanwhile, Maggie began to hallucinate. Sitting on the edge of the gurney, she started swatting imaginary flies.

Looking at her, the doctor shook his head negatively. "I don't expect any problems, but keep an eye on her respiration and heart rate. The nurse will give you instructions. If there's an emergency, you can always bring her back here or call nine-one-one." He jumped up from his metal and Naugahyde stool and quickly made his escape.

Sighing, I signed the discharge papers. Then I watched with resignation as my date tried to guide Maggie to his car. She reeled and staggered through the parking lot until she collapsed face down on the trunk of Lee's gigantic Oldsmobile. Seemingly nonplussed, Lee unlocked the back door, gathered her gallantly in his arms and placed her firmly on the back seat. Next, he opened my door and smilingly gestured me inside.

I definitely want to get to know this guy better, I thought.

"I'm starving!" Lee exclaimed as he got into the driver's seat, turned the key on, and started the car.

"Me too!" came a cavernous voice from the back seat.

I looked lingeringly at Lee, wondering when his tolerance would end. Would our relationship be over before it began?

Lee stopped at a Mexican fast food restaurant on the way home and bought takeout. When we arrived at my house, however, I realized Claire had my house keys, which were on the same ring with my car keys. All the doors were locked so we sat on the front lawn under the olive tree and ate taquitos while Maggie swatted invisible flies. Suddenly, announcing that she had to go to the bathroom, she dropped her slacks and urinated on the grass. At that point, Lee seemed to be struggling to maintain his composure, and I mentally kissed our future goodbye as I silently gave thanks that at least it was too dark for the neighbors to view this spectacle.

Finally, about thirty minutes later, the kids arrived. I guided Margaret into our living room where she tottered over to the couch and fell down on it.

"What's wrong with her, Mom?" Darroll wanted to know. He was dressed in his GI Joe fatigues, and I couldn't help thinking that his cartoon hero had never faced this kind of problem.

"She's been drinking, honey. That's what happens to people when they drink too much," I explained gently.

I hated for my kids to see this. Damn it! Somehow, some way, I intended to open a halfway house for these women, but, for now, if I didn't help them, no one else would.

The boys went to bed, and Claire went to her room to finish a book she'd been reading. Lee and I were left alone with Maggie and her flies. Because of the children and Maggie's condition, I didn't want to be left alone in the house with Maggie, and, since, after tonight's fiasco, I never expected to see him again, I decided I might as well take advantage of Lee.

"I know you'll think I'm crazy but is it possible you could spend the night?" I asked softly.

Lee looked a little surprised.

"I won't know what to do if Maggie's sick," I rushed to explain, "but you've been a paramedic. I have a sphygmomanometer and a stethoscope: will you stay? David has some pajamas you can borrow, and I'll make up the hide-a-bed in the office."

Maybe he felt sorry for me, or perhaps it was just too late to drive the twenty-five miles home, but he agreed. I felt more relaxed with him there and finally went up to get some sleep. Through the thin walls we could all hear occasional outbursts of incoherent speech from Maggie during the hours that followed. Eventually, morning came. Lee and I rose at dawn to drive her to the County Hospital. Once again we were instructed to wait while she was admitted through the emergency room.

I walked over to the vending machine, got two paper cups of the metallic tasting coffee, and brought one over to Lee. As we sat in the waiting room, I wondered what he must think of me. I was pretty sure he'd never had another date like this.

Just as we were finishing the sickly brown brew, Margaret exploded through the swinging doors. She stormed out the side entrance of the hospital with Lee and me in pursuit.

"Hey, Maggie, what's going on?" I called after her.

"They wanted to take my temperature again. I told them they took it last night, and I'm not sick. I'm detoxing!" she raged.

I understood her seemingly inexplicable response. Streetwalkers who were confronted by authority figures often fought them. To them, power meant abuse, as in molesters, pimps, and police. Unfortunately, that attitude spilled over onto other people like nurses, doctors, and teachers.

"Honey, they have to determine you physical condition before they admit you," I tried to explain, but Margaret would have none of it. She marched down a garden path between hospital buildings.

"Stay here," Lee ordered and followed my errant client.

Since I couldn't think of anything better to do, I sat on a cold stone bench. In a moment, I heard shouting from behind the building where Maggie and Lee had disappeared.

"Just give me my money, and I'll take care of myself!"

"We can't do that, Margaret. You're sick, and you need help."

"Then I'll go earn some money!"

"Have you looked in a mirror lately? No man is going to pick you up."

Silence.

Thirty seconds later, Maggie stomped past me and back through the emergency room entrance. Lee walked toward me, his hands held high in a gesture of non-comprehension. Before he could speak, however, my client burst out of the doors again.

"Well, are you coming?" she demanded, immediately turning and walking back inside.

Finally, Maggie was admitted to the detox unit. Lee and I started back to my house. All the way home, I looked at his handsome face, those green eyes, that pointed little nose, his thick brown mustache, and wondered if I had let a drunken prostitute ruin my chance with the most interesting man I'd met in a very long time.

In front of my house he opened the door to let me out. "If I hurry," he said, "I'll get to work on time." I nodded. Feeling I had to let him off the hook quickly, I thanked him and got out. As I reached the front door, Lee rolled down his window and called to me, "So what do you want to do tonight?"

My heart skipped a beat. "I'll make dinner!" I called back.

Lee nodded and drove off with a smile. As I opened the front door, I couldn't help the grin breaking upon my face like the morning sun.

6

I GET TO KNOW
MY ADVERSARIES

I was cheerfully doing my morning chores after we had left Margaret Holman at the County Hospital, thinking of tonight's dinner with Lee, when the phone rang.

"Becky," a tear-strained voice began when I answered. "This is Melissa Voorhees. Child Protective Services is going to take my baby away because she was born addicted, so I'm going to go to my sister's house in Reseda for a week to kick my heroin habit. I'd like to start your program when I come back, if that's okay."

By now, for me, it was a familiar story. Because of the efforts of the social service agencies, many of the drug addicted babies were being placed in foster homes.

"Sure. You can call me collect if you want," I offered. I knew she was probably going to return to her pimp, but, at least, I could offer my support if there was any chance she'd make a break.

A few hours later, Kaylee Mills, the chief social worker at the County Hospital, phoned. "We have Melissa's baby, but no Melissa!" she announced.

"She called to say that CPS wouldn't let her have the baby because it was addicted to heroin," I explained.

"No one told her that," Kaylee insisted.

In order to understand and help the prostitutes with which I dealt, I'd had to learn to put my middle class values aside. They live in a different world, with different rules, but in their environment their behaviors have a valid foundation, both reasonable and logical. Little Laura was a "trick baby," sired by one of Melissa's customers. In a prostitute's mind, the child of a pimp is wanted, valued, and loved, but the offspring of a john is one more abuse heaped upon her. This made Melissa feel ambivalently toward her infant. My client, unable to come to terms with her own rejection of little Laura, had convinced herself that the unwanted baby would be detained by the authorities. I fully expected Melissa to go back to the only world she knew.

To my surprise, Melissa returned the following week as she had promised, eager to begin her program. Without complaining, she made her bed on my living room sofa, because I couldn't get a shelter to accept a recovering addict.

This was the first time that I accepted one of the streetwalkers as a house guest on a long-term basis, but Melissa endeared herself to me and my children in a very short time. We called her "Missy Munchie," because she loved sugarcoated doughnuts. I assigned Darroll to teach her to make her bed and keep her living space neat. I figured she'd choose to do these things responsibly rather than suffer the embarrassment of having a nine-year-old show her twice.

Claire volunteered to drive Missy to visit her children in their foster homes. I appreciated my daughter's patience in taking time out of her busy schoolwork to show this important kindness to one of my clients. It gave me more time with David, which was especially important because, in desperation, I'd decided to home school him for his sophomore year. Like all parents, I'm sure my children are geniuses, but I couldn't have proven it of David by his grades, so I took matters into my own hands. While this added a tremendous amount of work to my schedule, it was very important to me.

Missy couldn't understand the need for taking medications as prescribed. Instead, she would ingest them in large amounts and far too frequently. My solution was to have David dole out her medications. I felt the responsibility would increase his self confidence. Since we were home schooling him, he was there during daytime hours, and he was bigger than Melissa. She accepted this with her usual good humor.

"Who's the kid, you or me?" she'd tease when he gave her the allotted doses.

Of course, this worked both ways. At times when I was called away from the house, Melissa took fiendish delight in seeing that my son did his schoolwork.

David's favorite pastime is "paybacks," a fact which Missy learned very early in their relationship. One night, when she had been with us for a week or two, David waited quietly in his room until he heard her turn off the television and go into the bathroom. He then rushed silently into the living room, snatched the remote control, and hid in my office with its open windows into the front room. When Melissa returned and laid down on the couch a few minutes later, he turned on the TV. When she sat up in surprise, he turned it off. On. Off. On. Off. Scared out of her wits, she ran to my room and walked in.

"Becky!" Melissa called in a frightened voice as she ran over to the bed in which I was asleep. As I awoke, she told me about the mysterious television.

A few seconds later, a laughing David joined us. "I did it!" he announced proudly.

"David! You scared me half to death!" she rebuked him. By now she was laughing herself.

I had no idea what was going on at that moment, but I assured myself that it meant Melissa was fitting in well with the family, and turned over to go back to sleep.

To the outside world our home life probably seemed strange with its unusual inhabitants, but helping others strengthened the bonds between Lee and me. We were now seeing each other every evening. During the summer months he liked to barbecue on the patio while the kids and I swam in the pool, but when autumn brought that activity to a halt we began to eat dinner indoors and then watch a video or help the kids with their studies, and take long walks together. Usually, Missy or some of my other clients were around, and they invariably shot Lee angry glances. One night when we were alone, he broached the subject.

"Why do your clients give me dirty looks?" he wanted to know.

"Because you're a trick," I answered candidly.

Deeply offended, Lee snapped, "I am not!"

"I know that, honey," I soothed. "But to the streetwalkers, all men are tricks, and they're afraid I'm going to marry a john."

Lee hadn't officially asked me to marry him. It was simply a foregone conclusion, and we talked about our eventual marriage naturally. This was extremely trying for my clients, because I was the first person besides their pimp who had cared for them, and they were afraid of losing my affection.

Melissa resolved her conflict with my love life by engaging in a romance of her own. She told me that she had a straight friend, a respectable psychologist in private practice, Dave Colchis, who was teaching her to read. Missy was quite impressed with him, but I soon began to think that he was a Harold the Helper, like Robert Kvale. Dave was an outspoken advocate of prostitution, and his comments were so articulate that he was solicited by the news media for debates.

I found out that Colchis had been dating whores up and down Wickersham Boulevard daily. So I gave no credence to his professed love for Missy.

Unfortunately, Melissa didn't realize what he was, and I

didn't feel I should tell her my observations. Her sweet nature, coupled with her illiteracy, interested Dr. Colchis immensely. He told her that his marriage had been "dead for years," promised to teach her to read, and someday, to marry her. Anyway, she accepted his infidelities as a part of male nature.

Since Melissa spoke highly of her family, I suggested to her that she phone her brother. Maybe, I hoped, if she renewed family ties, her relatives would encourage her to forget about the psychologist.

"My brother hates junkies," Missy told me sadly and declined to call him.

One evening in late September, though, I came home to find her grinning from ear to ear.

"I talked to my brother," she bubbled. "Twice in my life he's told me he loves me, and tonight was one of those times!"

I was deeply touched by her happiness, but when Melissa related that her brother was an Iron Eagle, known as "Cajun Devil" and that he wanted to visit her soon and meet the people who were helping her, I was less than enthusiastic. Denny Altmann was due to arrive at my home on October 9th for ten days of meetings that I had arranged, and the Iron Eagles had a contract out on his life.

On October 4th, motorcycles roared into my driveway. I ran to the front window and saw an assortment of bearded, tattooed riders, clad in tattered denim, making their way to my front door. Across the street, I saw my neighbor Alice White pull her curtains quickly closed. This business of helping prostitutes was taking an ominous turn. Nevertheless, I opened the door and weakly smiled a welcome to six dusty men covered with road grime. Melissa ran in from the backyard to greet her brother, whom she excitedly introduced.

I phoned Lee at work and informed him as calmly as I could that I had guests. "I'd appreciate your company as soon as possible," I said.

"And bring beer," I added, in what I hoped was a conspiratorial tone he would understand.

Claire came home shortly after the bikers arrived, and, with obvious delight at visiting with people so alien, joined us in the living room. Darroll, who had been swimming, dried off and made himself part of the unholy congregation. Lee and David left work an hour early and brought several six-packs.

Conversation during the ensuing evening was a bit rough, and my children learned some new words, but, otherwise, the bikers were the epitome of polite company. No one was raped, mugged, or murdered, much to my relief. Lee seemed to take it all in stride.

However, soon afterward, for Melissa's safety and our own, Jerry Hudson arranged for her to live with her girlfriend Audrey. While Denny Altmann visited, we didn't dare to take Missy into our confidence, but I'd assured her that Jerry would take charge of her program and that the change was only temporary because the house was too small to accommodate us all, and I had invited someone to visit before she'd come there. It was hard for her to change living environments, because we'd become family to her, but I thought it for the best.

Denny arrived with his bodyguard, Craig Cantrell, that Sunday. Lee and I met them at the airport. Although we'd never seen Craig, and I'd met Denny only once briefly, we recognized them immediately.

It was hard not to. Towering above the other passengers, Denny wore a Stetson under which his brown hair was pulled back in a pony tail. Cowboy boots added several inches to his already imposing six-foot-three frame. He was lean with granite-like features. Only the laugh lines around his eyes kept him from looking menacing. Craig was nearly Denny's height, but his body was muscular, his head was bald, and he wore one gold earring. I had a fleeting impression that I'd seen him in a cleaning product commercial.

That night Denny began talking about the current threat to his life. "I have never divulged gang secrets," he said, "but my knowledge of their inside operation makes me dangerous to the Iron Eagles." The former hit man had friends among various law enforcement agencies because he worked tirelessly to educate young people about the risks of gang involvement, and he spoke frequently to incarcerated juveniles to convince them to turn over a new leaf. I guess he detected my concern about our safety because he phoned an FBI agent whose name and number his local bureau had given him

"Okay," he said as he hung up the phone, "we got us protection."

We went outside where Lee was preparing the barbecue. Denny and Craig drank coffee at the picnic table while I chopped vegetables for a salad. We talked and got to know each other.

"I've spent many years as a high-ranking member of the Iron Eagles," Denny explained, looking over at me to see my reaction. When I evidenced none, he went on, "and Craig has been an FBI gang infiltrator." Together, they gave us a firsthand depiction of the almost unbelievable amount of power wielded by gangs.

Altmann's background included drug sales to dealers, gun running, control of his gang's prostitution and gambling rings, and training as a hit man. One of the most chilling aspects of Denny's cool, ruthless management of his state's chapter of the Iron Eagles was the invitation, by the club's national kingpins, to become a congressman. Gang funds, he was told, supported political campaigns. Denny had declined the invitation.

Craig had infiltrated the Iron Eagles and rode with them for eight years, providing information on their doings to the FBI. During the years that he traveled the Southwest with the club, he became familiar with their prostitution activities which helped finance their businesses: interstate and international transport of drugs and weapons. Prostitution money also helped pay for "protection" from many police agencies responsible for monitoring the routes, towns, cities, and borders through which gang members plied their illegal trades.

While Craig had always been on the side of the law, Denny's conversion was dramatic. "A bloody gang war erupted in Southern California between the Iron Eagles and the Speed Demons about six years ago," he told us. "The body count kept going up and up as members of the two clubs took vengeance on one another. I was brought in to commit two revenge killings, but when I arrived at the funeral of a brother Iron Eagle memories of my mother's prayers for me ran through my mind. By then I'd been a gang member for many years, and these murders were to have been my first 'hits,' so the other bikers were watching me closely. My escape from the brotherhood can only be termed a miracle." It was chilling to realize that only days before I'd entertained men who were sworn to kill him.

The next morning, Denny Altmann was scheduled to be the featured speaker on a local radio talk show. Lee, Craig, and I sat quietly in the studio as the calls came in hot and heavy for an hour before the show host announced a five minute break for news. As soon as the microphones were shut off the program director put through another call to Denny. He listened for a moment, then hung up and grabbed his hat.

"We have to get out of here right now. Agent Packard says the Iron Eagles are on their way over here!"

As we left, we could hear the announcer promising to continue the interview after the news break.

Lee ran out the front door of the building to get his car, while Craig herded Denny and me out the back. We sped away, down side streets, on a zigzag course to my house.

I said goodbye to Lee, who had to return to work, and put on a pot of coffee, but before it had finished brewing he was back.

"What are you doing here?" I asked, surprised.

"Four Iron Eagles entered the cocktail lounge across the street from the shop. Ted was afraid they were watching the shop for me! I told him it was probably just a coincidence, but he insisted I take the day off."

Denny and his bodyguard were inclined to agree with Ted's assessment. "I'm not afraid," I said in my usual naive manner. "Iron grillwork covers my doors and windows." Altmann laughed as he showed me how easily the gratings could be popped open. With that, our guests made other sleeping arrangements for the rest of their stay.

The week followed with meetings, radio programs, television shows, and SWAT team protection. On Friday evening, two corrections officers took Denny, Craig, and me forty miles out of town to a boys' detention facility, where eighty teenagers convicted of serious crimes were housed. For security, the FBI agent insisted that we take only one vehicle, so Lee stayed at the house with the kids. I was beginning to understand just how hazardous our situation was.

An agent in an unmarked car radioed our arrival at Highway 137, the long lonely road which ran five miles through wooded hills to the facility, where another agent greeted us and ushered us inside to the meeting room.

"What do you want me to do?" I whispered to Denny as he adjusted his microphone.

"Pray!" Altmann murmured.

Taking his advice, I sat on one of the folding chairs which had been placed against the wall while Craig conferred with the security personnel. It occurred to me that the meeting might run for an hour or more, but I was happy to have an ample opportunity to ask for divine assistance.

In a few minutes, teenagers began to enter the room. Some swaggered, with obvious chips on their young shoulders. Some looked around and, seeing Altmann, kept their eyes glued on him, obviously fascinated. Others sat off to the sides or in the back, attending obviously because they had been told to do so.

Denny brought the situation under his powerful sway in moments.

"You think you're tough because you're doing time here, but this ain't nothin'," he growled in his bass biker's voice. "If you go to prison, you'll find every guy in there wants to make you his girlfriend. If you're smart, you'll finish school, don't do drugs, and stay outta gangs. Let me tell you how it really is."

Ninety minutes soon passed, and as I looked around I saw every eye riveted on Denny. The boys went forward to speak to him afterward and told him what was on their minds. It was times like this that made me understand I was doing exactly what I was supposed to be doing, despite the dangers and the stress.

On our way back to the car, the warden stopped us.

"I want to thank you for telling it to these boys like it is," he said, shaking Denny's hand. "You may have saved them."

The next morning, I held a private meeting at my house for clients and volunteers of Project New Life. Lee and Claire had made refreshments the night before, and the boys were kept busy making and serving coffee as our guests arrived. Craig set up a projector while Denny got ready to deliver his most chilling presentation yet. When everyone had taken a seat, I introduced Altmann, then sat next to Lee. My children were waiting eagerly to hear our guest's story.

Denny spoke of his life as the president of the Michigan State Chapter of the Iron Eagles, and of his training as a hit man. Every person in the room paid rapt attention to what he said for an hour or more. Then he turned on the projector and began a slide show which vividly imprinted itself in our memories.

We saw a lovely young girl of about fourteen lying in bed next to a bearded biker, half her face blown away by the shotgun blast that left them dying in a pool of blood. A dismembered body lay stuffed in the trunk of an old Chevy, haphazardly covered with a sheet of transparent plastic. A whitewashed house, surrounded by a picket fence in a wooded setting, went up in flames, its eleven occupants only bits and pieces of flesh and bone in the aftermath of the explosion. The bodies of fifteen men and women lay strewn in crazy disarray, dead of machine gun fire. There were dozens more—all a pictorial testimony to the ruthlessness of gangs.

The slides had been taken by various law enforcement agencies as evidence of gang violence. Copies had been given to Denny Altmann by his supporters in law enforcement so that he could illustrate his comments when he spoke.

That evening, we attended yet another meeting with Denny Altmann and Craig Cantrell. Lee and I witnessed SWAT team members positioning themselves on the roofs of surrounding buildings as we entered the packed meeting house in a small mountain community. We took two of the last seats in the place and waited. By the time Denny walked to the podium, a crowd of eighty people stood in the aisles.

A hush fell upon the throng as Denny spoke in a steel edged tone. "Five years ago, I woulda soon as shot you as looked at you . . ."

It was inevitable that Melissa would learn of Denny's visit, because so many of my other clients attended his meetings. Missy understood the peril of entertaining a man with a price on his head, so she breathed a sigh of relief when he left and she was allowed to return to my house.

One afternoon in the week following Denny's departure, Claire drove Melissa to visit her children in their foster home. My daughter took a camera, and the two spent a happy afternoon with Missy's little ones. During the ride back to our house, in the best of moods, they giggled and chatted, but as they pulled into the driveway, their laughter stopped. The garage door was open, and David's body lay supine under it, with his head and upper torso at a grotesque angle. His skin was unnaturally pale, and blood dripped down his face from his mouth and nose. His sister jammed on the brake, and the girls sat for a moment transfixed. If they went into the house to call for help, would the same fate await them? Tense seconds passed as they hesitated. Fear grew upon them in a crescendo. Suddenly, a hand waved—David's hand. An impish grin broke upon his face, and Claire gunned the engine. My son lifted his flour-dusted and ketchup-stained face just in time to keep from meeting the windshield of my station wagon.

"Oh my God!" Melissa groaned, trembling from head to toe.

When I got home later, each of the trio related their version of the story, but my client added a tale of her own.

"There was a biker, a friend of my brother's," she confided, "who'd been an Iron Eagle for a long time, but he started shooting speed. The Iron Eagles don't let their members shoot drugs. They sell drugs, but they don't ever put needles in their own arms.

"One night, I saw him sitting in his pickup truck, drinking, so I said, 'Hi!' to him, and he said, 'Missy, they're gonna kill me 'cause I'm shootin' dope.' The next day, the police found him dead. They'd shot him in the head. When I saw David laying there all white, with blood on his face, I thought the Iron Eagles had killed him, and probably you, too, because of Denny Altmann."

She embraced me, her body wracked with sobs. My thoughts were churning. I had spent over a year working with streetwalkers and had hardly made a dent in the work needed. It was overwhelming and now, I was finding out, quite possibly dangerous. Should I quit while I was still alive? Was I placing my family in jeopardy? The memory of my prayers in the juvenile facility sustained me. I had to believe God's Hand was upon Project New Life.

7

NASTY PEOPLE

Thomas Reichmann approached the battered Chevy from the driver's side. He knew what he'd find: a whore bent low over the lap of her john, her blouse pulled up, engaged in a blow job. He watched quietly as the man, a skinny unkempt person in his early thirties with black horn-rimmed glasses, fondled the hooker's breasts. As the john groaned with his climax, Reichmann shined his policeman's flashlight in the window, which brought the couple immediately to an upright position.

"Let me see some ID," the officer thundered. It was all he could do to keep from laughing as the man fumbled for his wallet. He loved this game of interrupting while the john was cumming, before he paid the streetwalker.

"Here it is, Sir." The man's voice quavered.

Thomas shined his light on the proffered driver's license. He committed the name and address to memory. It might come in handy some day. Then he handed the ID back to the man and shined his light in the woman's face. "I need to see your ID, too."

"I don't have any," she spat defiantly.

"Get out of the car and step away from it, Ma'am," the bluesuit ordered.

Charlotte Coppersmith complied slowly. As she closed the door, Tom banged his flashlight on the roof of the car above the driver and said, "Get out of here, and if I ever catch you with a prostitute again, I'll run you in."

After the car drove quickly away, the officer turned to the woman. She was about nineteen, pretty, with dark eyes and auburn hair that fell to her shoulders. She wore no bra beneath her lacy blouse and her nipples showed plainly. She was in jeans and boots with a leather jacket for warmth on this cool evening.

"So what's your name, honey?" Thomas asked her as he moved closer.

"Carol," she said petulantly. She crossed her arms to hide her breasts from the cop's leering eyes.

He grabbed her hair and yanked her head back in one swift movement, which pulled her to his body. "I mean, what's your real name?" the bluesuit demanded.

"Charlotte," she said. She began to tremble.

Thomas liked the young ones. They struggled, but they were afraid of him, and he taught them to respect the law. "Do you want to go to jail tonight, Charlotte?" he asked her, his voice suggesting nothing.

"No," the redhead answered carefully.

"Get in the cruiser and gimme some head, and I'll think about it," Reichmann ordered.

They sat in the front seat of the patrol car, and Charlotte performed her fifth blow job of the evening. When she'd finished, Thomas let her go.

"See ya around, Charlotte," he said through his open window, as she stood hugging her jacket to herself in the cool night air.

A few evenings later, Officer Reichmann spotted Charlotte Coppersmith and another ho he knew well, Carrie Hope, in a fast food restaurant where they were talking together at a table. He pulled his patrol car into the parking lot, walked in, and joined them.

"Why don't you buy me a cup of coffee? Then we'll go for a little ride," he suggested to the pair as he sat at their table.

Charlotte paled a little, but Carrie answered, "I don't do that no more, Tom."

"You got religion or something?" the policeman sneered.

"No. I've got Project New Life. The people there are helping me get a job and get out of the life," she answered calmly.

Reichmann was interested in this. Who would help a ho?

"Tell me about it," he said. "Maybe I'll give them a call when I meet girls who want to get out of the business."

For half an hour, Carrie expounded excitedly about Becky Walden and her project, ending by giving both Charlotte Coppersmith and Thomas Reichmann Becky's phone number.

Carrie's story ended here, because she was going to live with her father the next day. Many of my clients who were illegitimate or came from families who'd split up fantasized that if only they could find their birth fathers (who had usually deserted the family), their father would take care of them. In the distant past, as small children, some had been "Daddy's girl." Then Daddy had left, and the stepfather or boyfriend who entered the picture had molested them. Most of these young women never found their fathers, but Carrie was one of the lucky ones. I would have preferred that she finish the program, because she'd be taking a long-term drug habit, lack of formal education, and fifteen years of street smarts to a small town in rural Oklahoma, but the most important thing was, she was getting out.

Both Charlotte Coppersmith and Thomas Reichmann phoned me that night. The cop was first.

"Is this Becky?" the deep authoritarian voice on the phone asked. I thought right away, police officer. Nevertheless, I wasn't taking any chances so soon after Denny Altmann's visit.

"Who is this, please?" I asked politely.

"I'm Thomas Reichmann, with the city police. Carrie Hope told me about your program. I see a lot of prostitutes on the street, and I'd like to help them. Maybe I can come by your place sometime," he suggested.

I always appreciated police officers who got involved. There were some terrific cops who brought girls to my door instead of taking them to jail. I agreed to meet Reichmann two evenings later.

Charlotte Coppersmith called me a few hours later. After introducing herself, she said, "By the way, did a cop named Reichenberger or Reichmann or something like that call you?"

"Yes. Did you tell him about Project New Life?" I asked, a little surprised.

"No way. He's bad news. Look, if we can meet tomorrow I'll tell you all about him."

"Do you want to come over tonight?" I asked.

"No, I'm beat. I have to get some sleep," she said wearily.

We made a date to meet the next afternoon.

At the meeting Charlotte related Reichmann's treatment of her.

"I know some cops will use their badges to get free sex, free drugs, and a lot of other things," I said disgustedly, "but this is the first time that I've been duped by one of these people." Still, there was nothing I could do about the meeting Reichmann and I had arranged. I couldn't let this guy know that I was on to him.

When the appointed evening came, Melissa had a dinner date with Dave Colchis. She was dressing when Reichmann, wearing his uniform, arrived. Although I already disliked him, I tried not to convey it as the officer asked about the women I was working with. As I still didn't completely trust my discretion, I let Lee explain what we hoped to accomplish with them. After ten minutes of conversation, the doorbell rang and Melissa came bounding out of the bathroom in a smart black dress, her golden mane a mass of soft curls. As she opened the door, Dave smiled a greeting to us, then a surprised look of recognition crossed his face as he saw the police officer sitting in the recliner. Missy grabbed his hand, and, without a backward glance, called "Goodbye" as she pulled Dr. Colchis down the garden path to his car.

An hour and a half later, the phone rang. It was Melissa, and she wanted to know if Officer Reichmann had left.

"Yes, he has, but how did you know who he was?" I asked.

"Dave told me. He wants to know if you're going to be awake when he brings me back at ten, because he wants to talk to you."

"Sure. Lee and I will both be here."

Two hours later, they were back. Dr. Colchis came right to the point.

"Thomas Reichmann is a sick and dangerous man," he told us. "He follows prostitutes when he sees them get a ride, and then he sneaks up on the john's car and watches him get his rocks off before he pulls his cop routine. That way, the ho doesn't get paid for her services. If they don't give him any trouble, he lets the john go and makes the girl give him head."

Melissa interrupted. "If Reichmann knows a hooker is gay, he rapes her with his nightstick or his flashlight. One woman I know said he used his gun to rape her."

My hand went to my chest, where my heart was beating rapidly. The doctor's eyebrows raised in an I-told-you-so look, and Lee turned pale, as I probably did.

"Why doesn't somebody turn him in?" I gasped.

"I know a couple of girls who threatened to, and he told them he'd kill them. I think he probably would, too," Colchis mused.

Needless to say, I avoided Thomas Reichmann like the plague, but that wasn't the last time I saw him.

A short time after Melissa returned to live in my home, I realized that she was using drugs again. It was no mystery to me where she was getting them. It had to be Dr. Colchis. He resided less than one mile from his office. Because he was home at odd hours of the day, he used a phone recorder to receive his messages. I strongly suspected that Missy left most of them.

She'd rise, eat breakfast, shower, and dress, all the while engaging in lively conversation. Then she'd go to the phone, dial, and, in a voice from the grave, moan, "Dave, this is Missy. Call me when you get home."

The psychologist always arrived in the late mornings or early afternoons to take Melissa to visit her children, keep an appointment with the social worker, or to work on her reading with her. When they returned a few hours later, Missy would want to take a nap. I allowed this to go on for several days before I decided I must confront them together.

"Well, I know I shouldn't buy her drugs," the brilliant, middle-aged psychologist confessed, "but it keeps her off the street!"

It sounded good but I knew it was to Dave's advantage to keep her hooked and dependent on him to buy her drugs. That way, she had to see him. It was ridiculous, because he had so many women, including the wife of his "dead marriage," but he wanted Missy.

"Look," I insisted, "you either stop buying my client drugs or quit seeing her." The psychologist promised to behave. Of course I had my doubts, but, as fate would have it, he didn't get the chance to go back on his word. Like most of my clients, Melissa had used so many aliases she had lost track of them. A week or so later when she went to the courthouse to set a date for a court appearance, she was confronted with old warrants which had popped up on the computer, sixteen in all. Fortunately for Missy, the District Attorney was happy that she wanted to turn over a new leaf and allowed her to plea bargain. She was sentenced to only four months, which would mean ten weeks in jail, with time off for good behavior.

With Melissa Voorhees in jail, the kids and I had our house to ourselves again. It was good to have more time with my children, because my marriage to Lee Usry would change the family makeup entirely. Claire had been my second-in-command for many years, and I hoped that she'd accept Lee. The kids hadn't seen my ex-husband since we'd left Alaska, so they thought of the four of us and their grandparents as all the family they had.

Lee and I planned to announce our engagement during Thanksgiving dinner at my parents' home. Then we'd phone Lee's brothers and sisters, who'd be gathered in Phoenix. My mother and her husband Tom approved of Lee 100 percent, and I knew they'd be delighted at the prospect of having him as a son-in-law. Things seemed to be going along swimmingly; however, David threw a monkey wrench into the works when he overheard us discussing our plans and broke the news to his sister. Claire declared, "I'm too old to have a father!"

Things weren't going as I'd hoped. Nevertheless, we convinced David and Claire to keep our engagement a secret until the time we'd chosen to announce it. Somehow they managed, although my son was ebullient and my daughter was acrimonious.

At last the exciting day dawned when we'd share our news with our families. Never had I felt so happy and content. Only one small incident marred the perfection. During the summer, before Lee and I had started dating, I'd been baby-sitting for one of my clients when my youngest son Darroll, watching me change a diaper, asked, "So, Mom, why are boys and girls shaped differently?"

My explanation was received with only and "Oh" to indicate that he understood, and the subject had not come up again. I wasn't even aware he remembered it until Lee and I broke the news of our impending wedding after Thanksgiving dinner. To our surprise, tears trickled down Darroll's freckled cheeks.

"What's the matter, honey?" I asked, alarmed.

"Are you two gonna have babies?" he demanded.

"Yes, we'd like to," I answered gently.

Sobs wracked his body, and he said miserably, "I know what you have to do to make babies, and I don't want you to get married!"

We respectfully quelled the laughter which welled up inside us as I whispered to Lee, "If he ever finds out what prostitutes do for a living, we're in even bigger trouble!"

When Virginia Eliason was killed, her murder received a couple of paragraphs in the back pages of the local newspaper. I wondered why the media would bother to mention the death of a hooker; it wasn't their usual policy. Then I began to talk with women who still worked the street.

Virginia had been a twenty-seven-year-old mother who worked the street at night while her neighbors watched her two children. She drove an old Pinto, which she parked on Wickersham Boulevard while she worked, and it was in this vehicle that her body had been found. The violence of the crime was ghastly, which was what had apparently caught the media's attention. Her body had been partly skinned, and her throat was slashed. She had been left to bleed a painful death.

The other streetwalkers were extremely shaken. Many of them began to carry knives for protection, which made me nervous, because I knew that an attacker could easily turn the weapon against a weaker victim.

Kathy Stevens was a young woman who applied to Project New Life for help about this time. She had been beaten, stabbed, and left for dead by a john shortly before she began our program, and one day she mentioned something which made me shiver.

"You know, Becky," she said, "I saw Virginia the night she died. She was with this cop named Tom Reichmann. He's kind of weird, and he wants us girls to give him head for free, and it always made Virginia mad. She told him she was gonna narc on him if he didn't leave her alone, but maybe if she would've went with him she wouldn't have met the john who killed her."

In the back of my mind I wondered if it was a john who killed her. The police never found out.

Lee and David's employer and friend Ted closed the machine shop for the four-day Thanksgiving holiday and took his family on a cold weather camp out. They offered to keep my sons for the end of the weekend so Lee and I could have some time alone after we made our engagement announcement on Thanksgiving Day. Lee and I were to drop off the boys on Friday. Claire had to study for her finals which were in two weeks, so she elected to spend the weekend at Grandma's house, where she would be thoroughly pampered for four days. When we returned to the city late Friday night, cold but happy, Lee kissed me good night and promised to come over early the next morning.

I was preparing a gourmet breakfast for him when he pulled up in his car. No sooner had he come in the door than the phone rang. It was Martin Carson, the founder and director of Good Start, a long term shelter for ex-offenders, drug abusers, and their families. Martin had been supportive of Project New Life, and my children and I had lent our backs to putting the Good Start shelter in shape for its grand opening.

"Becky, I need your help," pleaded Martin in his deep bass voice. "I have a husband and wife over here that I need to separate for a few days so I can work with the man. Can the lady stay with you?

"Martin, can't you put her in one of the shelters? I'm so busy. My house is crowded, and I always have to be able to take in a client if there's nowhere else to house her."

"Becky, she needs someone to work with her one on one," he pleaded. "I don't know where else she would have that."

"All right." I sighed. "I'll pick her up at noon."

He was probably stroking me, but I didn't know why until Doreen Neville, Martin Carson's client, got into my car. It was obvious to us immediately that she needed more help than I could give her. Her front teeth were missing, and she told us that they had been knocked out by her abusive husband. She talked nonstop, jumping from subject to subject. She was obviously emotionally ill and in need of psychiatric treatment. Shocked, Lee and I spoke earnestly with her about going immediately to a battered women's shelter.

"Sammy will find me. He always does." She shook her head. "It won't do any good."

Over the next two days we heard how for years she had been battered and bruised, locked in their apartment more times than she could count, and then raped by her husband. Like most abusers we had known, Sam Neville equated sex with power.

"He wants it all the time, but first he beats me. He don't give me no rest, even when I get my period," she said in a matter-of-fact tone. "I've left him lots of times, but it's always the same. It don't do no good. He always finds me."

On Monday I phoned Martin's office, but the Good Start director was in a meeting. I told his secretary that it was imperative that he return my call as soon as possible.

Good Start was supposed to be designed to meet the needs of the entire family. The organization was run by men except for one female house mother. They were fanatically religious people who had some very old-fashioned ideas about women's roles. Even Ralph Hobson, a social worker and the Neville family's case manager, was ill-informed about spousal abuse. It was Hobson who returned my call.

"Is there a problem?" he asked innocently.

"Doreen Neville has been severely beaten and abused by her husband. She needs psychological help, and she should be in a battered women's shelter," I said firmly.

"Well, you know how Doreen talks all the time, Becky. I can understand how her husband would get fed up and smack her, but we're working on that with him. We're hoping that you, as a Christian, can convince her that God doesn't want families to split up," Johnny answered.

I wondered if he knew that I was divorced.

"Johnny, have Martin call me," I insisted wearily. There

was no point trying to educate a jackass.

But Martin was no better informed about the issues of spousal abuse and sexual assault than Johnny. He, too, pleaded with me. "Let Doreen stay a little longer while we talk to her husband." He had me between a rock and a hard place. I couldn't insist that she move to a women's shelter because I had come to realize that she was too mentally ill to provide for her own needs. We couldn't find a mental health facility which would take her. They not only refused to take non-voluntary patients, but at that time they also denied access to those who requested help, unless they were committed by paying family members or had health insurance.

Trying to care for Doreen for even a few days was exhausting, because my work with the prostitutes did not conveniently come to a halt whenever I was busy with other things. I was deeply touched, however, to witness the tender ministrations of the streetwalkers toward Mrs. Neville, once I explained her situation to them. There was no need to mention her mental illness, for they could see that for themselves as she chattered incessantly without making sense, rubbed orange halves on her face, and performed other strange but harmless rituals.

Meanwhile, Missy sang my praises to anyone who would listen and managed to send me other hookers who were getting out of jail. One was Garland Friesen, who had had only a few days left on her sentence when Melissa had begun hers, and she listened eagerly to Missy's story of a project which helped prostitutes. When she was released from jail, Garland phoned Dave Colchis—he was well-known on Wickersham Boulevard—and Dave brought her to me.

Garland, a slim, dark-haired beauty, had entered the life five years earlier because of cocaine addiction. She was not a victim prostitute but she was rapidly losing her eyesight, and streetwalking was far more dangerous for her than for other people because she had already developed night blindness. Ms. Friesen had begun using drugs during her fourteen years of marriage to a real estate broker, but social use had degenerated into constant drug abuse.

Garland's husband had been awarded custody of their children during a messy divorce, and she had been left with nothing. She bore no ill will over this, for she realized that her drug abuse caused the breakup of their marriage, their family, and their business. Now that she had served time in jail, Garland Friesen earnestly wanted to start over but she had nowhere to go and no way to support herself while she made the transition. This made her a good candidate for Project New Life.

The first thing I did was to take her to an ophthalmologist. Unfortunately, he said, "Nothing can be done to halt Garland's eye disease, which is progressing rapidly." Like all recovering addicts, she was tormented by the siren's call of her drug, yet she was desperately afraid to give in, and her fear gave her strength. Employment was unlikely, because her training had been in office skills for which she needed her vision, but she was determined to learn to adapt.

I asked her if she would like to be my office assistant until we could find something for her. Enthusiastically, she agreed. I was deeply moved by Garland's efforts to reorganize my files and to help me run the office efficiently, because she obviously did so only with great effort. Her lack of visual acuity would not allow her to put my papers in order by herself. She tried to work with me on this, but the steady stream of phone calls, Doreen's incessant chatter, and my family's interruptions made her plead with me to hire a secretary.

Garland was understanding of Doreen's needs, but the opposite was not true. The ex-streetwalker patiently listened, comforted, advised, and repeated it again when she realized that Doreen Neville forgot everything moments after it had been said.

Although from the beginning I had tried not to bring clients to my home, some needed intensive help, and many times I had no luck finding that kind of placement. So, even though I wanted to keep my family private, my house often became a refuge. Samantha Rice was a guest whenever the mood struck her, which was often. When Sam met Doreen she treated the mentally ill woman kindly, as all the streetwalkers did, but she felt very much worried. After observing Doreen for a while she came to me. "I'm afraid caring for her is too much for you to handle," she warned. I protested, but she didn't know how close to the truth she was. I was very exhausted. Although they were rivals for my attention, Sam and Garland joined forces trying to convince me to send Doreen away. For a time there was no place for her to go, and meanwhile, it was Garland Friesen who made me realize that I couldn't help everybody.

One day not long after Doreen's arrival, I took Garland to her ophthalmologist, whose office was on Wickersham Boulevard. On the way home she asked me to pull over to the curb so she could speak to a friend whom she had noticed on the sidewalk. When I did, she rolled down the window of my station wagon and called, "Judy!" to a slim young woman in a dark blue nylon parka, with blue jeans and heavy boots. Red hair cascaded down her back, and over her shoulder was slung a duffel bag. She carried two paper sacks.

Garland called again, "Judy! Where you going?"

The redhead ran toward us, a smile on her freckled face. She put down her bags and reached through the open window to give Garland a hug.

"I'm just on my way to a friend's house at the other end of Wickersham," Judy told her.

"Can we give her a ride, Becky?" Garland asked as she turned to look at me.

"Sure." I smiled. "Hop in!"

"What's going on?" Garland prodded as Judy took her

place in the back seat. "I thought you had an ol' man."

"I did. I met a really nice guy, Richard Quick, at a bar a year ago, and I moved in with him. We were so happy. I stayed home and puttered around the house. Everything was wonderful for the first time in my life. Then we went to a cocktail lounge and one of my old tricks recognized me. He told Richard that I used to work Wickersham Boulevard, so he kicked me out."

I glanced in the mirror and saw tears running down Judy's cheeks. She reached into a sack and produced a Mason jar which held something red.

"I even had a garden," she continued. "Here's some tomatoes I put up last summer."

Garland accepted the jar with thanks, and Judy said I could let her off at the next corner.

"Is she going back to streetwalking?" I asked Garland when our passenger had closed the door.

"She'll have to," Garland replied reasonably.

"Maybe we should go back and tell her about Project New Life," I suggested.

"She needs time to grieve before she can make a new life, Becky, or I'd've told her," Garland assured me.

I'd learned to trust the women's judgment about such things. As I drove back to the house where Doreen was waiting, I rehashed the incident in my mind. Like Judy, Doreen Neville wasn't ready to change her life, albeit for different reasons. I couldn't care for her indefinitely, and she was unable to be self-sufficient, so a public shelter wasn't a viable alternative. What she needed was a long-term managed care home. Good Start would be perfect, except that her husband was a resident there. I had to talk this over with Martin Carson.

I phoned Martin and begged him to work with Doreen instead of her husband, and Doreen told him in no uncertain terms that she did not want to live with Sammy Neville. Carson was entirely insensitive to our pleas. Like so many well-intentioned people, Martin Carson thought that a woman's place was with her spouse. "If only," he observed to me privately, "she would learn to quit annoying the poor man, he'd probably stop hitting her."

The morning dawned cold and bleak. There was an unexpected knock at my door. I was alone with Doreen. David was in electronics class at our local high school, which supplemented his home schooling. I looked through the peephole and saw Martin Carson with another man whom I hadn't seen before. I opened the door, and, as the pair stepped inside, I heard Doreen scream. I spun around.

"What are you doing here?" she demanded of the stranger.

Martin answered for him. "Sammy misses you, Doreen. I brought him with me to talk to you about going home."

Doreen began to tremble and cry as the man reached for her arm with a smile.

"I want you to come home, honey," he told the quivering woman. "You're my wife; I miss you."

"Martin," I said, livid, "why have you brought Doreen's husband to my home?" No one in our social service community had dared to violate a safe house before, but it was typical of this male-dominated ministry to blithely disregard women's needs. "Doreen," I said, turning to her, "you certainly don't have to go anywhere."

Flashing me a dirty look, Sammy kept begging and entreating her, promising he'd be better.

Doreen looked over at me sadly. "I have to go, Becky," she said, sighing heavily. "Maybe he means it this time."

They left together.

I thought that the others who had known Doreen would be as furious as I was, but unlike me they received the news with equanimity. I should have realized they were used to this kind of treatment from men.

Garland, always practical and efficient, insisted that we use the time we now had without Doreen to finish organizing my office. I was delighted to have her help, but I felt that by throwing herself into this work so completely she was avoiding her own problems. I phoned a social worker, Ray Dobson, who was also blind, to discuss Garland with him.

Ray explained that "While it's crucial for Garland to learn to adapt to her vision loss, it's even more necessary for her to receive treatment for her addiction, despite the fact that she isn't presently using drugs."

"Why is the order so important?" I asked, puzzled.

"Well, if she adjusts to her blindness before she deals with her drug problem, she will eventually return to cocaine. She must enter a treatment program, Becky," Ray told me.

With mixed emotions, I related this to Garland. "I hate to lose you right now, but your personal needs have to come before the project's, or mine."

My work was absorbing, and I couldn't help but feel that it was important. As much as I loved Lee Usry, I was torn between marriage and work. One harried morning when we left late for an important conference on women and drugs, I exploded at Lee, "I want to change the world, and you want me to change diapers!"

I drew a deep breath and gathered my thoughts. "I'm sorry," I apologized. "It's just that our relationship is everything I've ever wanted, but my work with the prostitutes means a great deal to me, too. I really want to marry you and have more children and move to the country, but how can I do that without deserting my clients?"

Lee understood my divided loyalties. He assured me, "We'll work it out."

Somehow, knowing he understood was all that mattered.

8

WEDDING BELLES

As our wedding date drew nearer, a lot of people got the jitters. Claire was defiant. I understood that this was her expression of grief over losing our close relationship. Many of my ex-prostitutes were experiencing feelings of abandonment, too. I had the double burden of trying to reassure my own daughter and my clients that I still loved each and every one.

One day in mid-December I received a phone call from a very incoherent Sam. As she rambled on I broke in, "Have you taken something, Sam?"

"Just codeine and doriden but I'm afraid I might have overdosed, Becky," she slurred. "Will you come get me?"

Rushing downtown, I went into her motel room and helped her to my station wagon. When we arrived at the hospital, no one argued; they took her immediately to the emergency room. I was allowed to stay in the room as doctors and nurses inserted IV's, administered medications, and monitored her vital signs, all with an air of urgency.

"What's she on?" a concerned doctor asked me.

"Codeine and doriden. She phoned me and said she

thought she might have overdosed," I replied.

"Has she ever done this before?" the doctor wanted to know.

Despite the fact that I tried not to discuss my clients' past, I knew this was one time a full disclosure was necessary. "She's overdosed with heroin," I answered.

The doctor walked me across the room to a quiet corner and spoke in a voice too low for Sam to hear. "Look, if she uses drugs regularly and she overdosed, she could have called nine-one-one. The fact that she phoned you tells me that she's trying to get your attention."

I must admit that I missed this possibility. Sam was obviously taking my marriage plans very hard.

In a few days, Sam was released from the hospital, and I brought her home with me. She and Garland took the opportunity to confront me about getting married again.

"Every man's a john," Sam said. "Don't you know that?"

"We know you're in love with this guy, Becky," Garland told me. "We just want to warn you."

"I love you, Baby, and I don't want him to hurt you," Sam added.

"I love you too, honey," I assured her. "But not all guys are tricks. Lee isn't. He's good to me, and he loves me. We'll be happy."

I smiled to myself at calling her honey. I'd fallen into the habit of calling my streetwalker clients pet names, because it was so common on the street. When they wrote to me from jail, they would sign their letters with "all my love forever." Of course if one of them got mad at me, her promises of love forever would be forgotten immediately, because streetwalkers simply have no concept of enduring relationships.

In early January I found a treatment center in Phoenix, Arizona which would take Garland Friesen. She was disappointed that she would have to leave for the program immediately because she'd planned on attending my wedding in March, but it was important she take the spot before someone else did. A few days later we bid each other a fond farewell. I'd miss her, but she needed to deal with her addiction.

Lee was getting worn out from the twenty-five-mile drive each night and morning to his house in the country, because he always left me as late as possible and returned to see me before work each morning. It was an exhausting schedule, so he took an efficiency apartment in my friend Jerry Hudson's complex, which was only a couple of miles from my house. Sometimes in the evenings we visited with Jerry and his girlfriend, Audrey, and would go out for doughnuts to the shop across the street.

Shortly after Lee moved into his temporary home, the tenants on either side of him vacated their apartments. The efficiencies were rented again almost immediately, and there was something strange about his new neighbors. One was a woman with one child, and the other was the mother of two, but all the children shared the same father. The father baby-sat the little group each night while their mothers worked. It wasn't long before we realized that Lee's neighbors were prostitutes and the baby-sitter was not only the father of their children, but their pimp. In the quiet of the evenings, we could hear through the thin walls the father's distraught instructions to his children.

"Debbie, don't hit your sister! Lynnette, pick up your clothes! Winona, stay out of the cookies! Debbie, quit hitting your sister!"

If we hadn't felt so sorry for the children, we'd have enjoyed the pimp's discomfiture as poetic justice.

When Melissa was released from jail in February, she not only had to deal with her misgivings about my marriage, but she had to resist using drugs, too, because she moved in with me again. I was a little worried that we might end up having to take her on our honeymoon.

Lee and I didn't have much time to visit with Jerry and Audrey as our wedding day approached except one evening, during the second week of February, when we managed to spend some time with them. As we discussed Jerry's temporary role as head of Project New Life while I was away, the phone rang. Jerry answered, then handed me the receiver.

"It's for you," he said.

I took the phone, and Claire said, "Mom, Sam's on the other line. I'm going to make this a three-way call."

In a moment a thick voice slurred into the phone. "Becky? It's me, babe, Sam. I'm so loaded I'm gonna get arrested. Can you come pick me up?"

"Just a minute, Samantha. Hold on, honey," I instructed her; I repeated to my companions what she had said. Sam was not a client of Project New Life but we were all very fond of her.

"Well, Sam's never asked for anything like this before," Jerry pointed out. "I think we ought to go get her."

"Me, too," I agreed, although at that moment I wished I could have just one evening to myself. Then I spoke to Sam. "Okay, we'll be right there. Where are you?"

The address was that of an all-night fast food stand in the part of town where the illegal drug trade was practiced openly.

Jerry and Audrey piled into the back seat of my station wagon while Lee got into the driver's seat. I joined him up front. As we drove, Audrey commented, "It's a shame you two can't get any time away from the project."

"Maybe I should have Melissa baby-sit Sam," I joked.

Jerry looked thoughtful.

"That's not a bad idea," he said. "It would give Missy an opportunity to see how bad she looks and acts when she's loaded."

After a little further discussion the four of us decided to give Melissa the responsibility of monitoring Samantha for a few hours. We were only a phone call away, and we could return to my house from Jerry's apartment in five minutes.

When we arrived at the restaurant and saw Sam, we could see that her assessment of her state of discombobulation had been correct: she was very, very loaded. The men helped her into the back seat where she slumped between Jerry and Audrey. She tried unsuccessfully to carry on a conversation with us, and, when she lit a cigarette, it fell from her fingers into Jerry's lap. She bent over to retrieve it and seemed to forget where she was, because she began massaging Jerry's leg. Audrey and I stifled giggles as Jerry gently removed Sam's hand and put it on her own lap.

Finally we got home. Melissa and Claire were awaiting Sam's arrival with hot chicken noodle soup and coffee. As my daughter helped our friend get settled, I explained our plan to Missy who agreed to watch Sam until Lee and I returned. While we talked, Samantha was sitting at the breakfast bar, spoon in hand, trying to feed herself, but her face kept falling into the soup bowl.

Melissa watched Sam wistfully for a moment. Then she asked plaintively, "Do you know how much I want to feel like that?"

Somehow, though, she got through the experience and it seemed to have a good impact on both women.

Meanwhile, my other clients had their own ways of letting me know they were having problems coping with my impending marriage. Some were more successful than others.

Emerald Harbison never expressed any interest in other women, so it surprised me when she brought up the subject of my marriage.

"You know, Becky," Emerald said during one of our weekly sessions. "I've been thinking about you and Lee. I have a really hard time having sex with the guy I'm going with because when he wants me to give him head, I feel like he's a customer, and I resent it. I just hope it's easier for you and your husband than it is for us." She managed a wan smile as she patted my hand.

I realized then that her intelligence also encompassed depth. Knowledge without empathy is a lonely pinnacle. Emerald, however, had revealed a very personal emotion, and for that I was grateful.

A few weeks before our wedding, Lee told me that he and David were going to take a sewing machine to Mrs. McCutcheon that afternoon. Their employer Ted often had them make deliveries to elderly or disabled customers.

"Mrs. McCutcheon lives just off Wickersham Boulevard, so we might see some of your clients," Lee teased.

About four o'clock, I received a phone call from Melissa who sounded very upset.

"Becky," she began with a hint of tears in her voice. "I don't know how to tell you this. I just saw Lee drive down Wickersham Boulevard!"

"It's all right, Missy," I comforted her. "He was just delivering a sewing machine to an elderly lady."

"Are you sure?" she asked worriedly.

One of the most difficult parts of transition, both for the women and me, was when clients told me that they were certain they had dated some man or another whom they now knew in "civilian life." I could attribute some incidences to mistaken identity and a few others, like Lee's outing on Wickersham Boulevard, to my clients' tendency to think of all men as tricks. The fact remains that at least one in twenty males do "date" prostitutes.

Eventually, the prostitutes and I learned to deal with our feelings toward johns the same way we handled straight women's anger toward hookers. We chalked up their behavior to ignorance.

Christine Mayer seemed to be happy for me. She and Claire decided to plan a rather unique surprise bridal shower. At it, many of my straight friends met "working women" for the first time in their lives. For one night no one cared what anyone else did for a living—I wished it were always that way. In any case, it not only helped my clients feel a part of the straight community, but it also gave them a sense of participation in my wedding, which put them more at ease with it.

The next day I phoned Garland, partly to tell her about it, but more to hear how she was doing in her rehabilitation program. I expected to leave a message for her to call back collect, so when she answered the phone I was pleasantly surprised.

"It's so nice to hear your voice!" I exclaimed. "Did you just happen to be in the office when I called?"

"No. I'm the receptionist!" Garland informed me.

At last March 3, the day of our wedding, dawned bright and breezy. The church was located atop the highest hill in the city, and the parking lot was already filling with guests as I arrived with Claire and my friend Sharon Riner, who had made my gown. They helped me dress while my mother flitted nervously about. The organist began to play. Lee's family and mine were seated. The wedding march began. I took my stepfather Tom's arm and we walked down the aisle. Then Lee took my hand, and the ceremony commenced. When the minister pronounced us husband and wife, we turned to face our guests. They were our families, friends, and many former prostitutes—all the people we loved.

A limousine, a gift for the day from Ted, took us back to my house where about eighty people waited on our lawn. As we stepped from the car, rice, confetti, and streamers were thrown into the air over our heads.

Inside, we joined our family and friends for hors d'oeuvres and champagne before we changed our clothes for our trip. Dave Colchis was Melissa's escort, but Maxine Barr, her sponsor, would take her home. Maxine had agreed only two days before to let Missy live with her. I was thankful that I wouldn't be worrying about Missy on my honeymoon.

As we made our way to the front door and, turning, waved goodbye, I noticed for the first time Samantha, comfortably and sensually ensconced on the living room couch on a man's lap. Undoubtedly, the guy was a john, and I was very sure he had to be a Clinging Clem, because only a Clem or a Harold would attend a ho's friend's wedding, but Clem alone would be so overtly affectionate in public.

I breathed a prayer that our other guests wouldn't strike up a conversation with Sam's beau, because although a Clem's main interests are the vital statistics of nearby women and the latest prizefight, he's willing to monopolize the conversation on any subject. He's also the john most likely to marry a hooker, for wedlock provides him with his own private prostitute.

Slipping my hand through Lee's, I brushed aside all thoughts of my clients, and our honeymoon began.

The children joined us at Lake Tahoe for the second week. The boys rented fishing equipment and headed for the dock early the first morning. David returned to the warm cabin before lunch, but Darroll lay on the pier and kept his line in the water. Around one o'clock snow began to fall, but our younger son never moved. By 5:00 P.M. he was covered with several inches of snow, but still he dangled his fishing pole in the water. We insisted he come in then, but he returned to the pier the following morning, and we realized he had discovered his great love in life: fishing. From that day on he never missed a chance to cast his line.

The second week passed as quickly as the first. Soon it was time to go.

Lee and I relaxed on our bed, as we talked quietly on our first night at home. There was no need to lock the sliding glass doors of our bedroom and living room, because we kept the iron gratings shut and locked. But when we heard the outside door to our bedroom slide open we turned in surprise to look. Suddenly, the drapes parted slightly and a camera was thrust through. We couldn't see the photographer. Not only was he hidden by the drapes, but we were blinded by the flashbulbs which exploded into brightness again and again.

"What's going on?" demanded Lee.

David burst into a howl of laughter as he said, "Don't worry. It's not loaded!"

I suppose life with David prepared me for the vicissitudes of working with prostitutes, but there were times . . . !

About 2:00 A.M., just hours after David's candid camera session, the phone rang.

"Hello," I answered groggily.

"Becky, this is Lou Silverman of the city police," a deep, kindly voice informed me.

I usually hated getting calls from the police in the middle of the night. They always spoke in such sharp, clear tones that I was awake for hours afterwards, but I'd become friendly with Louis Silverman, a detective I'd met on the phone while he was investigating the theft of a john's car by a criminal prostitute working, as they all did, for drug money. Although I'd earlier refused to help this woman, she had had the temerity to give Silverman my name as a reference when he'd questioned her! Lou had a sense of humor, however, and let the hooker go when the john got his car back. Although we only talked on the phone he and I had become good friends.

"I have a young woman who was just beaten up by a john. She's fifteen years old, and Juvenile Hall doesn't have room for her tonight. Will you take her?" Lou continued as I struggled to consciousness.

"Does she want to come here?" I asked the policeman as my head cleared.

"I think she's willing to go anywhere I suggest. She's pretty shaken up," came the unwavering reply. I could detect a hint of desperation in Lou's voice.

"Okay. Bring her over. I'll turn on the porch light for you," I told him, and gave him directions to my house. The phone had awakened my husband so I explained the situation to him as I got my bathrobe on.

"I'll get up with you, honey," Lee offered.

"No. Go back to sleep. You might as well accept this now. You can't get out of bed every time I have to get up for someone. You have to go to work in the morning," I told him.

"So do you," my groom protested.

"I'm used to it," I insisted. When he saw I meant it he turned over and went back to sleep.

I got out linens for the hide-a-bed and made hot cocoa while I waited for Lou to arrive with his charge. In fifteen minutes he knocked at the door and when I opened it I saw Lou, a dark haired, well-built man, half hiding at his side stood a bedraggled teenager. I was always impressed when police officers brought women and girls to my door because I knew they saw the worst of the streetwalkers every day, and they still cared for these women enough to try to help them. Lots of lawmen are johns and some, like Thomas Reichmann, are self-appointed punishers of prostitutes, but the majority are decent human beings who truly want the women to find a better life.

Lou was very concerned about this young person, and I asked him to stay for hot chocolate while we talked. "I have to go back," he said, "but I'm really glad to finally meet you in person."

"Me too," I replied and poured his cocoa into a Styrofoam cup for "takeout."

After bidding him goodbye, I turned to talk with the girl who was curled in a small ball on my sofa. As I looked closer, I gasped. Her nose was bloody, and her brown hair was bloody, tangled, and dirty. She was about five foot two and was dressed in a cotton checked blue dress which was torn at the neck. Her windbreaker was several sizes too large, as if it had been given to her at the police station, and she wore nylons and heels, not very comfortable for walking hours on end.

"I'm Becky," I began with a smile. "I just want you to understand that I'm not a jailer or a foster parent, and you're free to leave at any time. The reason the officer brought you here is because I help people get out of prostitution, and if you want to change your life, I'll be glad to help you. What's your name?"

"Stormie," the girl answered.

Maybe, I thought, but I doubt it. Streetwalkers choose romantic sounding names as their aliases.

"You can sleep on the hide-a-bed. I'll help you make it up. There's some clean bedding on the chair over there," I told Stormie. I liked my clients to participate in their recovery by working together with me.

We rose to make the bed, and I continued my interview. "Do you want to go to the hospital? The officer told me a john had hurt you when he talked to me on the phone."

"Nah. I'm used to it. The guy tonight just slapped me around. One guy last week kicked me in the stomach. Two weeks ago some man held my arms while his buddy burned me with a cigarette."

Stormie was trying to make me feel sorry for her, so I knew that she'd be gone before the day was through because none of my successful clients dwelt on negatives. They very much lived in the present and hoped for the future. This teenager had a pimp waiting for her somewhere and she was only taking advantage of the police officer's well-meant kindness in not arresting her.

I bade Stormie good night, warned her that she would be awakened early by the various members of the household, and returned to my room. As I lay in bed, the man I loved so much beside me, tears welled up in my eyes for the youngster on the hide-a-bed. She probably thought she was desperately in love with her pimp, and it was likely she would never discover what love really is. The chances were very good that she would be dead of an overdose or killed by a john before she was thirty. Lee was snoring softly by my side. He turned over, put his arm around me, and I tried to put Stormie out of my mind. When I woke up early the next morning, she was gone.

A month or so later Sam phoned, certain that I would be as delighted as she was with what she had to tell me.

"Jim Thayer, the guy I was with at your wedding, asked me to marry him! Will you come to my wedding?" Samantha bubbled.

I wasn't thrilled. I'd had enough distasteful experiences with Clems to know that they expect a wife to keep the house clean and to cater to her husband's every sexual whim. They equate sex with love. The wife of a Clinging Clem is almost always a streetwalker who expects him to trade his paycheck for her sexual services and can't understand why she should be his maid, too. Nevertheless, I knew Sam couldn't comprehend my sentiments. After all, in her eyes, I had married a john.

"That's wonderful, Samantha! When's the big day?" I forced myself to respond cheerfully.

"Tomorrow. We're getting married at Mountain View Wedding Chapel at two o'clock. Don't be late," she teased.

At two the next afternoon, I met the happy couple inside the tiny wood frame turn-of-the-century house that was ending its days as a wedding chapel. Moth-eaten lace curtains covered the grimy windows, and pieces of the linoleum floor were missing. A pew against the front wall and some folding chairs provided seating for guests, and a tiny altar decorated with dusty plastic flowers occupied the back portion of the room.

The justice of the peace was a small portly fellow with greased-back hair and a missing front tooth. His wife, clad in a flowered house dress, doubled as cashier and witness to the weddings when necessary. The ceremony was short but rather effusive, and I was glad that Sam, at least for a short while, would have some happiness.

It was about this time that Lee changed jobs. Ted was sorry to see him go, but Josephson Appliance offered my husband a job as Department Manager for the largest of their five stores at a greatly increased salary and with chances for advancement within the chain, which he would not have had in Ted's one shop. David continued to work for our friend, however, and earned his highest praise.

Life seemed to be very good to us. All we wanted now was a baby to make our lives complete. I was still very concerned that I wouldn't be able to run Project New Life when and if that happened, but Lee said that, by the time we had an infant to care for, the shelter would be a reality and I'd have plenty of help.

May brought sunshine and blue skies. Birds on their way north stopped to sing of tundra and cool streams and berries growing wild. Classes were out for Claire, and she took a summer job.

David had done so well with our home schooling efforts that I encouraged him to take the admittance exam at our community college. Students who passed were eligible to take classes there while still in high school. It served as no mean boost to his ego when he passed the entrance exam, because he'd been several years below his grade level only nine months before.

A month later Darroll was given the "Most Inventive" award during his school's end-of-the-year ceremonies. This was hardly the prestigious honor the title implied. It was bestowed on him for making airplanes out of aluminum foil! After watching him be rewarded at the ceremony I began to seriously consider home schooling for this son, too.

It had been my belief that Christine Mayer had dealt with my marriage much better than the other streetwalkers had, but life is full of surprises. One of them came when Christine brought Vince Garzoni to meet us on a balmy June night.

Vince owned the Starlight Lounge where Christine had

worked as a nude dancer/prostitute, and he was her former pimp. It was rumored that the Starlight was run by the Mafia, but this only made it popular with the upper crust, who thrived on excitement. It was not a sleazy booze joint by any means, and its shows were surpassed only by those on stage in Las Vegas.

My clients sometimes brought their pimps to meet me, in hopes that I could help the "man they loved" change his life as they were doing. While they always thought the pimp and I would get along famously, we never even came close. It was always neither entente nor detente, but cold war. I knew that pimps came to meet me for one reason: to get their whores back. This was a field of honor, on which we dueled for the hand of the woman we both wanted.

Like the rest of my clients, Christine introduced Vince as her boyfriend. Although I was polite, I immediately put him on the defensive by asking what he did for a living. Street pimps hem and haw but Garzoni just explained that he owned a night-club.

"Did Christine work for you there?" I asked.

"She was a dancer," he admitted.

"She was a prostitute, too," I said candidly.

Garzoni shrugged.

"That's her business," he retorted.

"Do you two plan to get married?" I persisted.

"Maybe someday," Garzoni answered vaguely.

Christine was snuggled next to him, smiling benevolently. I understood that he'd been her "love" and her ego booster, but I wished she could see him as I did.

I made the evening something of an inquisition, but it didn't faze Garzoni. He was no street pimp who relied on threats, but a dangerous middle manager in the echelons of organized crime.

Most of my clients gave up on their pimps when they saw that they weren't going to change, but Christine allowed Garzoni to continue to court her. That he was the father of her son may have had something to do with her naive hope that she could change him.

Soon after this meeting, Christine phoned Mrs. Garzoni, who had a fifteen-year-old daughter with Vince, to ask her to give up this prize of a man. On the pretext of wanting the daughter to meet her half-brother, Vince's wife convinced my unwary friend to let little Judd go home with his daddy. Kindhearted as always, Christine allowed a visit.

Shortly thereafter, Vince Garzoni sued Christine for custody of their son, and won. The money and power at his command guaranteed his victory. There was nothing we could do.

In desperation Christine convinced one of her former johns to help her kidnap Judd but Garzoni's bodyguards foiled the attempt. The pimp took her to court again and she lost her visitation rights.

Tearfully, Christine came to me for comfort.

"What are you going to do now?" I asked hesitantly.

"I have to be an example for Judd," Christine replied. "I'm going ahead with my program."

"Good for you, Christine," I said, marveling at her fortitude and sorrowing at her loss. Sadness seemed to pervade my clients' lives.

In contrast to my personal happiness, Samantha's happiness was short lived. Her mother had been battling cancer for a year, and one of Samantha's greatest fears was that she would be in jail when her mom died. Although this woman had deserted her daughters when they were small and generally ignored them, my friend had never given up trying to make her mother love her. I worried that Mrs. Rice's death would be traumatic because of their unresolved relationship.

Sam's sister Debbie phoned me one afternoon in June to tell me that their mother had passed away that morning, so I wasn't surprised to find Samantha on my doorstep a few hours later, her face tearstained and her arms outstretched. As I embraced my friend and patted her on the back I spied three grocery sacks with her clothes in them on my porch.

"Mom died this morning, Becky," Samantha sobbed in my ear.

"I know, honey. I'm so sorry," I murmured.

"Can I stay with you for a while?" she asked hesitantly. "I left Jim."

"Sure you can stay," I said and ushered her inside.

Sam set the bags on the sofa and collapsed beside them. I handed her a box of tissues. Sitting down next to her, I asked, "Why did you leave Jim?"

"Debbie called me this morning to tell me about Mom," she began. "I've been so upset. I've been crying all day. When Jim came home tonight, I told him that Mom had died. He lay down on the bed and said, 'That's too bad about your mother, honey. Come here and give me some head.'"

9

SHOCKS AND SURPRISES

One of the most important rules of Project New Life was that clients had to work full time and go to school part time, or attend classes full time and get a part time job. Of course, sometimes that just wasn't practical. Melissa Voorhees desperately needed more education before she could find any kind of work, but the only classes available for her needs were held at night. I couldn't leave her alone all day, so she spent quite a bit of time at my house.

It's easy to understand why we loved Missy. A kind, considerate person despite her problems, she treated our family as if it was her own. She worried that David didn't have enough friends in the neighborhood and spent a lot of time with him. One of their favorite games was Sorry, a board game played with dice, a set of markers for each player, and cards which bore simple instructions. The game can be played passively or aggressively: individual players decide whether to attack their opponent's piece or move another of their own instead. This game was crucial to Project New Life's program. We played it often, because it forced the players to interact which was a skill greatly lacking in streetwalkers.

Not only did Melissa worry about my children's welfare but they worried about hers. My son Darroll offered to teach his friend to read. Daily, he would patiently help Melissa sound out words, and she would let him beat her at Sorry.

Still, boredom set in, and Missy asked permission to visit her brother for a week during which she would celebrate her birthday. Then she planned to return to Maxine's house.

The day before she was due back, I received a despondent phone call from Melissa. She was in jail. She explained that she'd decided to come back a few days early, party with friends, and then return to my house before either her brother or I found out. Instead, she'd been arrested.

"I only meant to party one night, Becky. Then I decided to ask Dr. Fox if I could have some codeine and just party one more night before I came home. When I got busted I was only doing codeine. Phyllis, the friend I was visiting, bought some heroin from a cop. That's what they found, and now *I'm* in jail!" She sounded *so* innocent.

However, my naivete had long since faded.

"What are the charges against you?" I asked.

"They're charging me with possession of narcotics. Dr. Fox wrote four prescriptions in some of my aliases, so the police think I bought the pills illegally," she complained.

"You did," I pointed out. "Do you want me to call your brother?" I knew she wouldn't want him to know she had used drugs again, but she had to come to terms with reality. I was not amused with her.

"I don't know, Becky. Do you think they'll drop the charges?" Missy was hoping she would escape punishment, but I knew better. She'd had too many convictions in the past.

"I doubt it, Missy. You need a lawyer. The court will appoint you one, so I guess I don't have to call Cajun unless you want one of his attorneys to defend you." I said this casually, but we both knew the court-appointed attorneys weren't likely to expend a lot of effort trying to cut the jail time of a drug-abusing prostitute.

There was a momentary silence, then Missy said, "I think you'd better call Cajun Devil. I don't want him to know I was using drugs, but I don't want to go to jail for a long time, either."

When I hung up, I thought I'd better tell Darroll about Missy's problems. He was swimming in the backyard pool with Ruth, the daughter of friends. I pulled back the curtains from the sliding glass doors and looked at the children, who were gazing into each other's eyes from opposite ends of a boogie board with rapt expressions. Puppy love had been blossoming between them for several years. They looked so cute and happy I decided the news about Melissa could wait.

At noon I phoned Lee.

"Hi, honey!" he said, pleasantly surprised by my call. "What's up?"

"I wish this were a happy call. Missy's in jail, Lee." I couldn't hide my disappointment. "She got busted for narcotics."

"I thought she was with her brother," he responded.

"She was, but she came back a few days early to party with friends. She wants me to call Cajun Devil," I told him.

"She must be desperate!" He chuckled. "Well, Becky, you can't stop her from using drugs, and I guess her brother ought to know. Maybe this will be the best thing for her."

"Lee, I love you," I said.

I felt so thankful for him. Lee tells me what I need to hear, and he's usually right. "It's just so frustrating not to be able to help Missy when I know she can make it," I said. "If only she didn't have two Harold the Helper johns, Dave Colchis and Dr. Fox."

Lee said sympathetically, "I know you take these things to heart, Becky, but you can only do so much. The rest has to be done by Missy herself."

When we hung up, Darroll was still occupied, so I phoned Melissa's brother. I had expected to hear a string of expletives

that would make a sailor blush, but Cajun only expressed disappointment.

"I wish she'd get off those damn drugs, Becky," he told
me. "Missy's always been a nice girl, and I don't think she's a
junkie. I just don't understand it, but then I've never been
addicted to anything but dinner." He sighed and I couldn't help
thinking that maybe being part of a street gang isn't addiction
but it certainly is a sickness of another kind. "Well," he said,
going on, "I know a lawyer, Willie Hayes, who'll help her. I'll
make an appointment and call you when I get into town."

Willie Hayes. The name was familiar. He was rumored to
be an Iron Eagle himself.

On the day of the appointment, I sent Darroll to my
mother's house and drove to the attorney's office which was located on a side street downtown. There were only two cars in Willie
Hayes's parking lot, a Ferrari, which I assumed belonged to the
lawyer, and a classic Mustang in mint condition. The Iron Eagles
seemed to have a penchant for nice cars.

Inside, Hayes's secretary ushered me into his office where
Cajun and three of his biker brothers sat in plush leather chairs.
Willie, a compact fortyish man, wore a gray pinstripe three-piece
suit. He gave my hand a brief squeeze but Cajun wasn't so gentle, and I wondered if the weights he lifted weighed a ton.

"My baby sister's in jail on a narcotics charge," Cajun
growled in his deep biker's voice. I always found it amusing that
cops and bikers use bass tones, but the former enunciate clearly
and the latter seem to snarl. Today's conversation, however, was
anything but funny.

"Has she been arraigned?" the attorney asked as he made
notes on a yellow legal pad.

"Yeah. Her bail's five thousand dollars. I ain't posted it
yet," Cajun told the lawyer.

I was shocked by the attorney's next statement.

"I'll find out who the judge is going to be. I may have

something on him, but if I don't it might cost you a couple of grand."

"Okay."

I looked at the lawyers and the bikers one by one. No one but me seemed surprised at these revelations. I kept up a facade of savoir faire but I swallowed hard, realizing that I'd probably just been a party to a conspiracy to blackmail or bribe a judge.

"Do you know what happened?" the lawyer asked Cajun.

"I'd like to know myself," he replied indignantly. "I put out word on the street that no one was to sell her drugs."

I started to tremble. Cajun Devil expected to be obeyed when he ordered all the street dealers not to sell drugs to his sister, even though he lived more than a hundred miles away. I stared at him for a long moment. I hadn't realized how powerful he was. I knew Cajun was part of the gang, but Missy hadn't mentioned that her brother was a top dog in the organization.

Nervously, I explained, "Melissa told me her friend bought heroin from a cop, but she got busted along with the other woman because she had a prescription for codeine. According to her, the doctor wrote several scrips in different names so she could buy more without being questioned."

Cajun gripped the arms of his chair so hard his fingers whitened. "She's got a damn hype doctor?" he exploded.

"You want me to take him out?" This came from Red Cat, one of Cajun Devil's companions. I looked over at him. He was about thirty-five with waist-length blond hair and a beard to match. Tattoos covered his arms, and he was wearing tattered jeans and a black T shirt which read, "Iron Eagles—Flying Heavy Metal." He didn't sound like he was kidding.

I'd just been made party to a conspiracy to commit murder! I had to think fast.

"Could you give me a chance to make a public example of him?" I interjected quickly. "I'd like to get them to pull his license as a warning to other hype doctors."

Fortunately, Cajun took my suggestion, at least for the moment.

"Okay, let me know what happens, but if nothing does, I'll take care of it my way," Cajun declared.

It was a mystery to me why Cajun was so incensed with Dr. Fox. Was it because the physician's actions had indirectly caused his sister's arrest, or was it that the doctor was a competitor as a pusher? In any case, I lodged a complaint against the doctor with the State Board of Medical Examiners. A few weeks later, I received a call from one of their officers, Dr. Harvey Gould.

"We've just closed an eight-month investigation of Dr. Fox which had been brought about by numerous complaints. Our investigation has found no justification in these allegations," Dr. Gould assured me. "Your friend's claim that he wrote a prescription in another name than her own can't be substantiated. Physicians don't demand identification when treating patients."

The good doctor had lily white hands as far as the State Board was concerned. I had a strong inclination to invite Dr. Gould to Dr. Fox's office, which was located on Wickersham Boulevard, and introduce him to the many drug-addicted street-walkers who could be seen in his waiting room on any given day. But a brotherhood, whether criminal or legitimate, tends to protect its members, and I knew that no amount of argument would persuade the State Board of Medical Examiners to reconsider Dr. Fox's qualifications.

Somehow, Cajun Devil's request that I keep him apprised of my progress slipped my mind.

Despite her brother's influence, Melissa didn't escape punishment. She appeared before a jurist known in our town as the "hanging judge," an apparently incorruptible individual who refused to be bought off. It wasn't often that Cajun Devil didn't get what he wanted, but he made his sister's stay in prison much more comfortable with well-placed bribes.

While Missy was in jail, Samantha asked to go to church with me. I was pleasantly surprised. Sam had never seemed interested in religion before. Perhaps it was her mother's recent death or her husband's callous treatment that drove her to seek solace in religion.

I chose an evening meeting in our church which had a congregation of about a hundred people. Most were adults in their twenties and thirties, and the services were full of joyful singing. When I picked my friend up, she was wearing a slinky low-cut black evening dress with high-heeled shoes and dangling earrings. To many of my clients, church meant dressing up, and dressing up meant sexy.

I swallowed hard and complimented her, "You look gorgeous!" And she did.

My family stayed home, so Sam and I had some time alone together. She listened attentively to the sermon which was about God absolving those who were truly repentant from their sins, and she seemed to enjoy the music. She shook hands with many of the shocked worshippers as we left, and I got the impression that she might like to return.

On the way home, Samantha said, "What the preacher was saying about God washing your sins away really meant a lot to me. Did I ever tell you about the first john I ever had? He was this old guy who wanted to kiss me. I could feel his false teeth with my tongue—it made me kind of nauseated. He had a little pencil-thin moustache and thick glasses. I still hate guys who look like that. Anyway, for days after we made love I kept taking showers, trying to get clean again."

I wished I could share what Samantha said with the minister. He had probably never delivered a more meaningful sermon or gotten such a heartfelt response.

However, the next week, the preacher took me aside as soon as I arrived for services, and several of the church elders joined us.

"Why did you bring that horrible woman last week?" the minister demanded. "She was dressed like a prostitute. She didn't belong here! There are churches downtown where people like that can go, but this is a house of worship for families."

"It won't happen again," I assured him indignantly. "Because you can be sure, I won't be back."

I never told Sam what happened in that meeting at the church, and I never took her again or went back there myself. As for the minister, I believe he'll have some explaining to do in the hereafter.

Not long after that I learned that my son Darroll's teacher had taken another position elsewhere. I decided to home school my son. Lee volunteered to lead a Webelo Scout troop for a year, so that Darroll would have companionship, and I also made sure that he had plenty of time to socialize at our new church and with other home school youngsters.

I carefully planned the week's lessons for my student-sons and spent as much time with them as they needed each day, which amounted to about ninety minutes each. If I was called away on Project New Life business during school hours they continued to do their work while I was gone. I could always tell if they goofed off, because I quickly learned to judge just how fast they could complete their assignments. If they had trouble in one subject, they simply worked on another until I returned.

In August a vacancy occurred in Lee's service department, and he hired David immediately. Our son was through with his school work at noon, and afterward I drove him to the shop. Some of the employees muttered about nepotism, but our boy's expertise soon impressed the most jealous of them.

On the tenth of September I submitted to my yearly PAP smear. I don't enjoy exhibiting myself to a man I've hardly met who pokes and prods me while telling me to relax—even if he is a doctor, but I do so for my family's sake. On September 13th the physician's nurse phoned me.

"Mrs. Usry, your PAP smear is a Class IV. Dr. Sein wants

to schedule an appointment to take a tissue sample for microscopic examination. Will tomorrow morning be convenient?"

I agreed to be at the doctor's office at 9:00 A.M. When I hung up I quickly dialed Lee's number at work. I felt as if my life were being ripped apart. I knew a Class IV meant possible cervical cancer. Now I might never have any more children.

When my husband answered the phone I blurted out the awful news. "Becky," he said, "I want you to be well more than I want our baby, so you can imagine how much that is." I took courage in his strength but twenty minutes later my husband came home with tears streaming down his face.

"I'm so afraid I'm going to lose you, Becky," he told me, holding me close.

Lee's mother had died of lung cancer fifteen years before. My husband had left college to nurse her through her final months. The frustration, pain, and sorrow he had felt made him sensitive to those who were sick or hurt, but he never completely got over his feelings of helplessness. Now cancer was threatening his family again.

The next morning we met with Dr. Sein, who explained the procedure, called a colcoscopy, to us. He would use a wicked looking tool with jagged teeth to remove bits of my cervix for microscopic analysis. The results would be known in a few days.

"How can you do this procedure in your office, Doctor?" I asked him. "Won't I need an anaesthetic?"

"There are no nerve endings in the cervix," he assured me. "You won't feel a thing."

In a few moments I lay upon Dr. Sein's examining table, with my husband holding my hand. The doctor removed instruments from the freezer and began snipping. Waves of searing pain radiated with each bite of the teeth, and I moaned aloud in distress.

"Be quiet!" the doctor ordered. "This doesn't hurt!"

Finally, the pernicious physician put away his instrument

of torture. Gradually, the agony diminished to a throbbing excruciation, and I passionately hoped that he would some day be reincarnated as a woman. Lee and I returned home to await apprehensively the doctor's call.

The results were both good and bad. I did have a carcinoma in situ, but it could be removed by a minor surgical procedure called a cervical conization. I would require twenty-four hours of bed rest at home afterward, and could slowly resume my normal activities over the following two weeks.

On October 10 I had the surgery. Evie took over the personal interviews I'd scheduled and Jerry did the driving for Project New Life. I only took a few days off to rest and even then I continued to take phone calls. I had planned my boys' school work several weeks ahead, and they were careful not to stress me. The only problem was the housework. I was incapacitated and no one else in the house had time, so Lee hired a maid from Rose Marie's Cleaning Service. She was to scrub the bathrooms, vacuum the carpets, mop the floors, and do any other cleaning I wanted done during the six hours for which my husband had paid.

"Thank you for coming," I said to Maria, a middle-aged Hispanic woman wearing a Rose Marie's uniform, as she arrived one morning in the middle of October. The boys headed for their rooms to do school work so she wouldn't have to step over them to vacuum, and I showed her what I wanted done. She filled her bucket and started down the hall for the bathroom just as the phone rang. It was a prostitute, so I excused myself and began my standard interview.

"What kind of prostitution do you do?" I asked as I reached for an intake form.

"Do you work the street?" I jotted "Streetwalker" in the "Type of Prostitution" blank.

"Do you have a pimp?" I asked next.

"How old are you, and how long have you been a prostitute?"

Out of the corner of my eye, I saw Maria walk past me as I assessed my caller's needs.

"Do you have any warrants?"

"What kind of drugs do you use?"

This continued for about an hour, as I made notes and began to determine possible goals. I called Evie to ask her to arrange for shelter for our new client and gave her my opinion of our most likely course of action for her. Shortly after I said good-bye to Evie, the phone rang again. It was Lee.

"How's the maid doing, honey?" he asked.

"I don't know, Lee. I've been on the phone for an hour. Just a minute and I'll go look."

I went to the hall bathroom but only the bucket was there. I looked around the house but couldn't find Maria anywhere. I picked up the receiver.

"That's funny. She was here but she's not in the house now," I said, puzzled.

"I'll call Rose Marie's," my husband said.

In a few minutes he phoned again, but I could hardly understand him through his laughter.

"Rose Marie's said the maid called them. She overheard you talking with a client and thought you were running a whore-house!"

"Did you explain . . . ?" I managed, astounded.

"Yes. The people at Rose Marie's thought it was hilarious. They're sending another cleaning lady now," my husband said, still laughing.

I had come to expect embarrassing situations in the course of my work.

After every media interview, at least one college kid, who had probably been told by his fraternity brothers that I ran a brothel, would call me to ask to hire a hooker. Nevertheless, I hadn't expected embarrassment to cause anyone to ask me for help.

When Paula Richardson phoned long distance that November, she sounded panicky. "You've got to help me!" she cried. "I don't want to be a prostitute anymore!"

When I heard desperation in the voice of a prospective client, it usually meant that she was in jail for the first time. Sometimes that provided the impetus to leave the life. Sometimes it didn't. There were no quick fixes.

"Okay. I need some information so that I'll know how to help you," I explained gently. "What kind of prostitution do you do—like massage parlor, streetwalking, or what?"

"I work for an escort service," she said. "I work out of my home while my husband is at work and my son is in school."

"How long have you been a prostitute?"

"Eight years."

"Does your husband want you to continue?" I asked. If he did, that could be a problem. There are housewives prompted by their husbands to work as prostitutes for a few hours a day. They earn far more than they could at any other type of employment.

"No! That's the problem. I've told him I'm at the club working out or with my girlfriends, and he just thinks I'm a great money manager. He doesn't know anything about this.

"You see, the answering service called with a customer this morning and gave me a room number at a motel where I was supposed to meet him. So I went to the motel, knocked on the door, and went in the minute it opened, because it's cold outside. I didn't even notice what the guy looked like. I just took off my coat and stood there in net stockings, black garters, and a teddy. When I turned around, the customer was my husband's boss!

"We just stood there staring at each other for a minute. Then I said, 'I think I have the wrong room,' and grabbed my coat.

"He ran to the door after me and called, 'Please don't tell my wife!'"

I was laughing by now but I couldn't let this lady know it.

I put my hand over the receiver and hoped she would keep talking until I got my hilarity under control.

"I've got to quit before my husband finds out!"

I referred Paula to a self help group of former prostitutes in a city near hers.

The Josephson Appliance Corporation Christmas party was to be held at the Gravel Lake Holiday Inn, one of the most exclusive hotels in town. Lee and David's employers were well-known for extravagant holiday celebrations and everyone dressed to the teeth for this lavish event.

To me, David was still a child at sixteen but his height, blue eyes, curly black hair, and straight white teeth made him appear a young man. Home schooling, however, didn't lend itself to him meeting girls, and David had no date for the party. His co-workers teased him unmercifully about not being able to find someone to take to the social event of the year.

I had an idea which I shared with my husband that might solve our son's problem with the Christmas party. Lee thought it was a great plan, so he suggested to David, "Why don't you invite Christine Mayer to the party?"

David didn't think Christine would be interested in dating a sixteen-year-old kid, but I knew she'd do it. In the three years since we had met, we had become dear friends, and she cared deeply for my children.

The night of the party, Lee and I left our son at Christine's house. Since he didn't have a car of his own, our friend would drive. We said good-bye and headed for the hotel.

The party was just getting underway when we arrived, with a live band providing a variety of music to accommodate the tastes of the different age groups present. The tables were set with crystal and linen, and people moved about, chatting with friends and co-workers. Lee and I chose a spot near the entrance so we wouldn't miss David and Christine, but there was no need.

Our son's date was so beautiful, every head turned when she entered the room. I heard several men mutter, "Where'd Dave get *her*?"

Our son introduced his date to some of the men he worked with, then led her to the dance floor. Her days as a nude dancer/prostitute had given Christine a grace and agility that drew all eyes to her. David was only a mediocre dancer, but her nimble rhythmic movements made him look skillful.

When men in the crowd tried to cut in on David and Christine, she gave them an innocent yet seductive smile and said, "Sorry, I've been waiting to be with David."

This former hooker considered my family to be hers, and she was going to make the men who had taunted David miserable. At dinner, my charming friend held the men seated near her enthralled with her witty observations and quick laugh, but she had eyes only for David. Never again would these impudent upstarts ridicule my son because he didn't have a girlfriend: she would make them drool.

Christine's suave elegance had exactly the effect she had hoped it would, and David's prowess with women was touted by his co-workers ever afterward.

Shortly after her one and only church experience, Sam had been arrested again for prostitution and had been sent to jail. I was sorry to see her on the same old merry-go-round, but glad that she continued to pursue her education during this incarceration.

"Only a couple more sentences, and you'll have a diploma," I teased her.

Unfortunately, when she was released just before Christmas, Sam once again began using drugs heavily. The emotional blows she had suffered during the summer had shattered her fragile ego, and she now turned to the solace she knew so well: she cushioned her emotions with layers of drug-induced euphoria.

A few days before Christmas, Sam phoned me in the morning to ask a favor.

"Could you give me a ride to my sister Debbie's house?" she asked.

"Sure, Sam," I promised. "I have to leave at noon to take David to work, and Debbie's house is on the way. Would it be okay if I picked you up about ten minutes after twelve?"

"Sure. Thanks, Becky," Sam agreed. "I'll be waiting on the sidewalk in front of the St. Mark's Hotel."

When we arrived at the hotel a few minutes after noon, Samantha was leaning against the building, her head sunk on her chest and the paper sacks which contained her clothes on the sidewalk around her. David and I exchanged looks of exasperation. "Will she never quit using drugs?" I said discouragedly. I parked the station wagon and put Sam's bags in the back while David led her to the car. She peered at us from under heavily-lidded eyes and slurred her thanks in slow motion speech. Then she slumped against the seat. David, worried that she might lose consciousness, kept up a steady stream of chatter. I had seen many people on the street in this condition, and I knew the hospitals weren't interested in helping them, so I decided to take our friend to her sister's house, as she had requested that morning. Debbie would watch her carefully and call the paramedics if they were needed.

I was glad it wasn't rush hour. The freeway traffic was moving at sixty miles per hour as I drove to Debbie's house. Suddenly, Sam opened the door and slid toward the pavement. David grabbed the collar of her jacket instantly, then undid his seat belt with one hand, while he held onto Sam with the other. Meanwhile, the car screeched as I hit the brake hard. With cars all around me I couldn't stop, only slow down.

"I dropped my cigarettes," Sam yelled incoherently as she tried to roll away from David.

David held her tightly as he leaned forward and brought

her back inside the car. Then he fastened her seat belt as my heart pounded and my hands shook. Somehow, my son managed to get the car door shut, then he sank into the back seat with a loud sigh. I could see his pallor in the mirror, and I glanced at Sam, but she was oblivious to the nearly fatal error she had just made.

"Maybe I'm in the wrong business, David," I suggested shakily as I started up the car again.

"No. We just need to be very careful," he responded breathlessly.

I don't know when my children had begun feeling the same determination I had that prostitutes should be able to choose a better life, but I was thankful that they did.

10

THE ANGEL OF DEATH

arah Flowers wrote glowing reports of her new home in Denver to Christine Mayers. She and the baby were happy, and she had a job at a day care center where she could take Justin to work with her. On the Saturday after Christmas I phoned Sarah. She seemed glad to talk with me, but there was a hollow ring to her usually bubbly tone.

After a few minutes, I knew something had to be troubling her, so I asked, "What's the matter, honey?"

Sarah's voice cracked as she replied, "Becky, I've got AIDS."

I struggled to maintain my composure but tears rolled down my cheeks. "When did you find out?" was all I could think of to say.

"Last week. I thought I'd gotten away from the life, but it followed me."

Sarah was trying to make a joke but I couldn't laugh.

When I hung up, I turned to Lee.

"Sarah's got AIDS," I whispered.

Lee put his arms around me as I sobbed. He said, "You knew this would happen to some of your clients. I know it's hard to accept but there's nothing we can do about Sarah. We have to help the others out there."

The specter of Sarah's future weighed on my mind. Some of my clients had told me about other prostitutes who'd worked the streets dying of AIDS but, until now, their deaths hadn't touched me personally.

On the following Saturday afternoon Jerry and Evie came over to watch Star Trek reruns with Lee and me for a few hours. We four Trekkies found solace and hope for the future in the little morality plays that were the theme of the show, and we occasionally got together on Saturdays to see a couple of back-to-back Star Treks. This weekend, though, Captain Kirk seemed unimportant. All we could concentrate on was Sarah.

"Don't johns worry about getting AIDS?" I said.

Jerry mused on this for a moment.

"I don't think so; have you ever seen the Central Park Loop?" he asked.

The rest of us looked at him blankly.

"At the northern end of the park the main road veers off in a long loop that's separated by pine trees from the rest of the area. I have a friend who's a paramedic who told me about the homosexual activity there," Jerry explained.

"The gays have adopted the Loop as their portion of the park, because it provides privacy from heterosexuals who object to their lifestyle. There's a lot of gay prostitution there."

We'd had a hard time reaching them because the male prostitutes aren't as obvious as the women, so we insisted that he drive us to the Loop. We piled into my station wagon, which Jerry drove. At the east entrance to Central Park he turned a corner and began explaining.

"There are the trees which mark the beginning of the Loop." He pointed to a pair of large fir trees, one on either side of the road. We could see nothing beyond these and the shrubs which formed a solid wall.

As we drove beneath the boughs of the two giant conifers, Jerry went on. "Look to our left."

Despite the damp, cold weather, three pairs of men were locked in embraces on the wet lawn. Two of them were kissing passionately.

"That guy's looking for action," Jerry said, pointing to a man who was laying supine on a plaid blanket. Evie and I were wide-eyed as we drove past him. The man was wearing sweat pants with a lump in the crotch that might have been a large potato. Lee and Jerry burst into laughter at our naive stares.

A few female twosomes sat on the trunks of parked cars, holding hands and talking. Two male couples in brightly-colored leotards and body suits necked side by side under the branches of a budding maple. A few lone men sat as if waiting for some- one to join them, and, as we watched, a young man dressed in a white miniskirt and pink blouse with white high heels and matching purse approached the solitary individuals one after another. When we drove around the Loop a second time, the transvestite prostitute still hadn't found a "date."

"Now look over there," Jerry told us.

The entire Loop road was lined with parked cars with men standing behind open driver's doors and leaning their elbows on the roofs.

"They're prostitutes," Jerry continued. "In daylight the open door is a signal that they're available. At night, they blink their headlights at passing cars. Now you see for yourselves the dual nature of prostitution."

"It's unbelievable," I said slowly. "I bet no one, neither gays nor straights, is taking AIDS seriously."

Sam had cleaned up her act shortly after her near-disaster at Christmastime. She went back on methadone which was not really a substitute for the drug combination she'd been using, but having regular urine analyses helped her keep clean. She was still hooking but being older and well-recognized in town she did most of her business before five o'clock, because the freshman cops arrested hookers in the early evenings.

When Marsha Majors, Sam's friend, had been arrested for prostitution in January, the women's jail had sent her immediately to the hospital because of her obvious physical debility. Marsha was diagnosed as having advanced tuberculosis, and, for once, the hospital didn't send the patient away just because she was a streetwalker: to do so would have been a death sentence. The prosecuting attorneys, long familiar with the thirty-four-year-old hooker whom they called "aging," recommended that the charges against her be dropped. They were probably hoping that the disease would give her a rougher sentence than they could get in court.

Prison inmates in the hospital were not allowed visitors, so as soon as her charges were dropped, Marsha phoned Sam to tell her. Samantha went immediately to see her. Thus began one of the most poignant episodes I've ever witnessed.

Every other day for the four months that Marsha was hospitalized, Samantha Rice took a two-hour bus trip across town to visit her friend. When visiting hours were over she made another two-hour trip home. This was no small feat because Sam had to earn a living. She couldn't work nights anymore, because her chances of being arrested were too high, so she had to compete with younger "babes" (her term) in broad daylight for tricks. Yet, she never missed a visit and when Marsha was well enough to leave the hospital Sam took her home and took care of her until Marsha was able to return to work.

During this period the frightening reality of AIDS came close again. Rosemary Johnson, who had once attended Harvest Tabernacle where Evie went to church, phoned the church pastor and asked him to send someone to visit her at Juvenile Hall. She was a sixteen-year-old girl dying of the disease. The minister phoned Evie because the girl was a prostitute.

"What should I say to her, Becky?" Evie asked me.

Sarah Flowers's chilling news at Christmas had been forever etched in my head, and now Evie's words fell like an icy mantel about my shoulders.

I shuddered and my anger rose, anger at this disease, anger at johns, anger at the molesters whose malefic actions had catapulted adolescent girls onto the street. I responded, "Ask her who at home molested her."

"What?" said Evie, taken aback. "Becky, I meant how can I comfort her? What can I say?"

"Evie, she probably didn't get AIDS from a john. She's only sixteen, and it takes time for the disease to develop. If we can find out who molested her, and if he has AIDS, which is likely, maybe he can be prosecuted."

Evie wasn't thrilled about my suggestion but she agreed to ask. Rosemary was being kept in an isolation cell so she was glad to have a visitor. She wore the gray cotton dress of an inmate although she wasn't being charged with any violations. The teenager had been brought to Juvenile Hall from the hospital by a social worker.

Evie visited the girl and came back to tell me, "Rosemary Johnson has been working the street since she was twelve years old. She's the victim of sexual molestation by her stepfather." I nodded. "I knew it was someone close."

Evie went on. "When she got sick, her pimp dropped her off at County Hospital's emergency room and left her there. Doctors say that she has AIDS."

"What a shame," I said. She nodded.

"Rosemary's mother refused to accept responsibility for her so Kaylee Mills at the hospital contacted Child Protective Services. A court order remanded the youngster to State custody, and when she was well enough to be released from the hospital she was sent to Juvenile Hall."

"Ordinarily, CPS would have been too overburdened to

respond," I said, "but the prospect of releasing an AIDS-infect-ed prostitute into the community frightened them into taking her into custody. Let me go with you next time and talk to her."

We went a few days later. "I wanted to ask you about your stepfather," I said to Rosemary when we got to her room. "You said he'd molested you when you were a little girl. I was wonder-ing if you knew what happened to him after you left home. Does he have AIDS?"

Rosemary's young face fell, her shoulders sagged, and she seemed to study the floor. It was a full minute before she answered. "My mom won't let me talk to my brothers and sister, but sometimes I call when she's not home. My sister says Doug has been real sick. He's lost weight, and he stays in bed a lot. I don't know. I guess he could have AIDS."

Plucking up my courage, I said gently, "Rosemary, maybe your stepfather gave you AIDS. I think we should get a lawyer for you and sue him."

The teen looked horrified. "I don't want to make my mom mad at me. She caught him in bed with me, and she thinks I made him do it. I really want to make up with her before I die of this disease."

And that was the end of it. Because Rosemary hoped for a reunion with her family before she died, she wouldn't pursue a civil suit against her stepfather. The reunion never happened. A few months later she passed away, a victim until the end of her life. Death of one kind or another seemed to go hand in hand with prostitution.

After Virginia Eliason's murder there had been no report-ed murders of prostitutes for several months. Then in March a sensational killing made the headlines. A streetwalker was found dead, her wrists and ankles tied, and gravel in her mouth as a cryptic warning. Police investigators insisted that her killer was a person or persons unknown.

In April two more hookers were found dead, one apparently stabbed and thrown out of a moving vehicle on the freeway, and the other choked and left to die on Lower River Road. Streetwalkers' dead bodies began to turn up about once a month after that. Some were left bound in motel rooms which had been set on fire. Several were found stabbed beside freeways. Another body appeared on Lower River Road. One woman's nude strangled body was found in a burning dumpster. Some were mutilated, and most were bound hand and foot. These killings took place in various incorporated and unincorporated areas in and around our city.

Kathy Stevens was choked, stabbed, and left for dead shortly after Virginia Eliason's body was found. The horrible event caused her to telephone me and I helped her enter our program. Several other streetwalkers I knew began reporting having been attacked by knife-wielding johns and managed to escape. When they spoke with detectives, however, little interest was shown in their stories, and none of them were asked to describe their assailants to a police artist. Many streetwalkers began to carry knives when they worked. This made me even more nervous, because I knew an assailant could easily turn a weapon on a weaker, untrained woman.

At this point the media began interviewing me frequently, wanting stories about the tension on the street. It made good copy, but as I pointed out no one asked why there were no suspects, why murders of prostitutes seemed to be acceptable.

The local police claimed that they were expending maximum man-hours on the cases, but no suspects were announced even after many months of terror and more bodies turning up.

Although tension remained high, there were no violent acts during the winter. The Chief of Police announced that the killer was believed to have left the area. However, my clients and I weren't as gullible as the police seemed to hope the public would be. We remembered that, during the summer, the cops had said there were at least two persons responsible for the killings.

In early June I received a call about a mysterious woman who had been living in front of a deserted shopping center on Poinsettia Lane. A man who owned the convenience store across the street had become concerned about this person when several of his customers had approached to offer help, but she'd neither look at them nor answer their questions. For days the woman, who looked to be in her forties, had sat motionless in front of the empty store surrounded by boxes and bags of clothing. The shopkeeper had called me because he had heard I worked with street people. I suppose he didn't know there was a difference between streetwalkers and street people. I agreed to try to help the woman.

I arrived at Poinsettia Lane at 11:30 in the morning. The sun was breaking through the clouds and shining down warmth, getting ready for its full blast of summer heat in a few weeks. The shopping center had once been a busy neighborhood mall, but industry now encroached the area. The only residents left were elderly men and women who hung onto their property tenaciously, perhaps remembering the neighborhood as it used to be, with neat lawns, trimmed hedges, and children playing in the streets.

The windows of the former grocery store were boarded up, and graffiti filled the walls. On the sidewalk in front, under the overhanging eave, a petite dark-haired Oriental woman sat surrounded by cardboard boxes and paper bags. Her head hung down. She took no notice of my car as I parked it and didn't glance at me as I walked toward her. I didn't want to give an impression of authority by talking to her from a standing position, so I sat down in front of her on the sidewalk, legs crossed Indian-fashion.

"I'm Becky," I began. "Some people I know are worried about you, and they asked me to come talk to you."

She made no response, not a blink, not a twitch. I continued.

"I know you don't belong here. Street people aren't as well dressed as you," I told her.

The woman's hair was piled neatly and professionally on top of her head. She wore Cleopatra-style eye makeup, elaborately painted and decorated fingernails, and an expensive silk dress in a form-fitting Eastern style beneath a heavy cotton parka which hung open.

"It's none of my business if you stay here, and I know it, but I just want to ask if you have enough to eat and drink, or if you need anything. I can tell that something has hurt you, so I understand that you might not want to talk to people, but I want to offer my help."

I continued to talk to her for twenty minutes without any response, not even eye contact, when suddenly she lifted her head, looked straight at me, and said, "I'd like some fried chicken and a Coke."

"Okay, I'll be right back," I told her. I got up and returned to my car, remembering that I had seen a Kentucky Fried Chicken restaurant a few blocks away. Fifteen minutes later, I was back, KFC in hand, with the largest Coke they served. I also brought french fries and cole slaw.

The woman had resumed her position, knees to her chest, arms wrapped around her legs, head down. I took the food to her. "I've brought what you asked for," I said gently and watched her eat the food slowly. I tried again to get her to talk to me.

"Do you need anything else?" I asked hopefully.

"You can get me a hotel room, so I can rest. I'm so tired," she replied. I noticed a slight accent this time.

"I'm sure the people who sent me can do that, but then what? You can't spend your life in a hotel room." I needed to keep her talking to me. If she drew back into silence I couldn't help her.

She looked up at me again. "All I want to do is rest. Who are you?" she asked.

"I help prostitutes most of the time, but I try to help other people, too," I answered. I assumed that was what she wanted to know, since I had already told her my name.

"I'm a prostitute." It seemed to take an effort for her to talk, and she spoke only a few words at a time.

"I want to help you."

The woman added, "I worked at a brothel for fifteen years, and now I have AIDS."

"I'll call the AIDS Crisis Center for you," I told her. "They can help you find a place to live."

"They won't help prostitutes," she said with finality. She rested her head on her knees again.

I found out that, in a way, the mysterious woman was correct: the AIDS Crisis Center couldn't provide free room and board for her. However, the reason was not that they didn't want to help a prostitute. They just didn't have the funding for long-term housing. There was no place I could send her. Never before had I failed someone so completely.

When I shared the day's defeat with Lee and Claire that evening, my husband was sympathetic but realistic.

"Well, you can't help everyone, honey," he soothed.

Claire saw things in a different light.

"Why didn't the brothel have health insurance?" she exclaimed in exasperation. She had a valid point.

11

SURVIVORS

Most of my street prostitutes, both male and female, had never held regular jobs. Few had been to school beyond the sixth grade. Our requirements of full-time employment and part-time education, or vice versa, caused tremendous alterations in their lifestyles. The change enabled them to see themselves in a different light very quickly. That new inner picture was all-important to making their transformation permanent.

Upper income prostitutes made fewer dramatic changes in their lifestyles. Many of these clients had college educations and moved through the community without the stigma of prostitution. Unfortunately, that meant their perceptions of themselves were also slow to change.

Christine Mayer worked at one of the local hospitals in the bookkeeping department. Since she had a college education, school was not part of her program but a full-time job was. After she had made a decisive though painful break with her pimp, she began to date romantic interests. Unfortunately, she didn't realize that the men she chose were johns, but I could see it plainly.

Christine phoned me to tell me all about the sweet young man in the accounting department whom she'd been seeing. Soon the calls began to be sprinkled with complaints about his interfering mother. By April she was begging me to have a talk with Mama.

Stanley was the type of John I call Mario the Mama's Boy. Typically Mario lives with his mother until she dies. He dates prostitutes because he's too immature to have a normal relationship with a woman.

I considered this sort of thing part of my job, because it was an issue of prostitution. Of course, I didn't usually speak with "Mama," but sometimes I let my clients talk me into chatting with the john/boyfriend. For Christine's sake, though, I went the rounds with everybody. Of course, my discussions didn't do a bit of good, but eventually my friend realized that I was right about Stanley, and she terminated the relationship.

Sally Michlovich was an alcoholism counselor with whom I shared several clients. When she phoned in May, she told me of a new client, Heidi Freeman, who had been a streetwalker and a heroin addict for fifteen years. Now Heidi was working as a machinist and was trying to change her lesbianism orientation, and Sally wanted me to talk her out of it.

"I'd be glad to talk to her, Sally, but I don't talk people out of or into homosexuality or heterosexuality. My goal is to get them out of prostitution."

Sally said, "Speak to her anyway. I think you can help her."

I called Heidi the next day and suggested we talk in person. I wanted to find out if she had really gotten out of prostitution. We agreed to meet at Harold's Donuts the next day.

The picture of that diminutive figure who awaited me as I walked into the donut shop remains fresh in my mind. Heidi was five-foot-two, with short, dark copper hair and warm brown eyes.

She wore blue jeans and a pink tank top fringed with lace. Tattoos covered her arms. She was the epitome of a tomboy, at once womanly yet virile. She wore no makeup on her beautiful face and her shape was utterly feminine.

We went to her tiny apartment where she showed me photographs of her two sons, Tyler, six, and Phil, eleven. Tyler's little face was still baby-round and sweetly dimpled. Phil was a handsome boy with curly dark hair and his mother's thick lashes surrounding big brown eyes.

"Oh, Heidi, they're darling!" I exclaimed. "Where are they?"

Her voice was soft but lively. Her eyes lit up, and her face took on that special glow that loving parents have when they talk about their children.

"They're with their father, Ethan Freeman. He was my pimp, and he won't let me have them. He won't send them to school, and they just run wild. But he's dying of cancer so I'll have my kids with me soon."

"Does your family help you?" I asked. I needed to establish whether she had any support base.

"Yes, my mom's helping me. Well, Evelyn Parker's not really my Mom but I've sort of adopted her," Heidi answered. She continued, "My real mother was a prostitute. She had eight kids and she gave us all away. I was in an orphanage with my brother until I was six and he was eleven.

"The day we were adopted was the only time my mother ever took us home with her. I remember she combed the lice out of our hair and gave us clean clothes. The next day she gave us a basket of fruit and kissed us goodbye.

"We'd been adopted by the same family. About three months after we got there my brother disappeared, and I never saw him again. He kept wetting the bed, and I found out later that they couldn't handle that, so they sent him away without telling me. I never found out where he went.

"My new mother made me do all the housework when I got home from school, and I never got out to play. I think that's why they adopted me, so they could have a maid.

"When I was fifteen, my adoptive mother thought I was trying to steal her husband, so she kicked me out. I didn't do nothing, though—she made it all up. 'Your mother was a prostitute, and you're nothing but a prostitute,' she used to tell me. She told the juvenile authorities that I had run away and was uncontrollable so they put me in Juvenile Hall for a year. Then they sent me to a group home. I ran away from there and met Ethan. I worked for him until I met my Mom last year."

I felt devastated that the innocence of childhood could be so ravaged and exploited. "Would you like me to help you find your birth family, or your brother?" I asked.

"No. I'm afraid to find out what happened to the rest of my family."

She was nothing if not honest, and I certainly couldn't blame her for her reluctance to search for her family.

Heidi had related her story in a straightforward manner. It was not as if she had rehearsed it, nor was she detached. This woman spoke as if she had become so accustomed to suffering she had learned to live with it. She revealed a lack of emotion in speaking of her life that I had seldom witnessed in other streetwalkers. A lot of the victim prostitutes imagine that their lives would be okay if only the stepfathers who had molested them would just go away. Then their families would be happy again. Others hoped to find their birth fathers, in the belief that they will once again be "Daddy's girl." Heidi Freeman had no pleasant memories upon which to embroider fantasies to sustain her.

"Sally Michlovich told me yesterday that you wanted to quit being a lesbian," I said. "Why is that important to you?"

She spoke candidly. "I started having sex with this girl who was a prostitute because she was so nice to me. Ethan was always mean to me, like my adopted mother was. Valerie, my girlfriend, let me stay with her when Ethan beat me up. She wanted to have sex with me, so I let her. I figured I owed her something. Now, when I want sex, I always want it with women, but I'm not a prostitute anymore, and I want to be straight."

"How did you feel about being a streetwalker?" I asked gently.

"I hated being a prostitute." Heidi continued quietly, "I taught myself to eat only every other day, so I wouldn't have to sell my body anymore often than that. I became an expert at pretending I was some place else, so I didn't have to think about what I was doing when I was with a trick.

"I started using heroin because it made me feel like I didn't care where I was or what I was doing. I haven't used smack [heroin] since I met Mom, but I'm having a hard time quitting beer. I like to go to the bar after work. I've cut down, though—I only drink two or three beers a night."

I looked searchingly at Heidi. Here was beauty of the inner sort—a crushed bloom which reopens, unfolding its delicate petals one at a time, slowly, testing its strength, fearing it will be crushed again. I hoped that I'd be able to watch her grow, and I wanted very much to meet "Mom." Who was this person who was so important to Heidi that she was able to drag her from the pit?

Since Heidi seemed sincere about wanting to change her sexual orientation, I gave her the phone numbers of several self help groups for people who were trying to overcome homosexuality, asked her for Evelyn Parker's phone number, and promised to arrange a few other details we both thought were necessary. As I got in my car, Heidi waved, hopped on a bicycle and rode down the street to her remedial reading class: she wanted to learn to read before her boys came to live with her. I watched her, feeling greatly affected by this brave and yet wistful young woman. I desperately hoped she would succeed.

A john, of course, is a person who pays someone to have sex with him or her. Not all of them pay in cash. Some, like Harold the Helper, trade room and board or meals for sex. Others, like Norman the Nerd, think they have to pay people to date them. The key is that the relationship isn't based on mutual respect and trust. It is based on trade.

Unfortunately, after Christine Mayer quit seeing Stanley, she hadn't learned a lesson. She began dating an ophthalmologist who turned out to be a Norman. At first, her glowing reports of romance with a physician made me happy for her, although his lavish gifts worried me. And the more she told me about him the more I worried. At thirty-eight, George Anderson had never married, hadn't even been engaged. This in itself wasn't a cause for concern, but coupled with the money he spent on her, it made me wonder if he might be a john.

As time went on my concern grew. Anderson seemed essentially self-centered. While he bought Christine gifts, they were either things she'd mentioned liking, or things that amused him, like jewelry and clothing. He only took her places where he could show her off, like the trendiest restaurants and nightclubs. She couldn't see the one-sidedness of the relationship, because this was the way she had always been treated by men. But I couldn't help seeing it. I always hated seeing my clients and friends go through these relationships even though I knew it was a natural part of their growth process. At least when they had troubles I was there to help them resolve their dilemmas.

Christine's eyes were slightly asymmetrical. One lid drooped a bit at the outside corner. This was unnoticeable to most people, but to Christine who'd always made her living by her beauty and whose self image depended on it, the tiny defect was enormous. Dr. Anderson told her he could "take care of it" with a minor operation, and she agreed enthusiastically.

George performed the surgery with a local anaesthetic in Christine's living room one Saturday morning. The next week he removed the stitches. The little droop was still there and now she had a tiny scar as well. At this point my friend poured out her disappointment to me.

"If he didn't know what he was doing, why did he even try?" she moaned.

"Christine," I said gently, "don't you think a man who really cared about you would have done this surgery under sterile conditions in his office, or referred you to another surgeon who was trained in that procedure?"

"I never thought about it," she confessed.

"George not only bungled the surgery, he's trading goods and services for your presence," I suggested. "People who love each other do give gifts, but Dr. Anderson is just giving you things so you'll do what he wants in every way."

"You think so?" Christine asked, not really ready to believe me.

"I'll tell you what," I replied. "Ask him to take you to the play at the Dinner Theater. I'll bet he refuses, because he can't show you off in the dark. Better yet, tell George you want to spend some evenings at home with him. You'll cook him dinner and afterward you'll play Sorry or Scrabble. My bet is he'll never go for it."

"But what if he just doesn't *like* to do those things?" she asked.

"If you find that the only things he likes to do involve showing the world he's got a beautiful woman with him, then you'll know he's a john."

It took Christine a month to convince herself that George Anderson was a john. When she came to the same conclusion I had, to her credit she ended their relationship.

We planned to try out our new camper after Claire's birthday in August, but I got a call from the Suicide Hotline the day before we were to leave.

A nude dancer/prostitute named Marcy Entwhistle phoned the hotline. The counselor, after determining it wasn't an emergency, transferred the call to the Project New Life phone. I spoke with Marcy briefly and wasn't as sure as the counselor about her state of mind. I decided to meet with her right away. My plan was, if she seemed stable I could determine a personal program for her, then have a volunteer help her start working on her immediate goals until I returned.

Christine Mayer was my first choice for a sponsor. Loving, kind, efficient, insightful and responsible, Christine always did a wonderful job. I phoned her before I left for Marcy's house, and she agreed immediately. I promised to call her after the interview.

Marcy lived with three roommates in a little white house surrounded by untrimmed rosebushes, which made me think of Sleeping Beauty's castle. When I rang the doorbell, she answered before the chimes had quit sounding, as if she had been waiting for me. As I followed her inside, I saw her long lustrous auburn hair and her dark brown, expressive eyes. I also noticed an elusive quality about this woman that I couldn't quite name.

"Oh, I'm so glad you've come! I can't believe you just came here right away!" Marcy gushed, a little too effusively.

I glanced around the room as she spoke. It looked like a bachelor pad. The furniture consisted of an exotic round velvet sofa, red and black wallpaper, and a stereo system with five-foot speakers. The place was messy with clothes tossed carelessly on the sofa, ashtrays full, and empty soda bottles on the gilt coffee table.

"Well, you called the crisis line, so I thought you were having a crisis," I joked gently.

"Oh, yes. Please sit down," she said and picked up the clothes on the sofa. "Excuse the mess. I live with three guys, and they're not very neat housekeepers."

What is it? I wondered. There's something about her that doesn't ring true.

"So, what's happening?" I asked casually, leaning back on the sofa with my knees crossed and my feet off the floor. "Do you want to get out of prostitution, or are you just thinking about it?"

"Well, I just hate being like this," Marcy answered. "I mean, even when I masturbate, I fantasize about hurting men. I want to have a lasting relationship with someone, but right now I hate men."

This threw me. None of my other women just plunged in and started talking about their personal sex lives. Probably, the things she was telling me had been bothering her for a long time, but it was unusual for new clients to manage the conversation like a cowboy leads a horse, and Marcy had a firm grip on where she wanted this to go.

I tried again, "How long have you been a prostitute?"

Marcy crossed her long legs and leaned against the arm of the chair opposite the sofa. She seemed to have a desperate need to be in control, judging from her response to my question, and the fact that she gained a height advantage by standing.

"Ever since I was very young. I worked the street until I was seventeen, when I became a dancer," she answered, with a toss of her hair, which fell in red-brown waves across her shoulders.

This sounded like early childhood molestation, so I said, "Tell me about your childhood."

"I always felt very different, like an outsider," Marcy began.

"I meant, tell me about your family and how you got along with your parents," I interjected.

She shrugged. "Well, I have nine brothers and sisters. My father deserted us when I was small and we lived in a one-room shack with my mother and grandmother. They hated my father, and they always talked bad about him. I used to run away, from the time I was little. I ate out of garbage cans. When I was eight, a man picked me up. It was raining, and I was cold and tired and hungry. He told me if I'd do something for him, he'd help me. He drove me to the back of a store and made me perform oral sex on him. Then he gave me two dollars. He didn't buy me food or give me a warm place to stay. He just put me out of his car in front of the store with two dollars. I began to hate men, but I didn't want to."

"You said you wanted to have a relationship with a man. Have you ever been married, or in love?" I asked, hoping my demeanor didn't betray my pity.

"Yeah, I've had boyfriends. Once I lived with a sailor for a year. I'm just so unhappy now. I hate being a prostitute, but it's all I've ever done," she told me in an even tone.

She was quite detached about discussing herself. Almost too detached, I thought. There was something else, though, some fleeting shadow that danced between us when she spoke. Something intangible.

"What are your goals? What kind of work do you want to do?" I tried to mask my distraction with professionalism.

"I'm interested in theater. I've taken some acting classes at the community college. I'd love to do Broadway shows!" Marcy replied, her voice taking on some inflection.

"Oh, that's exciting," I enthused. "Most actors have to do some other kind of work to support themselves, though, until they make a name for themselves. Have you ever thought about what else you could do, while you're breaking into show biz?"

I never discouraged the women from any goals they wanted to set. When you're at the bottom, the only way to go is up. I wanted to set no limits on their dreams.

Marcy hesitated for a moment. She looked me in the eye, as if trying to decide whether to trust me. With a sigh, she began, "There's a problem. I don't have ID."

"I'll help you get an ID," I said, brushing aside her concern. "I do it all the time for people."

"There's something I haven't told you." A pained expression crossed her face. She folded her arms as if to keep the world away.

"You don't have to tell me anything you don't want to, Marcy," I offered.

She covered her face with her hands. An uncomfortable silence fell upon us, like a fog descending on a forest. We were alone in her living room as time seemed to stand still. Neither of us knew what to say next. The hot August sun hadn't yet penetrated the cool darkness of Marcy's house, and the pool in the backyard splashed shadows on the ceiling. I became aware of a fan turning quietly in another room and tried to give her some time by concentrating on the sound.

"It's really terrible. I changed my birth certificate," she said.

"That's okay. We can order another one."

"No. I mean I changed my birth certificate." She paused, took a deep breath and then rushed on, "I used to be a man. I had a sex change operation when I was seventeen. I lied and told the doctors I was older, and I had to change my birth certificate myself, so they wouldn't know how old I was. I can't just get another birth certificate, because it would say I'm a man," she blurted out.

So that was it. As I tried to maintain my professional mien, thoughts passed helter skelter through my mind. How am I going to help this poor human being? What services are there for her? Is she telling me the truth? Why would someone lie about something like this? And, finally, Christine is going to kill me!

After her disclosure Marcy told me that she was not receiving hormones, that she needed follow-up surgery, and she needed to return to the sexual dysphoria (sex change) team for counseling. There was one thing for sure: career and education goals would have to be established after her medical and psychological needs had been met.

I explained to Marcy that I would be out of town for two weeks, and that Christine Mayer would be her sponsor. Marcy was glad to know that Christine had also been a nude dancer/prostitute, and I was relieved that I could leave my client with someone reliable until I returned. I knew Christine would be compassionate. Despite my confidence in Christine, when I called her I didn't mention the sex change.

It was hard to take a vacation at such a time but I knew my family needed my attention and that I should try to forget my work while I was away. Even so, when we reached San Francisco, I couldn't help calling Sadie Thompson, a career prostitute who had been referred to me as an interesting case of someone happy to be "in the life."

"When I decided to become a prostitute," Sadie told me, "it was because I was sick of the bullshit. I made about two grand a month as a teacher. I got tired of snot-nosed brats whose parents didn't care about them. I was just a glorified baby-sitter.

"At first I worked for an escort service. When some of the customers offered me more money if I would beat them, I decided to become a call girl. I wanted to leave Denver where I grew up, so I moved to San Francisco and began advertising in the lonely hearts column of the local newspaper.

"'The Love Queen will make you her prisoner. Slaves wanted for private dungeon.'" She laughed.

Sadie is a dominatrix, a prostitute who specializes in domination, and sometimes in sadistic sex. She uses whips and chains to rule the "despicable thralls" she holds in bondage. For her johns, the height of sexual fantasy is to be enslaved, beaten into submission, and bound to a bed or a chair.

"What I do is nobody's business but mine," she declared defiantly when we first met.

"I'm not trying to reform anybody," I countered. "I have enough clients who want to get out of the life. And it helps me understand other points of view to meet with prostitutes who don't want to leave the life. I hope I'm nonjudgmental."

By now I wanted to document every facet of this lifestyle, but how could I do that if I only talked with people who wanted to leave it?

Studying the unusual streetwalkers I found in San Francisco, I saw women and men dressed in leather, chains, and buckles. Their hair was cut and colored in punk-rocker style, and black lipstick covered their mouths. I wondered if the johns of this city liked their hookers to look that different, or if I was just missing the more common looking "hoes" because of my culture shock.

When we returned home, one of my first calls was to Christine. I was worried about Christine's reaction to Marcy. I should have had more confidence in her.

"Has Marcy had a sex change?" Christine asked as we talked.

With sinking heart, I replied, "Yes, she has," as nonchalantly as I could. I knew my casual tone sounded phony as soon as I spoke. I was afraid my friend would be angry at me for omitting to tell her such a major detail.

Christine wasn't at all perturbed, however. She said simply, "I know lots of dancers who have had sex changes. That doesn't bother me at all."

People who are or have been prostitutes are, as a group, the most empathetic folks I've ever met. I don't think there was a single straight person in Project New Life who would have worked willingly with Marcy, but here was a beautiful butterfly, with serious problems of her own, who would mentor this person, love her, encourage her. I could only marvel.

It was time to start Marcy on her program. I took her to her first appointment at the County Hospital where she was to be interviewed for placement in their sexual dysphoria program.

The social worker was a charming, charismatic woman who put my client at ease immediately. They talked for thirty minutes about the sex change program and the experiences

Marcy had had with her surgery and with her feelings. Then the social worker asked a question.

"Are you gay or are you straight?" she inquired.

Without a moment's hesitation, Marcy replied, "I'm straight. I date guys."

A silence fell upon us for a long moment as the three of us reflected on Marcy's answer. The social worker quickly changed the subject, but the question and her answer remains forever in my mind.

Christine Mayer, Heidi Freeman, and Marcy Entwhistle were all survivors. I felt good about their progress and what Project New Life was doing for their futures. My personal life was happier than it had been for a long time. I felt good about myself and confident about my abilities.

The next client I met was Kerry McCarthy. She worked for an escort service. She was married to a truck driver, and they had two children, hardly the image of a sexy, erotic prostitute. Her tastes ran to tailored suits and "sensible" shoes when she was off work, and I wondered if her customers would even recognize her if they should run into her on the street.

"I've been making plans to leave the life for years, but I've run into a snag and that's the reason I'm calling you. My husband's mother was recently diagnosed with Alzheimer's disease, and we don't have health insurance," she confided. "I have a degree in economics, and I'm ready to retire from prostitution, but now we can't afford it."

She'd hoped I could come up with a solution to her dilemma, but she had already done everything I would have suggested. Since Kerry McCarthy had mentioned that she was an AA member, I encouraged her to draw on her Higher Power for strength. For some reason she seemed to chafe at this. We spoke frequently and one evening after I'd suggested prayer again Kerry made her feelings on the subject quite clear.

"Becky, I do pray. You're always telling me to pray about things, as if you had a handle on God," she spat at me. "As a matter of fact, God means a hell of a lot to me!"

I realized then I still had a lot to learn about others and some substantive things to work on about myself.

Late one morning, after one of her appointments with the sexual dysphoria team, I drove Marcy Entwhistle to her job at Risque Rick's.

As she started to get out of the car, however, she saw a man approaching us. He'd just dismounted from a motorcycle and was wearing grimy jeans and a dirty T shirt marked "Iron Eagles." His beard was thick and unkempt and hung down over his beer belly, which spilled over his pants, and he was laughing.

"Oh my God," Marcy breathed, "why is he looking at us so intently and laughing?"

I shrugged it off, but it made me just as uneasy as it made her. However, in the busy afternoon which followed, the scene buried itself in my subconscious, and I didn't even mention it to Lee when we both arrived home.

The evening was one of those lovely autumn twilights which marks the passing of summer, with cool pine-scented breezes. I'd promised myself to spend this night with my family, but the familiar ringing of the phone told me early that I was probably going to have to change my plans.

"Becky?" a woman's voice asked when I answered. "This is Carol Bradley. Do you remember me?"

I had to smile. How could I forget? She was the first streetwalker Bob Kvale had recommended to Project New Life. When I'd picked her up, Bob had shown me his erotically decorated apartment. Unfortunately, she'd disappeared after an upsetting encounter with her father, and I hadn't seen her in four years.

"I want to try again to change my life," she said, "if it isn't too late."

"It's never too late," I assured her and made arrangements for her stay at a downtown shelter while she began working toward her goals once again. About two weeks later, as we were talking over her progress, she suddenly changed the subject.

"I really worry about Bonnie James' little girl Karen," she said.

"Why?" I asked. "I recently went to Bonnie's hotel suite with one of my other clients, and her ten-year-old daughter was sitting on the couch watching television. She looked okay to me."

Carol shook her head. "Well, Bonnie used to work the street but she's getting old. She and her husband live at the Highway 57 Motel, and she takes her tricks there. You've seen the suite. It has a living room and bedroom. Bonnie takes her dates to the bedroom while her daughter watches television in the living room," Carol explained. "The thing is, she has a hard time getting dates because she's gettin' so old so she has her daughter call up men and say, 'Do you wanna date my mommy?'"

This was against all the rules, both the law of the land and the law of the street. I frowned.

"Is Karen working as a prostitute?" I asked in dismay.

"No, not that I know of. Bonnie just uses her to get dates," Carol replied.

"She should definitely be turned in, Carol. That's an awful thing to do to a child. Do you want me to call Child Protective Services, or will you call?" I couldn't ignore this.

"You can call," she said. "I don't know how to talk to people. They might wonder how I know. I can't tell 'em I was a prostitute."

Although I phoned Booth Martin at CPS the next day, I was too late. Bonnie and her husband had moved from the motel a few days before. Carol's abhorrence of a using a child to attract johns was as great as mine. Together we began trying to track down the family. Within two weeks we learned that Bonnie was working Wickersham Boulevard in an area of seedy, disreputable bars. She took Karen to the taverns and sent her out on the street while she watched from inside. When a car pulled over to the child, Bonnie would run out and try to make a date.

I called Booth with this latest information. He told me that I would have to provide the name of the tavern, or CPS wouldn't be able to do anything about it.

"Booth, this woman is working Wickersham Boulevard. Can't you send a social worker out to investigate?" I pleaded.

"Becky, you know how committed I am to getting kids off the street, but look at the facts. Somewhere on Wickersham Boulevard, in one of dozens of bars, there is a woman with her ten-year-old daughter. It's not against the law for the woman to be on the street with her kid. We'd actually have to catch her in the act. Otherwise, it's hearsay. If I knew which tavern she was working, maybe I could do something about it, but I just can't arrest every woman with a kid who's on the sidewalk on Wickersham Boulevard in front of a bar."

I knew Booth was right, and Carol and I had both heard that Bonnie was working different bars at different times to keep from getting caught in just such a trap as we were planning.

"You know," Carol philosophized after I told her the outcome of my conversation with Booth, "there are kids starving in Africa every day and kids who are sick and homeless right here. Why does one kid mean so much to me? I don't even really know her."

I considered this for a minute before I answered. "Because if we ever get used to one child suffering, pretty soon we won't care about anyone."

We never found Bonnie and her daughter. Somewhere, Karen James is growing into a young woman. She has never had a home and never gone to school, but that's not because we didn't care. We did, but in her case, caring wasn't enough.

12

PROSTITUTION IS NOT SOLELY A WOMAN'S ISSUE

I had been having success helping streetwalkers change their futures, but I wanted the male prostitutes to know they didn't have to stay in the life, either. The challenge was to get the message to them. Males weren't often identified as prostitutes: so the professionals with whom they came in contact didn't refer them to Project New Life.

Spreading the word about our program wasn't always easy. Our posters were torn down and our pamphlets were destroyed when we left them in public places.

Even the telephone company tried to ignore us. I had asked them for several listings in the Yellow Pages under the headings for Women's Services and Rehabilitation Groups. And I asked for a new heading to be added, Prostitution Crisis Line. The phone company service representative kept asking me to wait while she spoke with her supervisor, who was clearly telling her that they couldn't print *that*. After forty-five minutes of bargaining, I informed her that if Cocaine Hotline, Alcoholics Anonymous, and Suicide Prevention could have explicit Yellow Pages listings, Prostitution Crisis Line would be listed, or they'd hear from my attorney. We got the listings.

But the boys and men on the street didn't seem to be letting their fingers do the walking. It took personal contact in most cases to make male prostitutes aware that help was available for them. Even then, they didn't often contact us. We had to go to them.

Jerry Hudson was talking with male prostitutes on the street one evening in August when he noticed a young and slender dark-haired man carrying a gym bag and sporting a telltale red bandanna in his right hip pocket.

"Hey, Man, what's happening?" Jerry asked.

"Be cool," the youth drawled, "I'm workin'."

"This ain't no way to make a living, Man. You're gonna catch AIDS from the johns," Jerry retorted with determination.

The young man looked Jerry directly in the eye and said, "I got me a wife and three kids in a hotel room. We got here from West Virginia two months ago, and I can't get a job. Welfare won't help us 'cause we ain't got our marriage license or birth certificates for our kids."

Encouraged because he felt the young father was the type of person we could help, Jerry extended his hand.

"My name's Jerry Hudson," he said.

The young man shook Jerry's hand and said, "I'm Clayton," but before my friend could tell him about Project New Life, the streetwalker spun around and muttered, "My ride is here."

A limousine pulled up to the curb, and Clayton got in. As he pulled the door shut, a smile of grim determination crossed his face, and he gave Jerry a quick wink.

"It was one of the worst moments of my life, Becky," Jerry told me later. "I knew we could help him but he drove off with that son of a bitch before I could say a word. I just wanted to pound that john into the pavement."

I knew exactly how he felt.

Among the peculiarities of gay prostitution are the johns I call "The Odd Couple." These are two homosexual men who bring a pair of male street prostitutes into their home for several months, while the hookers find other employment and get on their feet. Eventually, the "boys" move out, and the cohabitating couple find another pair of streetwalkers to "help." "Help" as in "Harold the Helper."

When Lee and I visited the home of Dennis Waite and Gary Spivers, an "Odd Couple" of our acquaintance, I was struck by the normal appearance of their house. In contrast to Bob Kvale's bawdy apartment, Dennis and Gary's home was neat, conservative, and tastefully decorated, with the exception of a room obviously used for "entertaining." After an hour's sparkling conversation, I excused myself to use the rest room.

"It's the second door on the right as you go down the hall," Dennis told me politely.

A red glow from a partially opened door on the left, opposite the bathroom, caught my eye, and I glanced into the room. Mirrors covered the walls and ceiling of the dimly-lit room, and I saw something that looked like a birthing chair at the near end. I hurried into the bathroom and wondered whether I dared sneak a better look as I returned to the living room.

When I exited the bathroom, I did so slowly. A peek into the room across the hall afforded a glimpse of a huge bed with lace pillows, some leather thongs or straps, various bottles, and some things unidentifiable in the three or four seconds I allotted to satisfy my curiosity.

As I returned to the living room, Dennis, with great amusement on his freckled face as if he knew I couldn't resist a peek, asked, "Well, did you see the 'game room?'"

"All that I cared to, anyway," I confessed, red-faced.

In the time that we knew them, at least ten young prostitute couples lived with Gary and Dennis, who later died of AIDS.

It was one of those dog days of late September when I finally got the opportunity to speak with Heidi Freeman's "Mom," Evelyn Parker. Streetwalkers didn't call much during this blast furnace weather. It would be a good time to watch Darroll and David splash each other in the pool while I relaxed in the shade and phoned Evelyn. We had heard about each other for weeks, but our hectic lives had so far kept us from communicating.

"How did you meet Heidi?" was my first question. I'd been dying to ask that since I'd met Heidi Freeman.

"I was going into my church one Sunday morning when I spotted a rough-looking young woman sitting on the lawn sobbing. I knew the moment I saw her that she was 'mine.'

"I walked over to her, put my arms around her, and invited her to come into church. She said, 'They don't want me in there,' so I promised to return after the service. When I went in, several people came up and told me that Heidi was no good. 'She's a prostitute, a lesbian, and a drug addict,' they said. 'And you should leave her alone.' As it turned out, her pimp's mother was a member of the congregation and that's how they knew.

"Well, Heidi came home with me and got cleaned up. She's off heroin now but she still drinks a little beer. A few weeks after she came to live with us, my husband got her a job as a machinist at Servco. He's a part owner, and he trained her on the job. Now she has her own apartment and, when Ethan Freeman dies, she'll get her sons back."

I came to believe that I was privileged to have met such extraordinary people. I thought of Heidi and Evelyn as a jigsaw puzzle, each of them pieces which would someday complete a rare and exquisite picture, one I would see and carry in my mind always.

Meanwhile, more and more pieces of other pictures emerged. Not all were in the future, I thought one day as I drew a deep breath and looked at the man across the table.

"Does anyone know you're here?" I asked.

My luncheon companion was Colin Nopson, a twenty-eight-year-old escort service prostitute who worked in Washington, D.C. He was impeccably groomed, with an expensive suit, manicured nails, and carefully styled hair. He gave the air of being used to fine restaurants and well-mannered people. He held my chair as I was seated and asked the waiter for the wine list, which he perused carefully before selecting an aperitif.

"I told Mr. Chenault's secretary that I was flying home for my aunt's funeral. They think I'm in Cleveland. In fact I did fly there before I caught another flight here. They expect me back Tuesday," Colin answered.

The tension of the moment was interrupted by a white-coated waiter with a linen towel over his forearm.

"Would you or madame care for dessert?" he asked my companion.

"We'd both like the white chocolate mousse with raspberry sauce," Colin said.

A busboy appeared to clear our luncheon dishes; then the waiter returned with our desserts before we could continue our conversation. This was one of those times that even the walls seemed to have ears, and I was terrified that someone might hear us. If I had known what Colin was going to tell me when he'd phoned that morning, I'd probably have chosen to meet him in an office rather than a high class club filled with society diners.

Earlier on the phone, Colin Nopson had told me that he was an escort service prostitute and that he wanted to get out of the life. He asked if we could meet at the Chart House, one of Gravel Lake's exclusive clubs, to discuss it. A little extravagance seemed a wonderful chance so I agreed cheerfully.

When I arrived, Colin was waiting in the lounge, watching boats sailing on the lake in the autumn breeze. He was about five-foot-nine, with delicate skin, a finely pointed nose, and thick, brown permed curls. He rose when the club's hostess escorted me over to him, shook my hand, and asked that we be given a private table.

After the waiter took our order, I asked Colin why he wanted to get out of the life. It was important that I understand, because I planned my clients' programs around their motives, goals, and abilities.

"I started thinking about it when my friend Kevin was murdered," he began. "We both worked for Raymond Chenault at Executive Escorts in Washington. Mrs. Usry, please promise me that you'll never repeat what I'm going to tell you."

"Okay, Colin. Just call me Becky, though." I hoped to put him at ease.

"Mr. Chenault has a clientele of international business-men, senators, representatives, important people. Kevin was dat-ing the vice president of a bank in New York, Walter Roemig, who had business appointments in Washington quite often. One evening, when I attended a cocktail party at Mr. Chenault's house in Virginia, I overheard Mr. C. on the phone. I was curious so I lis-tened in. He was saying, 'You'll approve the loan for Daniel Maynard, or the press will learn that Walter Roemig has been dat-ing a male prostitute during his trips to Washington.'" He leaned toward me. "Becky, I got out of the room before anyone knew I was there. I had no idea Raymond was blackmailing his clients.

"I wanted to tell Kevin but he was out of town that night. I was gone when he got home the next day. When I got home again, I found a note from him saying that he had gotten a call from Walter and that he was going to see him. It was very unusu-al, because our customers aren't supposed to have our phone numbers. Two days later the police found Kevin's body in the Potomac." Colin's voice cracked with emotion.

I rubbed my forehead with my hand. I could feel an intense headache coming on. "Colin, how can Raymond black-mail his own customers? Why don't they have him killed?" I asked. This wasn't making sense.

"Raymond's customers don't know him. They call the switchboard and talk to the operators. Raymond hires women to work the phones. He keeps the records of the customers," Colin explained.

"Colin, how did you happen to call me? You're a long way from Washington," I said. If Chenault traced Colin Nopson to this city, my name was sure to come up.

"My friend Jim Huber, who works at Personal Introductions, sent me a newspaper clipping about Project New Life. I used to work with Jim," he replied.

Personal Introductions was a prostitution ring which masqueraded as a dating service.

"You have three choices," I told him. "One, you can go back to work for Raymond Chenault. Two, you can go to the FBI or to the police in Washington, D.C. Or, three, you can go into hiding, assume a new identity, and have no further contact with your family and friends. I'd take the second option if I were you."

Colin Nopson was a good-looking man in an expensive suit, but suddenly he looked like a lost little boy as he considered my suggestions. When he responded, he was close to tears.

"I don't want to die, Becky. If I go back to Raymond, I'm afraid I might get killed one day. As for going to law enforcement, I've dated some cops, and I don't think they'd let me live to testify. I don't like the idea of going into hiding, but that's all I can do, I guess."

"Are you sure you can handle living in hiding?" I asked. "You might make five dollars an hour as a laborer. You can never see your family. You can't call or write your old friends. You certainly can't eat at expensive restaurants like this one."

My client was positive he wanted to escape so I agreed to help him. When the waiter brought the check, Colin first got out his credit card, then smiled and reached for his wallet.

"I guess I won't be using this anymore," he said, folding the credit card in half. "I used it to pay for my trip to Cleveland, but I paid cash for my plane fare here: foresight, I suppose."

I put Colin Nopson on the underground railroad. Afterward, I phoned Emerald, one of the "blue blood" prostitutes I knew to ask if she had dealt with espionage and blackmail.

"It's common for upper class pimps to engage in such extracurricular activities," she explained. "Even independent prostitutes are sometimes forced to participate in information gathering."

Emerald went on, "I now know that I can trust you, Becky, so I hope you'll understand why I've never mentioned this before. My life was at stake if I told the wrong person.

"When I was twenty-eight, I was working for an escort service in San Franciso when one night my date flashed a badge. I thought he was about to arrest me. Instead, he said 'Don't worry, Emerald, I'm not going to bust you. I need you to do something for me. Have you ever heard of Ralph Logan?'

"I told him I hadn't, so he said, 'I want you to date him. I'm going to arrange it.'

"I told this guy, 'Why should I?' And he says, 'Because you're going to jail if you don't!' So I said, 'Why do you want me to do this for another man?' He told me, 'Ralph Logan is a criminal lawyer who gets too many crooks off the hook. I'm going to be taking pictures, Emerald. The next time Logan defends someone who should be put away, I'm going to show him some photographs.'

"I didn't like it, but I didn't want to go to jail, either, so I agreed to do it. I told myself maybe I was helping get criminals off the street. But then the door was kicked open, and all these cops came flying through! It was awful! They set their man up. They took us both to jail, and the attorney was disbarred.

"That was when I moved out here and became a call girl. The only reason I could get out of the life was because I didn't date wealthy men and kept a low profile after that. I know quite a few women who work as call girls who have told me it's quite common for men to force them to spy on their customers. They think that some of the men are government agents, and sometimes they seem to be Mafia or something."

Then I phoned Sadie Thompson. I explained, "Some of the independent prostitutes said they're forced to spy or provide information for men who showed up at their doors. Has anything like that ever happened to you?"

This made Sadie laugh. "If someone dared to show up at my door, I'd have him on his knees begging for mercy!"

I laughed, too. She wasn't kidding.

As more time passed, I watched prostitution destroy a number of men, bit by bit. Some were male prostitutes who contracted AIDS. Some were johns who infected their marital partners. Some were fathers.

I'd known Derek Overby for seven years. His first wife had left him for another man several years before we met, and he had cared for his two young daughters for a couple of years, until his ex-wife decided she wanted them back. Derek wanted to do what was best for his children, so he sent them to live with their mother and threw himself into his work.

When Overby remarried, his younger daughter Kimberly began to visit regularly, but the older daughter Rebecca preferred her mother's more lax parenting. In high school, Rebecca began using drugs. Although Derek wasn't a person to discuss his personal problem, his new wife confided in me.

"Derek's put Rebecca into a drug rehabilitation program for teenagers," she told me one day. "I hope she sees it through."

I hoped so, too.

Several months later when I saw Rebecca at her father's house, I made it a point to talk with her. To my surprise, she was very up front with me about her problems.

"I'm sick of selling my ass and sleeping in the back of

cars to get drugs. I'm never going back on the street," the seven-teen-year-old informed me.

I hadn't known Rebecca had been prostituting herself, but then it wasn't something I would have expected Derek to discuss. I wished her luck in attaining her goals.

Six months later, Derek's second wife, Lois, told me that unfortunately, Rebecca was using crack cocaine again. Worse, she was pregnant.

Rebecca Overby gave birth to an addicted baby while in jail. Derek and Lois are raising their handicapped granddaughter while Rebecca continues in the cycle of prostitution, drugs, and jail.

At the end of October, Paul Williams phoned to tell me his wife Concetta was in labor and needed a ride to the hospital. I hadn't seen the family for quite a while, but I knew Paul would probably make his wife take a bus if I didn't pick her up, so I agreed to come get them immediately.

At the welfare hotel where they lived with dozens of other families who survived from check to check, I located their quarters quickly because their children were playing outside the open door. Paul Junior was nearly six years old, Gracie was just four, and Angelica was two and a half. In one corner of the neat little room was a bedroll which Paul and Concetta probably used for the children. A battered dresser stood inside a closet which had no door, and a bag of disposable diapers took up most of the floor space in the tiny bathroom. It was better than the van they'd been living in when Gracie was born, but I wondered where they intended to put a newborn.

Paul was wearing a long-sleeved shirt, and he looked glassy-eyed and swayed as he walked. He probably had just had a fix. I couldn't understand what charm he exuded that kept his whores working for him.

I carried Concetta's bags to the car and sped to the hospital, where she was hooked up to monitors while the staff searched in vain for someone to translate for them. Concetta's command of English seemed to have gotten worse since I'd last seen her. Perhaps it was the stress of labor that caused her to forget the language. After she was settled, I had to leave. I left my phone number with the nurses, in case they or my client wanted to talk with me.

On Friday, October 25th, two days after I'd left Concetta at the hospital, a labor and delivery nurse phoned to say that Mrs. Williams was asking for me. She was still in labor and was expected to give birth within the hour.

I hurried to the hospital where Concetta sat on the edge of her bed, moaning with each contraction. The nurses had opened her gown slightly in the back so that a doctor in delivery room garb could administer a spinal anaesthetic.

I was taken by surprise when a nurse asked, "Do you want to gown up for the delivery room?"

"Yes, if Concetta wants me there," I told her.

At this Concetta turned her head toward me.

"Si. Yes. Stay, please," she begged. Dark circles were under her eyes, and her hair was limp and damp with sweat. She looked as if she'd had no sleep in the past two days.

I scrubbed and got into the green delivery room clothes with paper slippers and a hair net. A nurse led me to a room tiled in pale yellow, with gleaming chrome fixtures and a huge circular moveable mirror in the ceiling. In the center of the room was a delivery table covered with soft white sheets, where Concetta was being transferred from a gurney. Her legs were put in stirrups and draped with clean cotton blankets. The scent of Lysol pervaded the air. I was directed to a stool beside the table, where I was to watch the birth. From a corner of the room, a green-masked physician appeared and seated himself between Concetta's legs.

After a moment, a nurse patted Concetta's hand and said, "It's coming! I see the head."

I stood to get a better look.

A tiny wrinkled face suddenly slid into view. A nurse slid a syringe into the doctor's hand. As he suctioned mucous from the little nose and mouth, another contraction pushed the shoulders into view. As he pulled the blood wet baby into the world, he exclaimed, "It's a boy!"

I turned to look at Concetta's face and saw that it had lost its tiredness. She was smiling, beaming, glowing. She tilted her head to get a glimpse of her tiny son, while I looked at each face in the room. Mouths were covered by paper masks but eyes showed delight. As the baby was weighed and placed in a warming bed with soft towels, I thought, This may be the best day of your life, little one, because I knew what awaited him at home.

Soon, one nurse took the baby to the nursery, while another prepared the delivery room for the next patient. There were no beds available in the recovery room yet, so I stood beside Concetta who lay on a gurney in the hall. I tucked the blankets around her as she shivered from the trauma of childbirth. Suddenly a tap on the shoulder surprised me. I turned around to see the doctor who had administered the spinal anaesthesia.

"Pardon me," the doctor smiled, "but when I gave your friend here the anaesthetic, I dropped the needle, and it stuck in my arm. She's a good girl, isn't she?"

A shiver went up my spine. I suddenly understood what physicians must feel when they discover a patient has a fatal disease.

"I'm sorry, Doctor. Her husband is an IV drug user," I answered. It was against Project New Life policy to reveal a client's personal background, but I had to say what I did, policy or no policy.

Funding for Project New Life came from my share left to me by my father of a family partnership in Alaskan real estate. A few days afterward a threat to our funding developed. My mother's husband Tom had become our business manager when he married my mother. He had reorganized the corporation as a partnership between himself, my mother, my brother, and I. My brother's seven children had inherited his share of the partnership upon his death. On February 9, Tom called us all together to give us a report on our property rentals.

"Our major tenant has notified us that he will not renew his lease when it expires next year. Conditions in Alaska may preclude finding another tenant, as you might be aware," Tom began.

As we listened, we realized that the crux of the matter was that the partnership, which had supported us all for many years, would do so no more. In a few months we would have no income from our Alaskan property, and we would, in all probability have a huge empty building on our hands. So much real estate was for sale at bargain prices in Anchorage at this time that there was little chance we could sell ours. We agreed that the best idea would be to let Tom continue to manage the property, even if it meant allowing a rent-free tenancy, so that the building might not stand vacant. Perhaps it would become salable in the future.

When I went to bed that night, everything Tom had told us became a knot in my stomach. I lay awake agonizing over what would become of Project New Life, if I lost the income I'd been using to run it.

"Don't worry, honey." Lee's voice was soft and sweet as he grasped my hand in the darkness. "We'll get by somehow."

His words comforted me, and I drifted off to sleep.

13

ANYTHING BUT FRANK

My altruism was tempered by anger and even annoyance at times. The following Friday morning was one of those times. Busy with housework and school work in the morning, I was making plans for the rest of the day when the phone rang. The voice on the other end was not one I wanted to hear.

"'Lo, Becky. This is Paul Williams."

"Hi, Paul. How are you?" I asked but I didn't really care.

"Concetta wants to come stay with you for a while. I'm gonna send the kids to her folks in Mexico for a couple weeks. Maybe you can get her some housecleaning jobs. She don't wanna stay with me no more."

Paul didn't bother asking if Concetta could stay with me. He simply told me she was coming. He was a manipulator, and he was also crazy. Trying to determine his real purpose or intent was like betting on the lottery. There were so many possibilities, it was unlikely I'd hit the right combination, and anyway, getting Concetta away from him had always been one of my objectives.

"Okay, Paul. Do you want me to pick her up?"

"Yeah. Can you get here pretty soon?"

"I'll be there in fifteen minutes. Give me your address."

If he sent the kids to stay with their grandparents, even for a few weeks, Concetta's parents would buy the children clothes, feed them nourishing food, read to them, and do fun things like take them to the zoo. Meanwhile, I'd have time to talk to Concetta. Since Paul wasn't mad at me at present, I wasn't afraid of walking into a trap, so I drove Darroll to my mother's home and left instructions for his school work with her and then drove on to the Williamses' hotel-of-the-month.

This most recent "home" was located at the top of a flight of stairs in a dilapidated downtown welfare hotel. The stairwell reeked of urine, and glassy-eyed men with several days' growth of beard stared at me as I passed. Women with greasy hair ignored crying infants and the small children who ran up and down the stairs. I grabbed a small dirty boy of about three as he tripped over a loose nail on the top step and broke what promised to be a nasty fall. The little brown-haired waif looked up at me as I set him on his feet, then turned and ran to a woman who sat in a doorway, a cigarette in her hand.

"I told you to be careful on them stairs!" the woman screamed at him.

When I knocked on the door of Room 16, Paul called, "Who is it?"

"It's Becky," I answered, sounding deliberately cheerful.

Paul opened the door himself, because Concetta was busy combing little Gracie's hair. They sat on the double bed, the only piece of furniture in the room besides some cardboard boxes which served as dressers. There was no bathroom or running water in the rooms. Eight rooms on each floor of this three-story pigsty shared a common bathroom. It was the Williamses' worst place yet. At least Concetta kept their room clean and the children washed, but they wore ragged and threadbare clothing.

"Concetta's parents will pick up the kids at the bus station at noon," Paul informed me. "You ready, Babe?" he said to Concetta.

He had conveniently forgotten to mention that I would also be taking the kids when I picked up his wife. Oh well, I would have driven them to Mexico to get them away from him.

Paul carried the baby to the car while Concetta and I struggled with various shopping bags and three small children. When we got outside into the light of day, I could see that Paul looked jaundiced and exhausted. The pimp was obviously sick. He knew I'd never agree to letting his wife work the streets, so he wanted her to do housework. It would keep her busy and bring in a few bucks. Never let it be said that Paul Williams let a perfectly able woman go to waste!

"'Bye, Babe," Paul said and kissed Concetta lightly on the cheek.

"'Bye," she responded without enthusiasm.

Concetta spoke little English and most of that was related to her prostitution activities. Paul spoke Spanish to her at home, probably to keep her isolated from her neighbors, which was a ploy typical of abusive spouses.

I drove my passengers to the bus station parking lot, where Concetta's parents, Juan and Elisa Domingo, were waiting. The Domingos had endeared themselves to my family by their patient, loving attitude toward their daughter and her children. They never uttered a word of complaint about Paul, and they had our sympathy.

The family hugged each other, and I stared at the passing traffic while my own tears fell.

"Becky!" Juan called. "We're so glad to see you!"

Juan Domingo was always a gentleman.

"I'm glad I could come today, Mr. Domingo. But what's wrong with Paul?" I couldn't help adding, "this time."

He turned to Concetta and they spoke in Spanish. Juan explained, "Paul has hepatitis. Concetta is not sure why he wants her to stay with you, but it is probably so he can get her back when he wants to. He blames her for his illness, but she says the Public Health nurse told her it came from using dirty needles."

"Wouldn't Concetta rather go home with you?" I couldn't imagine her wanting to stay here separated from her children.

Juan spoke to his daughter. Concetta vigorously shook her head as she answered her father.

"She says she doesn't want to anger her husband. He has come after her at our house before. It is better that the children are safe with us. She will find work here, as Paul told her to do."

Juan looked sad. Elisa paid close attention to her grandchildren. She wouldn't meet my eyes.

"Okay, I'm not in any hurry," I fibbed. "Take all the time you want to visit. I'll be in the coffee shop. Tell Concetta to come get me when she's ready."

I waved to the Domingos and left them to their family.

When we got back to my house, I phoned everyone I knew to ask for housecleaning jobs, but only three families needed help the first week. Still, they all liked her. Concetta was a good worker, and, despite the language barrier, she made friends wherever she went. I taught her some English, and she taught me some Spanish, but I had the better student.

On Saturday Concetta insisted on taking a bus to the hotel to pick up their welfare check, or part of it, so she could send money to her parents to help with the children's expenses. By words and gestures she made me understand that Paul had promised her the money. Despite my misgivings, she left, with assurances that she would return in the afternoon

Concetta didn't come back that day, or the next. On the day after that, not only was I worried for her safety, but also, she'd agreed to clean a house on Tuesday, and I hoped I wouldn't have to cancel because I had begged the people to give her a chance.

By Wednesday I still hadn't heard from Concetta, and I was very concerned. Darroll was at my mother's home with his school work while I tried to get some paperwork done, but I couldn't concentrate. I called Evie and suggested we go look for Concetta. I knew my husband wouldn't have been thrilled with the suggestion, because we didn't know what Paul would do if we showed up at his door uninvited. I called Lee at work to talk it over with him, but he was out. That was handy; I didn't want to argue with him anyway!

At the hotel we marched up the stairs to Room 16, where Evie knocked and called Concetta's name. For a long while, there was no answer, but we persisted. "Concetta, it's Evie and Becky. Open the door, honey."

At last, the door opened a crack, and our client's voice whispered, "I'm okay. Leave me alone."

Doggedly determined to see Concetta, I persisted, "Let us come in. We just want to visit for a few minutes."

Concetta allowed us to gently push the door open, and we stepped into the tiny room. A dirty blanket covered the bed, and sheets were hung over the window as curtains. The usual cheerful plastic flowers and old doilies were absent. The decor matched our client. Her eyes were black and swollen, and contusions covered her arms. She seemed to move painfully.

"Do you want to leave with us?" I asked.

"No! No! Paul come back here." She had the wild-eyed glance of a caged animal.

"All right. Do you need anything?" I pressed.

At that moment the door burst open, and there stood Paul. As in a horror movie where the monster refuses to die, this man who only a week ago was jaundiced with hepatitis now glared at us menacingly.

I kept my cool. "Hi, Paul," I smiled, while anger ate at my stomach. Evie gave him a cheerful grin, too.

"We thought maybe Concetta was sick. She left my house on Saturday, and she was supposed to be back that afternoon." I did the talking.

"Yeah, well, I been sick. I think she give me something. She don't keep the place too clean." He indicated the room with a glance around the dirty walls.

"Do you want us to take you to the doctor? Maybe Concetta should go, too. She's pretty bruised."

"Nah, I don't need no doctor. Concetta fell down the stairs. She'll be okay."

Perhaps Paul thought people believed his stories because they declined to challenge him.

I tried another tack. "Concetta missed a housecleaning job Tuesday, but the people said she can do it next week if she likes. There are some other families who want her to start on a regular basis. Did she tell you?"

I was promising more than I could deliver, but I had no inclination to argue.

"How come she only cleaned three houses when she was there a week? She ain't nothin' but a damn whore. What was she doin', sleeping with some guy insteada workin'?"

This was all part of the masquerade of Paul the injured husband, cuckolded, long-suffering, patient, and of Concetta the unfaithful, unclean, disobedient wife.

"It took us time to find work for her, Paul, but we have jobs lined up now. Why don't you let Concetta come back with us?" Evie suggested.

Let Paul save face and maybe he'd give in.

"Hey," he responded, "I just want my wife and kids. You know what I mean? I don't want her goin' off workin' and leavin' me alone. A man should be with his family."

"Let's be frank," she tried. Despite the circumstances, I nearly laughed: these two would be anything but frank. "You need more room. Concetta could stay with me, work for a month, and we'd help you find an apartment. You'd have a better place with a kitchen, and Concetta won't have to work unless she wants to. Welfare will pay for your apartment, once you have the first and last months' rent paid. Then we'll discuss the kids' arrangements." Evie was tenacious as a bulldog. She wasn't about to let Paul keep his wife here if she could help it. But Paul's mind was erratic as a moth in flight.

He indicated that the negotiations were now over. "Bring my kids home. I miss 'em."

I had no intention of bringing those children back to this madman.

"No!" I protested. "Let us help you get a better place, and you can get a job when you're well, or Concetta can work. Whatever you want to do is okay, except I'm not driving into Mexico to bring the kids back here. They don't even have beds here!" I retorted angrily.

That only infuriated Paul. "Get out of my house, you fucking bitch!" he shouted at me.

I left quickly. Evie, who had played the good cop to my bad cop, lingered while Paul hurled epithets down the staircase after me. I was sure that Evie was in no danger because her attitude had been conciliatory.

Evie exited the hotel as I slid into the driver's seat, and I unlocked the passengers' door for her. Neither of us spoke for a few blocks, as we gathered our thoughts. It was Evie who broke the silence.

"I gave Concetta my business card while Paul was yelling at you," she sighed. "I told her to call my home or office if she could get away from her husband, and we'd come get her. Let's stop by my office to warn my secretary."

On the way we debated whether Paul was crazy like a fox, or just plain crazy. We soon had more data to help us decide.

Evie's secretary Marilyn Perts was waiting for us at the office. She surprised us by coming running at us from behind her desk.

"Thank God you're here!"

"What's the matter, Mare?"

Evie, who was being gripped by Marilyn, patted the shaking secretary's back.

"A woman named Concetta just called. She was speaking English so fast I could barely understand her. She says someone named Paul has a gun, and he's going to kill Gracie and Manuel! He's going to take Paul Junior and Angelica away from her, and she'll never see them again! She begged me to go get her kids, Evie! I don't even know who she is!" Marilyn was sobbing by this time, and Evie was pale. I probably was, too.

For a moment, Evie and I stared at each other. Then I grabbed the phone and dialed Concetta's parents. Their phone service was usually erratic, and today was no exception. The phone rang twenty-five times before I gave up and phoned the police in their area. Several tense minutes passed while I waited for the operator to locate an English-speaking officer.

I asked for emergency assistance for someone to go to the Domingo home and warn them about Paul.

"No, Señora. We don't have enough officers to send them so far out of town. We cannot possibly do what you ask until tomorrow," came the polite reply.

I thanked the police officer, hung up, and explained the situation to Evie.

The Domingos lived in a pretty little village about twenty miles from the nearest town large enough to have a police force. In addition to sporadic telephone service, Mexico's impoverished economy didn't allow a large police fleet, so the reply was not a surprise.

"What are we going to do, keep calling them?" Evie wondered aloud.

"We have to warn them about Paul," I answered.

I knew exactly why Paul had said he would kill Gracie and Manuel: they had their mother's Hispanic features. Paul Junior and Angelica looked like their father. Concetta had told me Paul thought Gracie and Manuel were trick babies, but she insisted that all the children were his.

"We can't let Paul hurt those kids. I'll have to drive there," I said. "Evie, you don't have to go. Will you call Lee for me? I'll be back as soon as I can, but it will probably be after dark." I would have to drive to the border, cross it, and then drive an hour or so to the village. And do it all again coming back.

"What are you planning to do there?" Evie wanted to know. "Are you going to bring the kids back?"

"Not if I can help it. Even if I did, Paul knows where I live so I can't take them to my house. The best thing is to try to convince the Domingos to take them somewhere safe.

"Well, if you do bring them back, they can stay at my house."

Good old Evie! She was such a treasure. I hurried to my car and looked at my watch: noon. The gas gauge was nearly on empty, so I had to stop at a service station. Too nervous to eat, I bought a Diet Pepsi to go. There was a long drive ahead, in more than miles.

Very few streetwalkers returned to prostitution after an initial interview with Project New Life, and fewer still returned to the life after several weeks or months of trying to change. Those who did almost always did so because of their addiction to drugs or alcohol. Many of those I helped had gotten jobs, gone to school, or gone home. Except for Concetta. Here I was dealing with a battered wife as well as a streetwalker. I sincerely believe that of the two, the streetwalker has the better chance of changing her life.

Traffic was heavy, and the drive was slower than I'd hoped. Nevertheless, I arrived at the Domingo house at three o'clock. Paul Junior was playing in the front yard with children from the village. It was a beautiful, peaceful scene.

Elisa was surprised to see me when she opened the door in answer to my knock. She graciously ushered me inside. Little Gracie was riding a rocking horse, and Angelica let out a whoop of delight as she left the picture book she had been reading to come running when she saw me. She probably thought I'd brought her mama. It was so nice to see the children happy and secure, and so terrifying that it could all end in a bloody instant.

"Is Juan home?" I asked.

Elisa smiled and answered, "Si! Si!" She led me into the living room, then disappeared through a doorway when she was satisfied that I was seated comfortably. I called "Hello" to the children while I waited.

In a few moments, Juan arrived. He smiled and shook my hand as he took a seat next to me, and I hurriedly explained what had happened. When he heard that Paul had a gun, he shot up out of his chair as if it were on fire. He spoke rapidly in Spanish to Elisa, who ran from the room. Then he turned to me.

"We must leave here at once! My wife will take the children to a neighbor's house and you and I shall go to the police." He spun around and was gone.

The children sensed something was wrong. Little Gracie got off her horse and came to clutch my hand. In a few minutes Elisa returned with little Manuel, the baby I had watched being born.

Mrs. Domingo grabbed a diaper bag from a closet and herded the little ones out the door. I took Gracie's hand. Angelica was firmly attached to her grandmother's skirt. Elisa called to Paul Junior. The boy came in from the front yard immediately. Juan pulled their car to the front of the house and we strapped the children into their car seats and seat belts. Juan locked the front door as his wife drove away with the children. Then he and I left for the nearest police station.

Detective Padillo was a tall man with dark hair and eyes and a thick moustache. He would have been handsome but for the deep worry lines which crossed his brow. His wainscoted office was on the second floor of an old police station. From across his huge metal desk he smiled at us in the friendly manner of the Mexican people.

Juan Domingo spoke rapidly in Spanish. The detective's smile faded as he listened carefully and then picked up the phone. When he hung up, he turned to me, and said in perfect English, "I have something to show you. Perhaps you will understand why I suggest you take the children to the United States."

After a few minutes, a slim young woman in a police uniform brought a file to Detective Padillo, who opened it and removed some photos which he placed on the desk in front of me. "These were taken last May," he told me.

The photographs were of two battered and bruised people, barely recognizable as Concetta and Gracie. Welts striped the child's back, as if a belt or whip had been used to deliver the blows. Blood was matted in her hair, and a bruise swelled her right cheek. Concetta was a mass of contusions, and both eyes were black and swollen. I felt tears start to roll down my cheeks.

"Señora, Paul Williams is a wanted man here. A maid found these two locked in a closet in a hotel downtown. Señor Williams had left his wife and daughter there and escaped with their two other children."

"Elisa and I paid for a room at the Colinas Verde, an expensive hotel, for the family so they could visit us for a week. Paul did this and left them," Juan confided, imploring me with his eyes to keep this our secret.

"When Concetta and her little girl were released from the hospital," Padillo continued, "they went to her parents' home. My department issued a warrant for Williams's arrest, but we never found him. He apparently returned from the States. A few days later, he cut the phone lines at the Domingos' house and kidnaped Concetta and Gracie. That was the last we saw of him.

"I suggest that you take the children to the States if you have somewhere you can hide them. We cannot guarantee their safety here."

I was certain that Detective Padillo was stating facts, not making excuses for his police force. We shook hands with the officer and said goodbye.

"Juan, what do you want me to do? Paul knows where I live so the children won't be safe at my house." I paused. "Why don't you and Elisa take them to the States yourselves," I suggested as we trudged down the stairs.

"I must stay here with my mother and sister, in case Paul goes to their homes. If Elisa takes the children across the border, do you have some other place they can stay?" he asked.

"Evie Evans wants them to stay with her. She offered to take the children, and I'm sure she wouldn't mind if Elisa joined them. I'll give her directions to Evie's house. Maybe the police will arrest Paul, and Concetta can come home."

Maybe this cloud would prove to have a silver lining, but I had long since stopped seeing out of those rose-colored glasses.

"Elisa cannot see to drive at night, and it will be dark before she reaches Señora Evans's home. She will have to ride with you," Juan told me as we got into my car.

We drove a circuitous route to the house of the neighbor where Elisa had taken the children to avoid Paul.

It was a tense trio of adults who awaited us around the kitchen table. Elisa held Manuel, while the other children watched cartoons in the living room. When Juan explained what the detective had advised, Elisa seemed relieved. The neighbors were happy with the news: they most certainly had not been thrilled about sheltering the Domingo family from a madman. It didn't take us long to transfer the car seats to my vehicle and fasten the little ones in. Then once again we were on the road.

Juan told Elisa to phone him when she got to Evie's house. The phones in the Domingos' neighborhood weren't working that day, as I'd suspected, but because Juan's mother lived in town, we would be able to keep in communication. I prayed Mr. Domingo would be safe, but perhaps I should have worried about myself.

When we pulled into their driveway, Evie and her children poured out the doors like firefighters answering a three-alarm call. Elisa was welcomed warmly, and we were swept inside by the family. The Evans teenagers fussed and cooed over Concetta's little ones while I spoke with Evie. Mrs. Domingo phoned her husband to tell him we'd arrived safely. "Paul no come," she told us when she hung up.

We breathed a sigh of relief, thankful that Juan was all right for the time being, but we should have known better than to hope Paul had changed his mind.

I phoned Lee and told him I'd be home as soon as I called Child Protective Services. I didn't want to take any chances. The authorities needed to be aware that Williams had threatened to kill his children, and that they were safe for the present in the Evans home with their grandmother.

The Child Abuse Hotline answered my call on the second ring, and the counselor waited patiently while I identified myself and my organization, then told them the complicated story of Paul Williams.

"I have Paul Williams on the other line," the counselor said. "He says you kidnaped his children. He wants you arrested."

"*What!*" I was shocked beyond words. "We've been set up," I whispered to Evie.

Paul, wily, unpredictable, cunning, and dangerous, had tricked me into bringing his children across an international border so that he could have me arrested for kidnaping. I wasn't exactly one step ahead of him, but I was lucky that I'd had the foresight not to take the kids from the custody of their grandmother. It took a great deal of convincing to get the counselor not to telephone the police. However, we had some influential friends, and Evie used a neighbor's phone to call some of them for help.

Finally, the hotline counselor agreed to allow the children to remain in the Evanses' home for the night. The next day we were to meet Concetta alone. If she wanted the children, we'd have no choice but to give them to her.

It was ten o'clock when I arrived home and explained the day to Lee.

"How did Paul know you took the kids to Evie's?" Lee wanted to know.

"He probably had us followed. Remember, honey, he has a stable of prostitutes who work for him. Maybe he saw Evie hand Concetta her business card and planned this whole thing. We'll never know for sure." Suddenly, I was exhausted from the driving and the strain. "Maybe it will make more sense when we see Concetta tomorrow. Let's go to bed."

Just as we were pulling up the covers, the phone rang. Lee picked up the receiver and wearily answered, "Hello."

It was Evie.

"Paul just called here. He says he's on the way to your house with a gun!"

Lee loaded his shotgun and took turns with David sitting up all night, waiting for Paul to arrive. Williams never showed up, but my husband and son lost half a night's sleep. The little pimp had won this round, too.

The morning brought sad news. Concetta insisted that she wanted us to give her the children and that she wanted to stay with Paul. Elisa kissed her grandchildren goodbye and watched her daughter board a bus for downtown, trying to keep track of three small children and carry an infant. Evie comforted Mrs. Domingo, but both of them cried all the way back to the Evanses' house, where Juan was to drive up and meet his wife. I was too angry for tears.

In the week that followed, visions of Gracie and Concetta bruised and battered appeared in my dreams. I heard their voices calling for help as I slept. Yet I awoke safe in my own bed. By the following Friday I could stand it no longer. I phoned Booth Martin, my friend at Child Protective Services. Booth listened to my story, but since there had been no abuse that I could actually report because Mexico's documentation couldn't be used in the

United States, CPS could do nothing. When I mentioned that the children had no beds, however, Booth got the excuse he needed to visit the family, and he assured me he would go that very morning.

Booth Martin found Concetta, Gracie, and Manuel in the filthy room, covered with fresh bruises. Paul told Booth that Gracie and Manuel had fallen from their parents' bed and that his wife had tripped on the stairs. Concetta's English faltered in her husband's presence. Booth and the police officers who had accompanied him removed the children to a group home and took their mother to a battered women's shelter.

On Monday morning Booth phoned me with good news. "Paul was arrested Friday night when he tried to buy heroin from an undercover cop. Concetta is still at the battered women's shelter and has asked to go to her parents' home with the children. Becky, if you pick up Mrs. Williams, I'll have the children released to her, her parents, and you." I was elated!

I phoned Evie and afterwards, the Domingos.

I helped Darroll with his school work for the next few hours, since the Domingos wouldn't arrive until after six. At four o'clock I left to pick up Concetta at the shelter. She seemed genuinely happy for once and excited to be going home. I wished it were easier to communicate with her, but I couldn't find out what I so desperately wanted to know. When we got to Evie's, Concetta asked me to take her to the hotel so she could get her clothes before her parents arrived.

"What if Paul's there?" I pointed out.

"Paul een jail," Concetta assured me happily.

I wasn't so sure. It was likely he had been arraigned this morning and released on his own recognizance. Concetta insisted she needed her clothes. I phoned the jail.

"Yes, Ma'am. Paul Williams was arraigned this morning. He's in holding now, waiting for his paperwork to be processed. It'll be several hours before he's released," a deep voice, full of authority, assured me.

Evie said she'd accompany us to the hotel, and I called the police for an escort.

It was dark when we arrived at the old building. A squad car met us there, and Concetta marched up to Room 16 with two uniformed officers. I parked half a block away and chatted with Evie while our client went to gather her belongings. I was the first to notice a man leave the hotel and approach our car. He was about six-foot-three, with hair pulled back in a pony tail, and he was wearing a dirty T-shirt and grimy jeans. A bandanna was wound around his head as a sweatband, and he seemed to be addressing us.

"Lock your door, Evie!" I whispered urgently, as I bolted my own.

Polite Evie, however, was paying attention to the man and didn't hear me. She opened her door and stuck her head out so she could hear him better. She got an earful.

"Are you the fucking bitches that's been tryin' to break up this nice family?" the stranger demanded. He reached for Evie.

Just in time, Evie slammed the door and locked it.

"Ignore him," I said fiercely. "We're safe in here, and Concetta is with the policemen."

Eyes straight ahead, Evie and I awaited the return of our friend. The best-laid plans of mice and men often go astray, it is said, but perhaps some people just lay better plans than others. Within fifteen minutes, another police officer arrived to escort us to the hotel room, where Paul was out of jail and in the midst of an eloquent plea to the officers to release his beloved wife to him.

"Mr. Williams says you're holding his wife against her will," one officer told us.

I couldn't believe it! Williams wouldn't give up!

"Booth Martin, from Child Protective Services, asked me to take Concetta Williams from the battered women's shelter," I explained as calmly as I could. "She and her parents and I are going to pick up the Williamses' children from Juvenile Temporary Shelter."

The officer turned to Concetta.

"Is this true?" he asked.

Concetta replied in Spanish. Neither officer spoke that language, but a neighbor, the same man who had accosted Evie and me, appeared, and he provided a translation which suited Paul.

"Mrs. Williams says these two women tried to kidnap her children. She wants her husband to go get them," he told the officers.

Concetta shook her head vigorously, trying to communicate to the officers that she had said nothing of the sort. Evie tried to intervene.

"We're just trying to help Concetta," she began.

"You shut up!" shouted one of the officers, shaking his flashlight in Evie's face.

She complied.

If I hadn't been so scared and infuriated, I would have laughed. Evie was like an overstuffed suitcase, valuable, but unable to contain everything. Sometimes I felt like I was trying to cram in a few things on one side, only to have something else pop out the other side, when I was trying to get her to keep quiet.

"Sir," I interjected politely, "the children can only be released to Concetta, their grandparents, and me, together. Mr. Martin instructed me this morning what he wanted me to do. Mrs. Williams requested that I bring her here to pick up her clothing, because she intends to go to Mexico with her parents. I'll be glad to give you Booth Martin's phone number to verify this."

"There's no one in that office after five o'clock, as I'm sure you know. If Mrs. Williams wants to go with you, she can." The officer turned to the helpful translator. "Ask her if she wants to go with these women."

An exchange in Spanish took place between Concetta and Paul's friend. Then the man said to the officer. "She don't wanna go with them," he lied.

Concetta understood some of what was being said in English, although she couldn't express herself, especially when she was stressed, but now the realization of what was happening seemed to spur her to action.

"I go! I go!" she cried in alarm.

The officer looked doubtful, but Concetta stooped to gather a pile of clothes into a shopping bag. Paul stepped toward her and pulled a box of miniature chocolates from his jacket.

"Here, Babe, I got these for you."

He looked at his wife with a hangdog expression. Concetta ignored the proffered box, gave her husband a dirty look, turned on her heel, and marched from the room.

I stood tall as we went to the car, but once inside I could not stop myself from shaking. Evie was silent. Concetta leaned against the back seat and sighed heavily. A few blocks down the street, as we waited at a stop light, I asked, "Did we almost go to jail back there?"

Evie and I looked at each other, then turned and looked at our client. Concetta raised her hands and said, "Me too."

We laughed: so Concetta understood more than we gave her credit for. I smiled at her, but our good humor was short-lived.

When we returned to the Evanses' house, the Domingos received us with relief. Concetta told her parents what had happened at the hotel, and they hugged each other tightly, crying and laughing. After a few moments, Juan said, "We must get the children and go home now."

"I'll call the shelter to tell them we're coming," I volunteered.

I dialed Juvenile Temporary Shelter. It would be easier if the children were ready when we arrived. Also, I was eager to get home after our ordeal.

"The Williams children?" a friendly voice repeated my request. "Oh, yes, their father's on the way to pick them up.!"

"No!" I shouted into the worker's ear. "No! They are not to be released to their father! Check your release orders! Booth Martin, the social worker, ordered them to be released to the mother, their grandparents, and me."

"I'm sorry," came the reply, "but our computer is down. I have a note that they're to be released, but I can't stop their father from taking them without a specific order, and that would be in the computer."

I slammed the phone down and yelled at the Domingos, "Hurry, Paul's on his way to get them!" and ran out the door to my car. Juan and Elisa were in their vehicle before I had my door shut, and Concetta came running after them. We raced the five miles to the shelter, where we found the children dressed and ready to go. As the Domingos left with the little ones from the south side of the parking lot, I watched a battered red pickup truck with Paul and his helpful neighbor pull in from the north entrance. They apparently didn't see us, because Paul went in the entrance of the building, seemingly intent on getting his kids. As I drove away, I prayed he didn't have a gun.

At home, I related all that had happened to Lee.

"Isn't Frank Evans out of town for a week?" he asked when I'd finished.

"Frank? Evie's husband?" I muttered, too exhausted to perceive the connection.

"Yes. Maybe it would be a good idea if David stayed at Evie's while Frank is out of town, honey. Then, if Paul should watch her place, he'd see a man there, or if he called, a man would answer the phone. She may need protection."

Although still a teenager, David was already six-foot-one and one hundred eighty pounds of solid muscle. His dark hair and moustache, blue eyes rimmed with thick black lashes, and deep voice could make him seem intimidating. He had been going out with one of Evie's blond daughters lately, so the thought of protecting the family for a week would probably appeal to him.

I called Evie to discuss the situation with her, while Lee asked David if he'd like to spend a few nights with his girlfriend's family. In a little while, our son was on his way to the Evanses' house, where he was fed and pampered every evening for a week while he answered the phone and paraded in the front window.

David had been back from the Evanses' house for two days when I got a call from Evie, who sounded panicky.

"Becky?" she quavered tearfully. "I didn't molest David!"

"Molest David?" I was thoroughly taken aback, and the absurdity of the suggestion made me laugh. "How could you molest David?" I giggled. Evie was five-foot-two and weighed a hundred pounds.

"Becky, a police officer was just here. She read me my rights!"

This was serious, but I smelled a rat. Not only was it physically impossible for Evie to molest David, but it was morally implausible. This smacked of Paul Williams.

"Evie, tell me exactly what happened. I know you didn't molest David, but we've got to get to the bottom of this," I insisted.

"A police officer came to my door. She said someone had complained that I'd molested David. I didn't do it, Becky!"

Evie was too upset to give me a lucid explanation. I'd have to calm her down first.

"Evie, what was the officer's name?"

"Her name's Carol Walker."

"Did she give a phone number? I'll call her."

"She didn't give me a phone number because she's not in her office very much," Evie replied, her sobs lessening somewhat.

I'd have to speak with the officer or her supervisor before this went too far.

"Where's she stationed?"

"I don't know," Evie answered, panic beginning to rise in her voice again.

"Was she driving a black-and-white or a State patrol car?"
I asked.

"She was driving a blue Toyota pickup truck," Evie
replied.

"A pickup truck?" I murmured. That could be either a
detective or a social worker from Child Protective Services. "Was
she wearing a uniform?" was the next logical question.

"Yes. She was wearing red pants and shirt, and she had a
heart-shaped badge."

Evie sounded disoriented.

"What did she say to you?" Maybe now she could explain
more clearly.

"She said she was from the Sex Crimes Division of the
Children's Unit of the City Police and that she'd had a report
that I'd molested David while he was staying here last week."

"Okay, Evie, stay on the phone. I'm going to three-way a
call to Detective Silverman. He'll know what's going on."

"No. I don't want anybody to know I was accused of child
molesting. It might ruin Project New Life," she protested.

"Evie, listen. Detective Silverman will help us find Carol
Walker so we can get this straightened out. No one is going to
believe you molested David, but we can't ignore this. Everything
will be okay, I promise," I assured her.

Louis Silverman was the policeman with whom I'd established a telephone friendship. His presence, even on the telephone, demanded respect. He was an honest cop, and he could be
trusted to guide us through this sticky affair. He kept an eye on
me, I knew, because he always seemed to know what I wanted to
talk about before I called, but I surprised him today.

Louis listened to my summary of Evie's story. There was
a moment's silence on the other end of the line, and I assumed
he was making notes. Then the detective's voice rumbled, "There
is no Sex Crimes Division of the Children's Unit in the city
police or in any of the police forces around here. I put the name

'Carol Walker' on my computer, but there's no one by that name employed by the police, the city, or the county. Can you describe this woman, Mrs. Evans?"

Evie couldn't tell him much more, except that her visitor had light red hair and was about five-foot-six and a hundred and twenty pounds.

"I'm cutting an order for a tracer to be put on your phone calls. Give me your numbers, both of you," Louis ordered.

When we'd given him the necessary data, Silverman added, "I want you to pretend to cooperate with this woman if you see her again, and let me know immediately if she contacts you."

That Friday, April 4th, Darroll and I were working on his math at the kitchen table when the phone rang.

"I'll get it, Mom!" Darroll said as he leapt from the table. He was always ready to take a break from his studies.

Still cautious because of all that had gone on, I said, "Let me answer it," and reached the phone first.

"Mrs. Usry, this is Officer Walker of the City Police. I have had a report that Evie Evans molested your son David. Do you know an Evie Evans?" I felt a chill run up my spine.

"Oh, dear God. Is David all right?" I asked in the most theatrical voice I could muster.

"I don't know. Did he stay at her house last week?" the "officer" asked.

"Yes. He was there all week," I told her confidentially. "But he didn't say anything to me about being molested."

"That's what usually happens, Ma'am. Kids don't tell because they're too ashamed. I'd like to have a meeting with you and Mrs. Evans this morning."

"Of course," I agreed, my voice quavering. "Do you want David to be present?" I was laying it on thick.

"I'd like to speak with you and Mrs. Evans first. I'll talk to David later. Will you be alone about ten o'clock? We can meet at your house," the polite caller suggested.

"Yes, Officer. I don't know what to say. Nothing like this has ever happened to us before. Whatever you think is best." I hoped I sounded properly shaken.

"I'll see you at ten," she said.

"Do you have a phone number, in case I can't get hold of Mrs. Evans?" I asked.

"I won't be in. I'll pick up Mrs. Evans myself," she replied, hanging up.

I quickly walked Darroll to a neighbor's house where he'd be safe. Then I phoned Detective Silverman.

"Louis, it's coming together! The phony cop wants a meeting with Evie and me at ten!"

"I'm going to order unmarked vehicles to surround your neighborhood immediately," he said. "She'll be in custody before she ever reaches your door." For once, I didn't stop to wonder what the neighbors would think.

I'd meant to phone Evie as soon as I finished speaking with Detective Silverman, but she called me first.

"Becky! Carol Walker called me. She wanted to take me to your house for a meeting. I told her I'd drive myself, but she said, 'You don't drive.' How does she know that? She hung up on me! How does she know I don't drive?" Evie's voice was quaking.

Before I could reply, a call beeped through.

"Just a minute, Evie, I've got an incoming call. This could be important."

I hated to put my friend on hold when she was so distraught, but it might be Detective Silverman. I switched to the other line.

"Becky," the now-familiar voice of Carol Walker threatened. "Evie won't come with us, but you tell her we're going to get her yet!"

She hung up before I could reply, so I got back to Evie.

"You seem to have scared her off," I told my friend.

We three-wayed the call to Louis Silverman and explained what had transpired.

"I wonder how she knows you don't drive, Evie?" Louis wanted to know.

"How did she know David spent last week at Evie's house?" I added.

No one had any answers. Louis called off the unmarked cars but promised extra drive-by surveillance for the next few weeks. The Usry and Evans families were very, very careful in the days that followed.

Louis Silverman eventually discovered that Walker's calls had been made from a public telephone booth.

Evie and I grew almost certain that the phony police officer was the work of Paul Williams. Since she'd left us with a threat, we felt it was in our best interests to learn the outcome of Paul's heroin charge. If he went to jail, we might be safe for a while.

Williams's trial date was set for Monday, April 14. We didn't really want to face the little pimp again, even in a courthouse, but the clerk of the court assured me that we wouldn't otherwise know the outcome of his trial for thirty days afterward.

Thus it was that Evie, David, and I found ourselves on the steps of the county courthouse at 8:00 A.M. one bright and breezy spring morning. We found the courtroom where Paul's trial had been assigned about one hundred feet to the left of the main entrance. We made our way through the crowded hallway lined with benches and entered Courtroom Four through a wide wooden door. Inside, folding chairs were set in neat rows from the low divider separating the small trial area from the audience to about six feet from the benches along the back wall, where we chose to sit beside the door, which opened toward us.

By 8:30 A.M. the courtroom was nearly filled, but there was no sign of Paul. David, tired of waiting in the crowded room, excused himself to go sit in the hallway. Evie and I scooted closer together as two people shoved into his vacated space.

Minutes ticked by slowly as people poured into the court-room. My eyes drifted to the clock, which read 8:45. Suddenly, Evie nudged me with her elbow. Coming through the door were Paul and a woman with light red hair.

"That's the so-called cop!" Evie whispered.

Paul scanned the folding chairs. The only seats left were at the front, and they had to pass us to reach them. He saw us. Grabbing the woman's hand, he pulled her quickly along the narrow aisle, whispering in her ear. She shot us a rapid glance as they took their seats, then spoke to Williams.

Options ran through my mind. Call the cops? That would take too long. Confront them after the trial? But what if Paul was armed?

As I mused, the door opened again, and a ragged unwashed man stepped inside the courtroom. As he passed, hands waved delicately in front of noses and heads turned quickly away. Someone muttered, "He needs Right Guard!"

"Forget the Right Guard. He needs Raid!" Evie quipped half under her breath.

The tension of the moment broke, and Evie and I dissolved into laughter. We looked toward the front of the room. Paul and the redhead, obviously wondering if the joke was on them, stared at us in horror and disbelief. The woman rose and strode past us toward the door, her only means of escape. She turned her head away and covered her face with her hand as she exited the room.

"Wait here," I whispered to Evie as I rose impulsively. "Find out what happens to Paul. I'm going to follow the redhead."

"Red" ran out the main door toward the huge parking lot. I reached the door only seconds after she did, but she had disappeared into the crowded lot. I searched through the rows for a blue Toyota pickup but there was no sign of either the woman or the truck. I returned, disappointed, to the courtroom. Evie looked at me expectantly. I shrugged my shoulders.

Evie leaned toward me and whispered, "The clerk read a list of names and said, 'If you're supposed to be here today, and your name isn't on the list I just read, you may leave the room and return in one hour. We'll get to everybody today.' I saw Paul leave. Do you want to wait?"

"Let's," I said.

At 10:00 A.M. Paul returned to the courtroom, which was less crowded now. At 10:15 the clerk read about twenty more names, one of which was Paul Williams. At 10:45 he stood before the judge, who inexplicably dismissed the charges against him. That guy had either the most incredible luck or he had connections. I suspected the latter.

As he left the courtroom, we followed close on his heels. With any luck on our part, we'd at least get the license number of the redhead's truck. David, still seated on the hallway bench, stood and followed us when he saw the odd procession. When Paul reached the door of the courthouse, he broke into a run down the stairs and across the parking lot, darting between cars. I briefly considered telling David to chase him but I had second thoughts when I realized Williams might indeed have a gun. Instead, we watched his flight from the top of the courthouse steps.

Williams ran straight through the parking lot and across the street where a blue Toyota pickup waited at a meter. The redhead sat in the driver's seat, and, when Paul got in, she gunned the engine and sped away. They were too far away for us to see the license plate.

I turned to the building and pounded my fist on the wall in frustration. Evie groaned.

"Well, I found out one thing," David said.

"What was that, honey?" I asked as the pickup drove down the long street and out of sight.

"Paul doesn't know who I am. He sat beside me when he came out of the courtroom earlier and asked me for a light for his cigarette. I guess he thought I was older. He told me he was being tried on a bogus charge and asked me what I was there for. I told him, 'Pretty much the same as you.'"

"Did you know he came with the phony cop?" Evie asked.

"I figured as much when I saw him in the hall with the redhead," David said. "So someone must have told him that I was staying at your house. He probably thought they were talking about Darroll."

We stared at one another for a moment, then, grumbling, we walked to my car, discussing the possibilities of what could have happened. There was only one reasonable conclusion: one of our clients had told Paul or one of his whores that Becky's son was staying with Evie Evans. The thought of a spy amongst us was chilling. We never saw the redhead again, but Paul Williams continued to explode like a minefield whenever we crossed his path.

14

THINGS GET OUT OF HAND

Fattie Patty and Kvetchin' Gretchen were two prostitutes who worked the street as a team, performing unusual sexual acts. I'd heard about the pair for years from street-walkers who spoke of them with disdain. I went to see Carol Bradley, who had mentioned them often.

"Do you think they'd talk to me?" I asked her.

She looked at me aghast.

"Becky, you don't want Fattie Patty and Kvetchin' Gretchen in your program!" she exclaimed, horrified.

"No," I agreed with a grin, "I probably don't, but I sure would like to meet them to try to understand that element of prostitution."

Eventually Carol agreed to contact the duo for me. I told her to tell them I would buy them dinner if they would answer some questions, and I guess that sounded okay to them, because they met me at Sal's Steakhouse downtown two days later.

Fattie Patty was about thirty years old, 5 feet 4 inches tall and weighed about 250 pounds. She had waist-length black hair which she wore in pigtails, with blue jeans and a tank top.

Gretchen was a slender 5 feet 7 inches tall with curly brown hair and brown eyes. Although she was only twenty-eight, she looked older from years of heroin use.

We took a table away from the other diners. After we had ordered I told the women that I had heard they "specialized," and I wanted them to tell me a little about how their work differed from that of other streetwalkers. It was a kinky question. Fortunately, they had both heard of Project New Life, and they accepted my explanation that I was doing research.

"Well, we work together most of the time, for one thing," Patty began. "And we service men who like pain. We don't let anyone tie us up, because it's too dangerous—some of them will kill you—but we tie *them* up a lot of times."

"One of our customers has us walk him around on a leash like a dog and spank him for being a bad boy," Gretchen added with a wicked grin. I had the feeling she enjoyed that.

"Oh, a lot of tricks want to be spanked. That ain't nothin'," Patty interjected. "Like I was sayin', we don't let them do stuff to us; we do it to them. Some guys want to be hurt real bad, like having us bite his dick until he cums. Some of 'em just like having two women at a time."

"Why do you think they want to be hurt?" I asked.

It was Patty who answered first. "'Cause they feel guilty about having sex, and it turns them on to get hurt."

"Not all of our dates want us to hurt them," Gretchen said. "Some of them just like to watch me and Patty get it on. Others like us to pee on them or worse." She watched my face to see if this had an effect, but after my years of helping prostitutes there wasn't much I hadn't heard. Disappointed that she didn't shock me, she tried again, "There's one dude who pays us to do it with his dog."

Patty seemed to regard dinner as fair trade for information, but Gretchen apparently came just to harass me. It wasn't what she said, but how she tossed out her tidbits, as if waiting with relish for the straight broad to recoil in horror at her stories. I wasn't about to give her a minute's satisfaction.

"How do you do that?" I dead panned. "Most dogs only get horny from the scent of a female in heat."

"He licks us till we cum," she informed me, losing interest.

Our waitress brought our dinners then. Patty and I had steaks, but Gretchen ate only a hamburger, probably because her rotting heroin addict's teeth prevented her from chewing anything tougher—and Sal's steaks were far from tender. I watched Patty wolf down four dinner rolls, then ask our server for more. She had two helpings of salad, a baked potato, and a hot fudge sundae for dessert—I presumed she had to keep up her professional appearance. I waited while the pair poured sugar into their after dinner coffer, like most druggies do, then returned to our conversation.

"Does any of the stuff johns want you to do ever bother you?" I asked.

"Sure. If they want to hurt us, we tell 'em no," Patty said.

"I don't turn down nothin' but the sheets," Gretchen answered. "Listen, some motherfucker wants me to shoot his dick off, I'll do it. All he has to do is pay me first."

Obviously, the lady's saturnine disposition had earned her nickname.

"We don't do kids, unlike some," Patty added. "Sometimes guys ask us to make a movie with little ones—eight, nine years old. We won't. We tell 'em to get someone else. I just hate goin' in a guy's apartment and seeing pictures and magazines of little kids having sex. I feel sorry for 'em."

"Bastards!" Gretchen muttered half under her breath.

"Listen, Becky," Patty apologized, "we gotta go. We have a date at eight o'clock. Would you like to see some of our equipment? You could come to our apartment if you want."

"No. I gotta get home," I replied casually. No way did I intend to visit these two on their own turf!

Concetta Williams and her children were still in Mexico with her parents, but the little ones were United States citizens, and they had medical coupons from our state, so when Angelica was scheduled to have surgery for a herniated navel, it was necessary to bring her to the States. Unfortunately, Concetta was no longer able to cross the border because her visa had expired, as Paul hadn't completed the paperwork to get his wife a green card. When Concetta's father telephoned me in late July, it was to ask that I meet Concetta and her mother and daughter at the Mexican side of the border. The Domingo family car was not working, and the grandfather would not be able to drive the girl to the American hospital. Juan warned me that Paul Williams knew of the surgery, so I was to be careful at the border, where he might be waiting.

I didn't mind the long drive, but when I arrived at the border Paul was waiting on the American side, among the pedestrians who would take the bus to town. He didn't see me, so I sank down in the seat and drove across the border into Mexico, where I picked up Elisa Domingo and her granddaughter. Angelica did not want to be separated from her mother, however, and, as we drove away, she began to cry, "Mama! Mama!" at Concetta, who was waving from the sidewalk.

It took several minutes for us to reach the border patrol station, where the American guard looked at me askance, then at the crying child, who very obviously was being taken from her mother. We were immediately directed to a fenced area where my station wagon was searched and we were questioned. Mrs. Domingo had her green card, but she, too, was under suspicion of international kidnaping. This happened as the clock was striking twelve in the tower of the little adobe church on the American side of the border. When the border patrol called the hospital to check our story, they were told that the doctor and his staff had just gone to lunch. So for two hot, dusty, thirsty hours we sat in the office of the Border Patrol and tried to convince

"La Migra" that we were on a mission of mercy, not child selling. Finally, the guards were able to reach the doctor's office, confirmed our story, and let us go.

As we drove away at long last, I began to laugh. Mrs. Domingo looked at me curiously, but I couldn't explain to her, in my poor Spanish, that I almost wished Paul knew how much trouble he had caused just by his presence. If the family hadn't expected him to be at the border—indeed if he hadn't come—Concetta could have walked to the pedestrian gate with her mother and daughter, explained to the guards, and the grandmother could have taken a bus the few miles to the hospital. I just couldn't get away from this guy.

Brian Tolbert, who had worked in one of the many gay bathhouses in our city, decided to try to convert his former pimp. His sponsor Christine Mayer, objected vigorously.

"I tried to tell him, Becky," Christine related. "But I don't think he believed me. What should I do?"

Like Christine, many of the former prostitutes tried to convert their pimps and/or johns to their new lifestyle but were largely unsuccessful.

"You'll just have to wait," I said. "It's not easy, but Brian has to learn for himself."

As well as time, it nearly cost Brian his life to discover that the "love" the pimp had offered him was nothing but a ploy to keep him working. Two weeks later the pimp had Brian beaten brutally to teach him obedience.

Not long after that Christine called to ask me to meet her new sweetheart, I was more than a little surprised.

"He's just wonderful!" she enthused one sunny afternoon. "His name is Michael Dover. I want you to meet him."

"But what if I don't like him?" I teased.

"You will!" Christine said, bubbling. "I just love him so much!"

"Does he know you used to be a dancer?" I asked, trying to be tactful.

"Michael used to pick up prostitutes on the street," she confided, "so he understands. He says it was like an addiction, but we've forgiven each other."

The last thing Christine needed was a street john. What was going on here? I felt she'd come a long way from her prostitute's mind-set. Well, if she could reform, maybe this guy could, too. I hoped so.

"When do I get to meet him?" I asked. I tried to sound delighted, but I didn't feel that way.

"How about tonight?"

That evening Christine introduced me to Michael Dover, a polite quiet man of slender build. Michael seemed caring and gentle: perhaps I was being overly protective of Christine. I decided to keep my mouth shut and wish my friend well. Besides, I had a lot of other people to think about.

Shawn Tate was a local talk show host who invited controversial guests to talk with opinionated audiences. When his show's producers invited me, they invariably put me in the audience, probably because I had neither a degree nor a "pedigree." If I'd been a professor, or, better yet, a whore, I might have been asked to be a guest speaker.

The subject of the show one August evening was the legalization of prostitution. Members of Progress, a group in favor of modernizing morality, and a national women's group, the Women for Old-Time Traditions, would be in the audience, and my views would be appreciated, the producers said.

When I arrived at the studio, I saw some women I knew from Progress, so I sat in the middle row with them, opposite the Tradition ladies, to chat a bit before the show began. Before I knew it, every seat in the audience had been taken, and the cameras were rolling.

Carla Simpson, the call girl who was tonight's guest, began the program with a defense of her career choice. Audience questions were allowed in the second of the five segments, so we all listened while she expounded on the glories of her calling. After the first commercial break, Shawn Tate brought his microphone into the audience, where the Traditioners eagerly awaited their chance to speak, and I turned to hear their informed comments.

"You sleazy, two-bit whore!" vituperated a Traditioner. "Where's your brain—between your legs?"

As I stared incredulously, these "ladies," educated members of a national women's organization, continued their emotional battery of Carla, who politely answered as many questions as she could. No wonder I had trouble getting support from the straight community, if other women felt as they did. "Well, you must be without sin yourselves," I said to them before we left, "to cast so many stones."

"Let's give Sam a graduation party!" Claire exclaimed when Samantha had called collect from the women's jail to tell me that she would receive her high school diploma before she was released that Monday. She'd studied for her graduation certificate with each incarceration, and she'd finally finished!

"You're right," I agreed. "Let's take her to the Nite Lite. She'll love it!"

Lee and the boys were excited about having a party for Sam's high school graduation. Claire and I shopped for gifts during the weekend and bought a silk blouse and a wristwatch. We bought cards and colorful paper for Darroll, who took over the artistic portion of the gift wrapping. David picked up the graduate at her sister's house Monday afternoon in his lean, green, mean machine, and escorted her into the restaurant as the rest of us arrived in my station wagon.

The Nite Lite, furnished in Art Deco style, had parquet floors, fresh lilies on the tables, and linen tablecloths and napkins.

It gave the place an elegance which attracted families as well as the singles set.

We sat next to the front wall in the family section. The tablecloth and napkins were salmon color, which, under the lighting, threw off a soft cast and seemed to erase years from Samantha's face: she looked as fresh as a teenager. Soft rock music wafted through the air from the dance floor, and we watched people file past our table to join the gaiety of the cocktail lounge in the next room.

Sam was moved almost to tears, and she said, "Oh, you guys!" again and again as we dined.

Most of my clients made their break with the life immediately, and, within six months, went on to get their own apartments and work a nine-to-five job. Samantha had taken much longer. I knew how hard it was for her to make her transition, so I had no complaints. In fact, I admired Sam's persistence: it was remarkable that she'd never given up.

"Now that you've got your diploma," Lee teased, "you have no reason to go back to jail!"

Sam replied with a grin, "Geeze, you're right. What do you think I ought to be?"

"Maybe you should be a doctor, with all you know about drugs," Claire offered tongue-in-cheek.

"Actually, I was thinking of becoming a nurse," Sam told us, suddenly serious. "I'd like to help people."

"You can help me," David told her. "I need a dance partner."

Sam was not the graceful dancer Christine was, but she looked beautiful to me as she swirled and swayed to the music of the band with my son.

"WASHINGTON, D.C. BUSINESSMAN ARRESTED FOR HAVING SEX WITH YOUNG BOYS," read the headline. I took a sip of coffee and perused the article with interest. "Raymond Chenault, well-known owner of Chenault Imports, was arrested yesterday on charges of having sex with teenage boys . . ."

Well, well, well, I mumbled to myself. So the wheels of justice do grind, albeit slowly.

Chenault had probably been set up, but I didn't feel the least bit sorry for him. Raymond Chenault was the invisible pimp who blackmailed his clients: he'd been Colin Nopson's employer. Colin's roommate Kevin had been murdered after one of Chenault's blackmail attempts.

It was early September when Concetta called. Except for the trip to the hospital, I hadn't heard from her since she'd gone to live with her parents in the spring. Juan Domingo had called me in August to tell me that Paul had forced her and the children to return to the United States with him.

"Paul seek. I have keeds. Chu come get me?" she asked in her thick accent.

"Do you want to leave him?" I asked. Dumb question, but she needed to say it.

"Si."

I didn't want to go another round with Paul Williams, but I couldn't refuse to help because of the four small children. Concetta gave me her location. I phoned battered women's shelters until I found one that had room for the five of them. Perhaps they would be more successful than I had been at protecting the family.

Concetta was waiting for me at a downtown street corner, trying to carry a baby, a diaper bag, and several paper sacks, while holding the hand of a toddler who was grasping the hand of her sister, who in turn was gripping their brother's hand. The scene reminded me of a television sitcom, but the humor ended there. As usual, the shelter considered my referral to be my client, and I had to be responsible for their welfare while they stayed at the shelter. I hoped Paul wouldn't come looking for me.

At the end of September Heidi Freeman phoned me with the news that her ex-pimp and the father of her children, Ethan, had died. I hated to acknowledge being glad about someone's death but this time it was true. Evelyn Parker and I had awaited this day eagerly, because Tyler and Phil would be able to live with their mother. The boys, however, were terribly upset. Ethan Freeman, pimp and white slaver, was also their father and, unlike the rest of us, they loved him.

Freeman had been so formidable a tyrant that even while he lay upon his deathbed no one had dared to cross him. Ethan had drifted in and out of consciousness for days: still Heidi didn't take her sons, for fear that his bloodthirsty lieutenants would kill her. When the long-awaited day came and the evil man died, it was his mother who told the boys that their father was gone.

"No! You're lyin' to me!" screamed the younger brother. "He ain't dead!"

As his grandmother tried to hold and comfort him, little Tyler kicked and struggled. He broke away from the older woman's grasp, ran out the front door, and disappeared around the corner into a nearby junkyard, where he hid for almost two hours.

Phil, five years Tyler's elder, punched his fist through the wall in angry defiance.

Three hours after Ethan's death, Heidi came to take her sons home. Their grandmother had packed their few belongings in a battered suitcase which had belonged to their father, while Freeman's whores and his lieutenants carried out the furniture and everything else to sell for drugs.

Heidi lived in a tiny U-shaped apartment, about 15 feet by 20 feet. Directly behind the entry sat a small bathroom and closet, only four feet in width. The rest of the apartment was divided almost in half by a wall which separated the kitchen from the living room where the boys slept. Their mother now bedded down on a rag rug next to the bathroom. One dresser held clothing that wouldn't fit into the closet.

When Evelyn phoned to apprise me of the situation, I asked if there were anything I could do to help. Because of their established relationship, I felt it was my place only to assist Mrs. Parker, her adopted mother, although Heidi had become precious to me.

"The boys don't have a stitch of clothing that isn't torn or completely worn out, or too small for them. I'm buying them clothes for the funeral and helping Heidi to enroll them in school. They've never been to school, Becky," Mrs. Parker told me.

It was Evelyn who found them larger living quarters. A week after the funeral had been held at the church where she and Heidi had met, Mrs. Parker helped them move into a one bedroom apartment in a four-plex. One person donated a hide-a-bed, someone gave the boys twin beds, and soon the little family moved into the rundown place which was to them a veritable palace.

"You should apply for Social Security benefits for the boys, Heidi," I told her brightly during my first visit to her new home.

She just stared at me for a moment. "Ethan was a pimp. He's never worked a day in his life, Becky," she explained with a shrug of her shoulders.

It had been a long time since I said something so stupid.

Christine Mayer continued to be a jewel, a sparkling diamond with many facets. It was too bad that she kept picking lousy settings.

One evening in September, I received a tearful call from her.

"Becky, I just don't know what to do. When the men I'm sponsoring call me, Michael yells, 'Your queer boyfriend wants to talk to you' loudly enough so they can hear him. I've told him how important this is to them, and to me, but he says they're nothing but a bunch of faggots," she sobbed.

This was one of those awful moments when I wanted more than anything else in the whole world to be selfish. Christine was as dear as a daughter to me, and I felt like telling her to dump the creep, but I had to be professionally detached.

"Well, if Michael feels that way," I forced myself to say, "You'll have to give up either the Project or give up Michael."

Then a sudden flash of insight gave me inspiration.

"I think it's time you started attending meetings with the other former call girls, Christine. Many of them have had problems with their boyfriends and could give you good advice. I'll call Emerald and tell her you'll be there, if you want me to," I offered cheerfully.

Christine agreed; so I phoned Emerald Harbison.

"My friend Christine Mayer will be at your next meeting," I began, but Emerald interrupted.

"Give me her phone number and I can call her, Becky. I have to leave for a BLT meeting in a few minutes."

"BLT? Like the sandwich?" I asked, confused. I added, "Christine's phone number is 555-4367."

"No, BLT. Birthparents Lifesearch Together," Emerald answered. "I always attend their monthly meetings."

"Who are you looking for?" I suppose I was being nosy, but she'd taken me by surprise.

"I gave up a baby for adoption when I was seventeen, and I hope to find him someday. I try to keep this separate from the other part of my life, because people think unwed mothers are prostitutes, anyway, and I don't want to give them ammunition to shoot birth mothers down. I gotta go now, Becky. I'll call Christine when I get back."

I was glad she'd finally told me. This was probably the reason that Emerald was so self-reliant: she would never allow anyone to get close enough to hurt her again. I wondered if her decision to give up her child had somehow precipitated her entry into the life. In any case, her bond with other people who were looking for their birth families was touching, for it was the only close personal relationship I ever discovered in her life.

Samantha Rice phoned in September, shortly after my conversation with Emerald, to give me good news: Sam had enrolled in practical nursing school! She would take a bus to the methadone clinic ("So I won't be tempted," she confided) early in the morning, then catch a second bus to the nursing school. It was a seven-month program, and she would graduate in April. Her news was one of the high points of my work.

Concetta was happy to be free of Paul. She found a nice two-bedroom apartment not far from our house, and Jerry's girl-friend Audrey checked on her often.

One morning Concetta phoned me. She seemed very upset.

"I dream there is a hand on my shoulder," she said. "I turn, and there is Paul!" She was close to tears.

"There's no way Paul can find you," I assured her. We had taken every precaution, and no one had heard from him.

However, the dream tormented my client nightly, and I was sorry for this sweet young mother who wanted only to make a better life for her children.

When the call came from Jerry's girlfriend, Audrey, I knew immediately that the panic in her voice portended trouble.

"Please come right away, Becky," she pleaded. "Jerry's so sick, and he won't go to the hospital. Maybe you can talk some sense into him."

I rushed to the car and drove as fast as I dared to drop Darroll off at Sharon Riner's house, then raced to where my friend lay—close to death, although we didn't know it then.

When I reached the apartment building, Audrey was pacing the walkway in front of Jerry's flat. As I parked the car, she ran to meet me.

"Thank God you're here, Becky!" the plump brunette panted. "I'm afraid we're going to lose him!"

I didn't know why Jerry refused to go to the hospital: he was quick to take a sick client to the doctor. Although Audrey and I were of different faiths, we murmured prayers as we ran toward the apartment.

Inside, Jerry Hudson lay upon his hide-a-bed. As sweat streamed down his face, he held his abdomen and groaned with agony.

"C'mon, Jerry, we're going to the hospital," I said. I added, "And no argument."

"I don't have insurance," he protested feebly.

"Well, we've been working together for three years. I love you but I can't afford to pay for your funeral," I retorted.

Jerry was too sick to argue any further. Audrey and I helped him into my station wagon, where he writhed and moaned on the back seat during the mile to the hospital. Quickly, I pulled into the emergency parking lot, then ran inside to get a wheelchair, because our friend could no longer walk.

Several tense hours later, Audrey and I spoke with the physician who had rushed him into surgery. Jerry had a ruptured appendix. "If he hadn't been brought to the hospital, he would have been dead by now," the doctor said. "As it is, the prognosis is guarded. He is critically ill."

But as the days passed, he grew stronger. Soon it became clear that Jerry would live. However, he was terribly weak from the infection, and the doctor prescribed rest at home. Frank and Evie Evans asked Jerry to stay with them when he was released from the hospital, and, much to everyone's relief, he agreed.

At times, when we were alone, Lee would pat my tummy and say, "I wish I had a watermelon."

I did, too. Why I hadn't gotten pregnant was a mystery and a source of sadness. We both loved children, and we really wanted a baby, but even after two years, we'd had no luck.

It was about the first of October when Christine phoned to tell me she was pregnant. She was thrilled, and although I didn't mention it, at last I understood why she was romancing another john. It had nothing to do with seeing herself as a prostitute. This time, she'd made the choice because of her lack of respect for men as tricks. It was Freudian, subconscious, and canny.

Prostitutes who have had children taken away, whether they've given them up for adoption because of social pressure like Emerald Harbison, or whether their children were forcibly removed, such as by Child Protective Services or violently removed by kidnaping, tend to do one of two things. Either they have one baby after another to "replace" the missing child, or they never have another child, because of the pain they've suffered.

Emerald Harbison never had another child. Samantha Rice has an "open adoption," wherein she speaks with her babies' adoptive parents and receives letters and pictures, so she hasn't felt as much pain of separation as Emerald and Christine, who, I could see now, was going to try again to replace little Judd.

Christine saw johns as disposable people, much as they view prostitutes. Use the guy to get pregnant, and when she felt like it, she reasoned, get rid of him. On a conscious level, she had to have a romance, because she no longer viewed herself as a prostitute.

I didn't rule over my clients. I couldn't force them to make decisions based on my experience. All I could do was observe, lend support when they wanted it, and pray for them. Christine was happy, and I wasn't going to interfere.

"Becky, this is Margaret. I'm in jail," came the rubbery voice one October morning. I could almost smell the alcohol over the phone lines.

"Maggie! What happened?" I demanded.

I felt like jumping up and down with anger. Margaret

Holman had been doing so well. I just couldn't believe she'd been stupid enough to drink again.

"I'm sorry, Babe. I was just gonna have a few beers with this guy, and that's all I remember. But it's okay. They told me I'm here for jaywalking and being drunk in public. I'm being arraigned tomorrow morning," she assured me, as if she expected me to rejoice.

"They'll probably drop the charges, Maggie, but that's not the point. You need to get back in an alcohol rehab program right away," I insisted. "You want me to three-way a call to the Women's Alcoholism Council? I can pick you up and take you to one of their shelters tomorrow after court."

I couldn't cut her any slack. If she walked out of the jail without supervision, she'd pick up her binge where she'd left off when she'd been arrested.

"I do want to go back to a program, Becky, but not right away. I need some freedom," Maggie complained. "I've been in programs forever."

"Listen to me, Margaret. You know what the doctor told you last time. If you keep drinking, you'll be dead in two years." I was almost shouting.

"I'll call you when I get out," she hedged. "I gotta hang up now."

As I stared at the receiver, the connection broken, my tears began to flow. I couldn't force anyone to leave the life, but Maggie meant so much to me. I'd watched her stretch her boundaries as she learned to read and write, got a job at a fast-food store, and made friends in the straight community. She had been sober for over a year. Why drink now? She could make it—I knew she could.

It's the alcohol, I told myself. You're not dealing with just prostitution. Maggie is a victim prostitute, but she's crossed the line between victim and criminal prostitution because of her addiction, and there's nothing you can do about it.

I don't know why I decided not to mention Maggie's call to my family. Maybe it was because I hoped there was still a chance that she might change her mind.

Gayle Laytona was to be the guest speaker on Reed Porter's talk show, and I was invited to participate from the audience. Gayle had been a call girl. She had been arrested for pandering, but while she awaited trial, she was in the race for State Senator of California.

After the show we went to a coffee shop where Gayle, her husband, and supporters quaffed hot chocolate. There were nine men in her party, including her husband, but Mrs. Laytona treated them all as if they were the sexiest, most important people in her life. She touched each man sensuously, with little pats on the arm, a tousle of the hair, a light massage of the shoulders. As different as the professional sports figure is from the weekend athlete, so was the prostitute Gayle from the people who only work as hookers. Most of my clients never behaved seductively when they weren't working, but this woman spent every moment in siren song. Each man responded to her as if she had eyes only for him, and seemed to fantasize that she was secretly his. I was fascinated.

"I gave it away to so many cops," Gayle said, "I thought, How's that different from prostitution? One of the women who used to work with me at the police department asked me how she could start working as a whore. I set her up with a good-paying customer, and she busted me for pandering. I was set up!" the call girl/candidate complained.

Sympathetic tongues clicked around the table at this, then Gayle changed the subject. "Do you want to see my campaign photos?" she asked.

Heads nodded and several men panted, "Yes!"

Mr. Laytona laid a large brown briefcase on the table and removed several eight-by-ten glossies of his wife posing wrapped only in bright crimson tape.

"ELECT GAYLE ANN LAYTONA," read the caption, "AND CUT THE RED TAPE!"

Shortly after my interesting evening with Gayle, Lee came home from work visibly upset.

"I saw Margaret Holman today, honey," he began

I had a sinking feeling.

"She was working the street, so drunk she could barely stand up. I thought maybe I should stop and try to get her to come home with me, but I didn't want to get arrested for picking up a known prostitute. Did I do the wrong thing?"

There was pain in my husband's eyes. He'd convinced Maggie to get help for her drinking problem the second time we had dated, and she had become a sort of treasure to him: he always asked about her progress and took pride in her accomplishments.

I told my husband, then, about Maggie's call from the jail and her refusal to get help.

"You should have told me when she called, Becky. You don't have to shield me from problems," Lee retorted angrily.

"I'm sorry, Lee. I was hoping Maggie would change her mind before I had to tell you," I replied.

The stress of this project on my personal life was overwhelming. I had started with my office in our home, but now we sort of "lived in my office." We received phone calls at all hours from people who wanted help, and we didn't turn anyone away. With Jerry sick, I had more to do than ever. I thought about having our home to ourselves with only the kids and ourselves to worry about, but I couldn't leave my prostitutes.

15

SURROUNDED BY THE ENEMY

One of the organizations to which I had applied for grant money called to say that we'd receive ten thousand dollars within a few months, which meant we could finally open Project New Life House.

Melissa Voorhees was released from prison on November 5th. She was to arrive by bus, and Darroll and I were to meet her. Dave Colchis, the psychologist she dated, said he was disappointed, but he wasn't able to sneak away to see Melissa for a few hours.

Missy's bus was fifteen minutes late, and Darroll was fidgeting.

"Do you think she missed her ride, Mom?" he asked for the third time. They'd been such good friends before she went to prison.

"No, honey," I assured him. "She'll be here."

Just then the PA system broadcast the arrival of Melissa's Greyhound, and we ran to the gate. The third passenger to get off was a golden-haired beauty whom we recognized instantly. When Missy saw us, she dropped her bags and opened her arms wide.

The three of us hugged and cried and laughed while the other passengers made their way around us.

"Oh, it's so good to be free!" Melissa exclaimed again and again. She took a good look at Darroll and added, "You've grown a foot since I last saw you!"

"C'mon," I urged them. People were shooting us dirty looks for obstructing traffic. "Maxine's waiting dinner for you!"

I'd arranged for Missy to live with Maxine Barr, who'd been her sponsor when she first began her program. They were good friends, and had kept up a correspondence while Melissa was in prison. Our greatest concern was her old struggle with addiction, because she couldn't use drugs and remain in our program. We'd just have to wait and see what happened.

The call from Detective Lou Silverman was a pleasant surprise until I heard what he had to say.

"Becky," Lou began, "could you make an important decision even if it might have unpleasant results?"

The detective was aware I was able to deal with life as it came to me, but if he had to ask I knew something crucial was in the offing.

"Sure, Lou. What do you have in mind?" I answered.

"One of your contacts, Booth Martin, may be a pimp," Lou replied. "I need your help to bust him."

"Booth? No, not Booth," I protested. He was the social worker at Child Protective Services who had done so much for Project New Life.

"What makes you say that?" I demanded. "He's been a terrific help, and he tries to help prostitutes on the street. I've never seen him be anything but professional. I just can't believe he could be a pimp!" I went on in an anguished tone.

"During an investigation last year, I discovered that some-one at Child Protective Services is placing teenage boys in the care of a man who runs a homosexual whorehouse, and I think it may be your friend, Booth Martin. I'd like you to help me set him up. If he's not guilty, no harm will have been done, but if he is, then I want to stop him."

"Look, I know Booth," I interjected. And I liked him. Middle-aged and balding, he spoke gently with a Southern accent. "Did you know that Booth is gay and that as a teenager he'd worked the street?" Lou asked.

"Of course, but he's been able to leave prostitution and become a social worker. He's very concerned about juvenile prostitutes."

"But," continued Lou, "he often places professed homosexual juveniles with gay foster parents," the detective said.

"Yes," I agreed, "and I know one of the biggest problems with juvenile prostitutes of either sex is that they sometimes climb uninvited into their foster parents' beds because they're confused about what adults expect of them."

"Nevertheless, Becky, he's got a perfect set up for a pimp to run an underage whorehouse."

"You're stereotyping him," I protested.

"But what if I'm right?" Lou persisted.

I sighed. After all, I'd been fooled by a psychologist who was also a pimp.

"What do you want me to do?" I finally said.

"Introduce me to Booth as a gay friend who's interested in foster parenting. If he's involved in exploiting boys, this will provide him with the opportunity to do so, and we'll have him. And, Becky, I know you like him," Lou added gently. "I hope I'm wrong."

"I know you're wrong," I said resolutely, but I couldn't help being afraid.

I did as Lou asked. He promised to call me as soon as he knew something definitive.

Meanwhile, other worries came to fill my mind. Later that same evening, Christine Mayer called to say she'd had a miscarriage.

The sense of loss she was experiencing was enormous, and I wondered how it would affect her relationship with Michael.

Also, I was more than a little worried about Chrissie. The fact that she was in the care of a street john while her mother was in the hospital, even for a day, was alarming. I had to remind myself that johns are human, and no matter what I thought of them, they could be responsible. In fact, Michael did take good care of the baby, and I had to admit that my view was becoming jaded.

Late that night I went to sleep out of complete exhaustion but a few hours later I shot up like a bolt, my heart pounding with fear: something had happened to my son David! I looked at the clock: midnight. Lee was asleep beside me, and I reminded myself that I had no idea whether David was even home from his date. I fought the urge to go into my son's room to check on him. I told myself I'd probably had a nightmare that I couldn't remember, but fear washed over me like waves on sand, and I could do nothing about at. At 12:15, I heard the front door open and close followed by David's footsteps going into his room. I told myself how foolish I had been. Then my heart slowed, my eyes closed, and I drifted off to sleep.

In the morning, I was in the dining room with Lee and Darroll when David came in. When I turned to greet him, I saw that his left eye was swollen shut, and a purple bruise covered his cheekbone. Before any of us could ask, he wisecracked, "Some guy insulted me, so I hit him with my face!"

David took a seat at the table, while I poured coffee into his cup. He took a long slow sip before he began.

"Sherrie and I went to the movies last night, and as we were leaving the theater, some older punks standing together on the side of the road started calling me names. I just ignored them and walked to the truck, then we drove to Carnival Sundaes for an ice cream soda. They followed us to Carnival's, and when we left, they came out of a bar next door, and followed us to the truck. I unlocked the door for Sherrie, and went around to get in myself, when this guy nailed me from behind, just as I got the door open, then he swung at me again. He hit me so hard I fell back against the seat, so I grabbed the first thing I felt, my baseball bat. I pulled that sucker out of the truck and whacked the dude across the side of the head. He dropped to his knees, and when I looked around, I saw his buddies running toward me, so I jumped in the truck and jammed out of there. I dropped Sherrie off at her mom's house, and came home."

"What time did that happen?" I asked, as I remembered my midnight intuition.

"We left the restaurant at twelve."

I didn't like it. Older punks meant possibly a gang. Did the incident have any relation to my work with prostitutes? I shuddered.

It was unavoidable that my mother and her husband, Tom, would learn of David's fight, for as luck would have it, we were to have dinner with them that night.

After she'd heard David's tale, my mother confessed that she'd been worried about our safety for some time.

"I'm afraid you'll wake up dead in your beds," she told me tersely. "I have a feeling one of those prostitutes is going to murder you someday."

I'd deliberately kept my mother and her husband in the dark about the more dangerous aspect of my work. She had no idea how likely it was that pimps had contracts out on us. Prostitutes? Probably not, but it's always a good idea to listen to one's mother. In this case even I felt she was right. Serious trouble was coming. It was just a matter of time.

Tom was concerned about my work, too.

"Becky, you say you're going to put Darroll back in public school this year, and I wonder what the other kids will say about his mother helping prostitutes. I don't think it's fair of you to embarrass him like that."

Tom is a Southern gentleman. The word "prostitute" would probably never cross his lips in female company. While he admired our work, it was a source of discomfiture to him when my name appeared in our local paper.

"And," my mother added sensibly, "now that there's no income from the building, how are you going to support your project? Lee can't support you and all those women when his job comes to an end."

They both had valid points, but I'd come too far to quit.

"We'll get our first grant in the spring," I explained. "I know you're worried, but we've worked too hard to abandon our cause now. I promise you we'll be careful."

Nevertheless, I felt suddenly apprehensive.

"I think we should move, Becky," Lee said one evening several days later. "Why don't we live in the country? Our rent would be less."

I had to agree with my husband. It was getting harder and harder to pay rent and have enough money to run the project, too; so we began to look for another place to live. We soon found it on a mountainside overlooking the city. Claire, in college now, moved in with Sharon Riner and her family.

Moving many years' accumulation out of a four-bedroom house was no easy task. We had to rent a storage locker for the donated items since our new place wouldn't have room for them. When moving day arrived, Lee and the boys began driving our belongings to our new home. We'd spend only one more night in the comfortable house we'd grown to love. If it had been the warm season, I'd have had one last swim in the pool. I put Misty out while we ate dinner, and took one last wistful look around the old place. When I returned to the patio door to call my dog, she was already there, retching, her neck extended, her eyes bulging.

"Lee!" I screamed.

As I knelt beside her, Misty fell on her side and tremors

shook her violently. My husband scooped up her little furry body in his arms, ran toward the front door, and yelled to me to phone the vet that they were on their way. David went with him, and Darroll watched as I frantically dialed Dr. Dixon's twenty-four-hour number. The veterinarian promised to meet Lee within ten minutes.

"Is Misty going to live, Mom?" Darroll asked. His face was pinched, and his brown eyes were filled with tears.

"I don't know, honey. She was poisoned. The only thing we can do is pray," I answered honestly.

I loved that little mutt as much as the kids did. She was my receptionist, my guardian, and my companion. We'd had so many happy times together. She let me know that I had calls on the phone recorder, and even managed to tell me when someone familiar called. She chased the neighbor's cat, but howled and grieved disconsolately when it was run over by a car. She greeted visitors with an outstretched paw. She followed me from room to room and waited patiently outside the door when I bathed. I would miss her terribly if she died.

". . . and, please, God, make her well. Amen."

Darroll prayed while I thought about our times with Misty. I wasn't as confident as he was that God intended to heal our dog; I'd never seen an animal that sick before.

Rrrring.

We knocked the receiver off the hook when we reached for the phone at the same time. I picked it up and answered breathlessly, "Hello."

A deep muffled voice answered, "Your dog's been poisoned. Who's next?" it said.

I felt a violent trembling spread through my body.

The next day, our veterinarian called to say Misty was going to be okay. The vet was certain that it had been a deliberate poisoning, and promised to call the sheriff's office to see if there had been any reports of similar incidents in the neighborhood.

He called me later to say that the only dog to be assaulted was ours.

Despite our worries, the move to our new house proceeded smoothly. Our new house was a quarter of a mile from the nearest neighbor, and we greatly enjoyed the peaceful panorama and the quiet which prevailed. Nights were spent in front of the wood stove, where we watched the lights of the city with our recovered pet at our feet. I found I had to go into town only three or four days a week, so I caught up on paperwork during the first weeks in our new home. Darroll began classes at the local school.

As soon as we were settled, I contacted Lindsey Baxter, and he began an investigation.

"Greg and I will come to your place to check the security," Lindsey informed me. "I want to do it right away. How's two o'clock this afternoon sound?"

"Great! I'll have coffee ready," I responded cheerfully. I liked the two detectives. Greg played Lindsey's valuable side-kick.

At two o'clock, I met the private eyes' car at the end of our half mile long, winding driveway and guided them through the fog past various dead ends, to our house. David and Lee gave our guests a tour of the property while I poured coffee and set a plate of cookies on the table. Darroll was in school until three fifteen.

When the men came in, Greg, as usual, let his boss do the talking, taking his turn when Lindsey gave him a cue. Despite their charming innocence, these two were canny investigators.

"Lovely place," Lindsey commented as he sipped his coffee.

"Thank you," I replied politely.

"You know," he continued, "if anybody wants to kill you, this would be a good place to do it."

I felt a chill go up my spine. Lee looked unsettled and David listened intently.

"Country road, trees and bushes, no close neighbors. You're out of the city, but you're still in jeopardy, Becky," Lindsey warned me. He turned to my husband. "Until we find out for certain whether, as we suspect, the attack on David and Misty's poisoning are related, you ought to keep a gun loaded, and make sure Becky knows how to use it."

"I will," Lee promised.

"The picture window presents a prime target for a sniper," Greg picked up where his boss left off. "You have a terrific panorama of the city, but a gunman would have a great shot at anyone in the front of the house from across that ridge." He pointed to the hill to the south.

"I don't want any of you to be here alone," Lindsey warned us. "It's too dangerous."

Later in the month, we invited Jerry, the Evanses, and Alan, an ex-con who was now semi-reformed and had offered to help Project New Life, to see our new home. We also wanted to let them know about David's assault and Misty's poisoning, as well as discuss the coming grant.

"What's to prevent all of us from becoming targets?" Evie asked.

We were familiar with our friend's penchant for stirring up excitement where none existed, but, thankfully, her husband intervened before I had to come up with an answer.

"Let's leave the matter of threats to the detective for now," Frank interjected. "What I've been wondering is how you can run the project when you're living thirty miles out of town."

Frank Evans had taken an interest in our group for a long time, but Jerry, Evie, and I still did all the work.

"You're so far from the action, Becky, maybe I should run the project from my house," Alan volunteered. "I have a phone in my room, I have a car, and I'm working nights now."

I replied to both men at once. "Well, I'm doing fine with

the phone, the paperwork, and the clients, but if there's an emergency, would it be all right if I called you?" I asked Alan.

"I think it would be a good idea if Alan did more," Frank offered helpfully. "He lives downtown, and he could take the clients to their appointments."

Apparently, Frank thought that all the prostitutes needed was a ride. I wondered if he'd let Alan transport his kids. The look on Jerry's face told me that he was thinking along the same lines as I was.

"One thing that you could do, Alan, if you have time, is to go through all the donated items in the locker Lee and Becky rented," he said. "We need to get rid of the things we can't use, like clothes that are ragged or stained."

He was trying to make "busy work" to keep our ex-offender out of trouble, and I fervently hoped he'd succeed.

Alan ignored Jerry's suggestion.

"I can do the TV interviews for you, Becky," he offered helpfully. "I know it's a long way for you to drive."

"Let's talk about the grant," Lee suggested. "We need to decide how we can best use it to accomplish our original goals."

The meeting ended with promises from everyone present to participate in such things as delineating a list of house rules; procuring furnishings; hiring a housemother; and establishing a greater funding base. This was very encouraging for me, because, heretofore, I'd been the one to do almost all of the paperwork.

While I was getting help with my paperwork, the work with my clients was still overwhelming. Heidi, who finally had custody of her children, was despondent about her older son, and called me constantly. Phil proved to be too much for his mother to handle. Not only had Phil lost his father, but at eleven, he was in school for the first time. The educators in their district didn't consider the child's emotional state, and placed him in a kindergarten class with his six-year-old brother. Angry and humiliated, Phil started fights with the other students and even struck his teacher. The principal phoned Heidi daily until, finally, he expelled Phil, who then had no place to go during the day.

"Ethan used to hold me down on the floor and tell the boys to kick me," Heidi explained. "So when I try to reason with Phil, he hits me and kicks me, because he thinks that's how he's supposed to treat women. Ethan's mother wants Phil to live with her, and if she can control him, I guess I'll have to let him go, but I don't want to."

Mrs. Freeman took Phil to San Francisco to make a new life for them. She hoped that a change of locale might keep her grandson from entering the life his father had so recently departed, but he soon got in trouble at his new school. Shortly thereafter, he was committed to a group home for boys on the recommendation of a counselor. Heidi called her son twice a week, and told him each time she spoke with him that she loved him. Heidi was an abused, neglected woman who had absolutely no example to emulate. Yet, what she did, or tried to do, for her boys was the tenderest illustration of a mother's love that I have ever seen.

As I mulled over Heidi's problem, trying to give her good advice as to what she should do, I also was worrying about my friend Booth. It was very difficult to wait for Lou Silverman's investigation of Booth to be completed. I felt deeply that Booth was the man I thought him to be: caring, truthful, and a positive force in Child Protective Services, but my heart ached at the thought of the possible alternative. Although I was busy with the project and my family, he was constantly on my mind.

On December 23, as the sun went down, I sat beside the Christmas tree that Lee and the boys had decorated and watched the flickering lights go on and off. The phone rang, and Misty ran to listen, but I answered before the phone recorder did.

"Booth Martin's okay," Lou Silverman informed me cheerfully. "I checked him out in every way possible. I think we're safe with your friend Booth."

As I hung up the phone, the purples and grays of twilight crept out of the trees and onto the driveway. I sat thinking of Booth, I felt the joy of the Christmas season fill my heart. I was so thankful that Booth was "clean." Misty came over to nuzzle me, so I took her chin in my hand and stroked her soft fur. I was thankful that my dog was alive and my son's wounds had healed. Yet I feared there would be more violence and against whom? I wondered apprehensively.

"Merry late Christmas," said the voice on the phone. It was two days after the holiday.

"Hi, Christine! Did you have a nice holiday?" I asked as I sat back to enjoy the conversation.

"Well, sort of. I threw Michael out."

There was a little grief mixed with impudent humor in her voice. I knew Christine Mayer well enough to understand that she was sad she hadn't captured "true love" yet, but she'd definitely enjoyed getting rid of Michael Dover. My analysis was right on target: he was a john, and he was disposable. Still, she'd believed that he was really a love interest, and "breaking up is hard to do," as the song says.

"I'm sorry things didn't work out for you," I sympathized.

"That's okay. He was a selfish prick, and I knew it all along. I should have done it sooner," Christine told me.

"Is there anything I can do?" I asked.

"You can say goodbye," she replied impishly.

"Goodbye? Where are you going?" She'd taken me by surprise.

"My sister Jeannie owns a restaurant in Rhode Island, and she's asked me to manage it for her. I'm going to drive back there January first. I'll stop in Denver and see Sarah Flowers on the way," Christine enthused.

My little butterfly. It was time she tested her wings, but I wasn't sure I was ready.

"I'm so glad for you!" I managed to say. "I'll see you before you leave."

As we hung up, I felt a bittersweet joy at Christine's announcement.

Well, "Mom," I thought, your "babies" are growing up!

Dressed in a blue gown, Claire was attending her first real prom. How could she have grown up so fast? I thought looking at her. I wondered if I'd been missing my youngsters' childhoods while I was so busy with my clients, and I wondered if Lee and I were lucky enough to have another child someday, would I miss that child's growing up, too? Not for the first time, I felt torn between my "two families."

Soon afterward Gayle Laytona lost her race for State Senator, and in January she was sentenced to three years in prison. I wasn't surprised: she'd foolishly flaunted her prostitution in the face of the Los Angeles Police Department. I only hoped that Gayle would survive her incarceration, for she'd be surrounded by enemies.

16

DANGER ON THE MOUNTAIN

On January 3, the telephone jarred me from sleep. By then I had been working with prostitutes for many years and should have been accustomed to the early and late hours. My mind was, but my body rebelled.

"Hello," I answered, groggy and grumpy. I wished I could sleep one night through without someone else's emergency to deal with. A moment later, though, I was ashamed for being so selfish.

"Becky! There's something wrong with Sarah!" Christine, calling from Denver, whispered nervously. "She's having a hard time walking, and her speech is slurred. She seems to have a high fever, too. What should I do?"

"Find a neighbor to watch the kids and get her to a hospital, or call 911," I replied. "And call me later."

When Christine phoned again that night, she sounded exhausted.

"It's a good thing I was here, Becky," she said. "Or Sarah might have died. That's not to say she's okay, though. The doctor thinks she has some kind of pneumonia that AIDS victims get."

"Why was she having trouble walking?" I asked.

"It was because the fever was so high. It was a hundred and six degrees. But, worse, when I asked the neighbors for help, the first one refused because Sarah's son is mixed race, and the next two refused because they'd learned she had AIDS. Finally, an elderly lady who lives upstairs took Dustin. I've been at the hospital most of the day. They kept Sarah—she's in isolation—and I came back here to take care of the baby. The old woman seemed to have taken good care of Sarah's little boy, thank goodness."

"What's going to happen now?" I asked. "Do they expect Sarah to get better? What happens to her son if she should die?"

"The doctor says that if she makes it through this she may have another year or two. Sarah says her mom will take Dustin," Christine told me. "I can't understand why her mother isn't here to help her now. Sarah can't take care of the baby much longer."

There wasn't much else to say about Sarah's mother. We both knew that the families of victim prostitutes could usually be expected to let them down, no matter what the circumstances. I wondered angrily if there were a legal precedent which could be used to force Sarah's stepfather, who had molested her and indirectly caused her to become involved in prostitution, to pay for her medical treatment and for child support for Dustin.

Suddenly, I was very thankful for my two loving parents.

Heidi's son Tyler tried very hard to atone for his brother's supposed sins. He was the model student insofar as behavior, but he learned nothing. Evelyn Parker picked him up after school each day and patiently worked to teach the little boy the alphabet and numbers, but, try as he might, he couldn't identify a single letter or numeral.

"I've had my oldest daughter, who's an educator, work with Tyler, Becky, but he's not learning anything," Evelyn told me one cold January afternoon, her voice fraught with concern. "If I give him tools he can take his bicycle apart and put it back together, but letters and numbers elude him."

"What does his teacher say?" I asked.

"She just insists he's not trying hard enough," she sighed.

"What do you think?"

"That's not right. He really tries. He's a good little boy, and he almost never gets in any trouble. The other day he was being naughty, so I told him, 'I'm gonna spank your butt if you don't straighten up!' and he was just as good as he could be after that," Evelyn replied, adding, "I talk that way to him because that's how Heidi talks, and I don't want to undermine her authority by making him think other people don't use that kind of language."

Despite Tyler's difficulties, I had to smile. Evelyn Parker understood that it wasn't our job to make clones of ourselves of the people who came to us for help, but to encourage them to stretch their own limits, to expand their own abilities.

During the next few months, Lee worked late many evenings because the appliance chain was closing many of its stores, and David often helped him. On the nights that they were gone, I locked the doors and windows and told Misty to "Guard the house," which meant she was to growl if anyone came near. Lots of beings—not human, we hoped—seemed to pass our home in the dark woods, for the dog frequently let out rumbles deep within her throat. We saw animal eyes glowing in the dark, which made our imaginations run wild, but no human tried to break in, and we told ourselves that we were being silly to worry.

One night, Lee and David were late coming home. Usually they arrived by eight, but this evening it got to be nine o'clock with no sign of them so Darroll and I put away the checkers game we'd been playing, stoked the fire, and climbed into our beds. We had to rise early the next morning for the long drive to my son's new high school.

About ten o'clock, a beam of light awoke me. As I sat up, I could see that the glow came from truck headlights, which shone through the picture window in the front of the house and down the hall into our bedroom. At first I thought my men were home, but when the headlights stayed on I began to worry. Why would Lee and David leave the truck running? Who was out there? The sliding glass door in the living room opened slowly, then footsteps sounded on the carpet. I trembled as I grabbed the shotgun beside the bed, just as the shadow of a man appeared in the headlights. In my loudest, most authoritative voice, I commanded, "HOLD IT RIGHT THERE!"

The man came to an immediate halt, and I could see him raise his arms in the shadow cast on the door.

"Becky, it's me, Lee," called my husband's familiar voice.

I dropped the shotgun and ran to him.

"Thank God you didn't come through the bedroom door, honey!" I exclaimed. "I was so scared. I might have shot you!"

"I knew you had that shotgun beside the bed, and I heard you cock it. No way would I have stepped through the door!"

"At first I thought you and David were home, but I got scared when I heard the truck running and someone come in. Why didn't you turn off the engine?" I asked, relieved in a way, but even more frightened at the thought that I could have shot my husband.

"David dropped some change. He kept the motor running, so he could turn on the interior light to look for his money," Lee explained.

We were both shaking by now. David turned off the truck and came in. "'Night, Mom and Dad," he called as he went to his room, unaware of the drama that had almost taken place.

If someone were trying to scare us, they'd just succeeded, and they weren't even here to enjoy it.

Melissa Voorhees was trying very hard to behave herself. She got a job at a doughnut shop, just the place for our "Missy

Munchie!" Maxine told us that she still dated Dr. Colchis, but she always came home sober.

She probably wasn't aware of how much my family loved her, because I absolutely insisted that she obey the rules, and she thought I was terribly strict. The problem was that she was exceptionally beautiful, and men would do anything for her.

Missy had so many good points: her tender ministrations to Darroll, and her consideration; her sense of humor; her determination to learn to read; her indomitable spirit. We all fervently hoped she'd succeed. Nevertheless, when Melissa took a bus downtown to report to her parole officer, she ran into old friends, two addict-prostitutes.

"They offered me a couple of hits of heroin for old times' sake," Missy related afterward. "I told them I don't do drugs anymore, but it sure was hard to walk away from free dope!"

The siren song of narcotics played steadily in her ears, however, and when she saw "druggies" buying doughnuts at her shop, temptation reared its ugly head. Missy confided that she was on shaky grounds at times, but so far she was holding tight.

It was February 24, many years after I'd become involved in aiding prostitutes who wanted to change their lives, when the violence against my family escalated to the critical point. That night we noticed that one of the sheds on our property had been ransacked. Immediately we called the sheriff, who took a report. Then we phoned Lindsey Baxter and Lou Silverman who warned us again to be careful.

Several evenings later, my teenage son David was working on his copper wire sculptures in another outbuilding when he thought he heard voices in the woods.

"I'm going to sleep in the camper tonight," he announced. "I want to keep an eye on the sheds."

Our neighbors had cautioned us not to venture into the forest after dark because of wolves, coyotes, and mountain lions, so I wasn't happy to let my young son spend the night outside, but my husband, Lee, reminded me that David wasn't a little boy anymore. I elicited a promise from David that if he saw trespassers he would do nothing but get a good description, and I admonished him to lock the camper against wild animals. Then I gave him a thermos filled with hot chocolate and bade him good night.

When Lee and I went to sleep, the darkness of the forest was complete; not a thing could be seen outside on this cloudy night. At three o'clock we were awakened, startled by a strong light coming from the window. I got up and peered outside.

"My God, Lee, it's a fire!"

Grabbing our robes and a fire extinguisher, we rushed outside only to see the sky darkening again. We were running toward the camper when suddenly a smoke-blackened apparition staggered toward us. David's head, arms, and torso were covered with soot. Only two blue eyes peered out at us. He coughed and gasped.

"David!" Lee cried. I was still half asleep and only now realized it was indeed my son who stood before me.

"What happened? Are you okay?" I yelled.

"Just bring the fire extinguisher," David exclaimed.

"If the fire starts to spread, the whole forest can go up in flames. Let' s go," Lee said and followed him. I was right behind him. "Stay there," Lee called back. Now he was at the back door of the camper. As he opened it, red flames shot out. Lee sprayed orange foam through the back door, then clambered inside and sprayed some more.

About fifteen long minutes later they were back. "We put it out," David said.

"What happened?" I asked David again, as Lee climbed down from the camper.

"I was sleeping, Mom. I don't think it was an accident; I think someone set it on fire," our still-shaking son answered.

Suddenly, we became aware of the chill in the air. It wasn't just that we were in our nightclothes: the cold seemed to emanate from a grave—ours, perhaps, I could not help thinking. Not long afterward the clouds passed, and stars twinkled brightly overhead. The glowing silver moon lit the ground around us. I couldn't take much comfort from the lovely scene: it would have been easy, too easy, for an arsonist to set fire to the house by that bright moonlight.

"Let' s go inside," Lee said. "We'd better get some sleep."

After a quick shower David went right to bed, and soon we heard him snoring. I turned to Lee and asked, without much hope, "Do you think the fire could have started by itself?"

"There was no electricity hooked up in the camper tonight. David had been asleep for hours—how could a fire start by itself?" he muttered angrily. "I've been trying to think of every possible way it could be an accident, but all I can come up with is that someone set that fire."

I responded then with the question that neither of us wanted to consider. "Do you think they knew David was in the camper?"

Lee put his arm around me. "Shhhh. Let's go to sleep," he wearily whispered.

But I couldn't sleep. I kept thinking that it was my involvement with Project New Life and prostitution which had brought fear and now peril to my family.

Still awake at the first grey light of dawn, I phoned the County Sheriff's Department. About nine o'clock, two officers arrived to investigate. They took our report and scrutinized the camper.

"You can see footprints on the right side of the camper, near the window. Did you folks walk around here last night?" one officer asked.

We assured him that we had only entered the camper through the door in the rear.

"There was a little rain after midnight, enough to make the ground muddy," the deputy told us. "There are footprints here." He pointed to the dirt beside the truck and camper. "Come on over here, folks. Let's match your feet against these prints."

One at a time we walked up to the footprints and showed the officer our shoes. Satisfied that the prints weren't ours, the officers looked inside the camper.

After a few minutes the second officer asked David, "Did you have the window opened, son?"

"A couple of inches for ventilation," he replied.

"That's how they did it!" the officer exclaimed. He pointed to a pile of burnt matches and a charred rag which had apparently been thrown, burning, through the window to a cushion which lay next to the bed where David had been sleeping.

"Do you have any enemies that you know of?" the first deputy asked.

"My wife is the head of Project New Life," Lee began.

"You mean the group that helps prostitutes?"

"Yes," I replied.

The deputies seemed to lose interest then. One of them closed his notebook, and the other told us, "There's not much we can do, Ma'am. There's probably a lot of people who would like to put you out of business. Let us know if anything else happens."

After they left, David looked a little dazed. He asked, "What happened? One minute they were investigating and the next minute they were leaving."

"Apparently, they think that if we're crazy enough to help prostitutes," Lee surmised, "they're not going to worry about our safety."

There was no point in filing a complaint with the Sheriff's Department about the deputies' conduct. They would only insist that the men had made a thorough investigation. And I knew some officers of the law could have been involved in prostitution as pimps or johns themselves, or maybe they were on the take.

Was someone trying to murder us, or was David's presence in the camper when arson was committed only coincidental? We went to Lindsey Baxter for advice.

Seated in his office amid gleaming ultramodern equipment, I couldn't manage to drum up the homey image that he and Greg Landers projected elsewhere. Here, Batman and his faithful sidekick Robin were the epitome of high tech investigators, efficient, electronically-assisted, and computer-enhanced.

"Well," Lindsey said when we had told our story, "let's sift through the evidence. So far, there have been nuisance incidents. Your dog could have died, but that couldn't be construed as a murder attempt."

A glance at my face made him amend his statement. "Not by the police, anyway," he added. "Someone beat up David, burglarized a shed, and set your camper on fire. It wasn't murder."

"It could have been," I broke in.

"No." Lindsey shook his head. "More like a warning. Otherwise, they would have set the house on fire trying to kill everyone." He paused. "And they still might."

I shuddered.

"So what do we have?" he continued. "Apparently a person or persons unknown are harassing you. They must believe you know why, because they're only scaring you. They haven't contacted you to tell you what they're after. Who do you know who would want to send this kind of message?"

My husband and I glanced at each other. I looked at Lindsey and admitted, "There's probably a lot of people."

Lindsey's professional demeanor hid his thoughts from me. We left the office a little while later with another admonition from him to be careful and a promise that he would investigate further.

Concetta's nightmares continued unabated. The worry began to wear on her, as the dreams came at first once nightly and then many times a night, despite our prayers together.

Jerry Hudson, still recuperating from his operation and unable to work, had given up his apartment and continued to live with Frank and Evie Evans. His girlfriend, Audrey, was the only person we had who could check on Concetta and her children daily, and she did so willingly. She phoned me every afternoon, always with reports of a neat and happy household and no threat of the little pimp. But still Concetta had those dreams.

It was about eleven thirty in the morning on March 13, that Evie phoned, her voice panicky but firm.

"Becky, this is Evie. Get over here right away."

"What's the matter?" I shot back, worried by her tone.

"Just get over here, now," she commanded.

I waited only long enough to phone Sharon Riner to ask her to keep Darroll again. Sharon never refused, although we hardly got to visit since we had moved. Soon I was at the Evanses' house.

Evie ran out the front door as I turned into the driveway, pulling on her coat.

As she got in, I asked again, "What's the matter?"

"I've been raped!" she sobbed. "Just take me to Kaiser Hospital."

"What! What happened?" I asked in confusion as I drove.

"I was doing the dishes about ten o'clock when I heard someone knock at the door. Frank had taken the girls to a soccer game, and I was alone in the house. I peeked out the window. Paul Williams and a man I didn't recognize were there, so I didn't open the door, but I called, 'What do you want?'

"'Where's Concetta?' Paul yelled. I told him I didn't know, and to go away. When I saw them walk away, I thought they were gone and I went back to finish the dishes. A few minutes later a man's hand came over my mouth, and the next thing I knew I was on the floor, and he raped me."

"You mean Paul Williams raped you?" I asked, upset what to say to my friend.

"No, it was the man who was with him."

"What did he look like?"

"He was about six feet tall, Hispanic or Italian, and he was wearing jeans and a red jacket. That's all I remember."

"Have you called the police?"

"No, and I don't want you to either. I don't want anybody to know."

"Have you told Frank?"

"No. He won't let me keep working with Project New Life if he finds out, Becky. Don't tell anybody. Please," Evie begged.

When we arrived at Kaiser Hospital, Evie asked me to wait in the car while she went to the emergency room. I understood the confusion and stress that result from being raped, so I would have stood on my head if it made her feel better. At one forty-five, my friend pushed open the swinging doors of the emergency room and said, "Let's go."

"Evie, you've got to tell Frank," I suggested gently when we were driving.

"I can't," she protested insistently.

"What if you're pregnant?" I decided to try a dose of reality, painful though it might be.

She turned to look at me thoughtfully, "I'll tell him his vasectomy slipped," she replied.

"After four years?" I responded incredulously.

Still, my friend insisted on keeping this a secret. I simply couldn't force her to tell anyone about it. I was to wonder, in the weeks and months to come, if it was a mistake not to insist that she go to the police.

Three days later, little Gracie Williams had a doctor's appointment. Because it was so difficult for Concetta to manage four children on a bus, I offered to drive them. When I pulled up to their complex about ten o'clock, I noticed a rented moving van in front of the building. Two men were loading furniture, and one of them looked terribly familiar. My heart sank as I realized Concetta's and my worst nightmare stood before me.

"It cost me a lot of money to get a social worker to tell me where you hid my wife," Paul Williams screamed as I got out of my car.

I saw Concetta carrying boxes down the stairs to the truck, so I ignored him and shouted, "Concetta! You don't have to go if you don't want to. Do you want me to call the police?"

Tears streamed down her face as she shook her head emphatically. "No! I go!"

Paul hissed, "You can't keep my family from me! You owe me. I had to pay off the social worker and rent this truck!"

Paul Junior and Gracie were crying, and Angelica was huddled in a corner near the front door. I was helpless. The income his whores brought in made Williams almost invincible. We both had "inside connections," but mine were based on respect and trust while his came from cold hard cash. I knew I'd never be able to track down the social worker who had betrayed Concetta, unless, I thought with sudden inspiration, I could get Missy's boyfriend to help me.

Madeline Colchis, wife of the respected psychologist Dave Colchis, so familiar to streetwalkers up and down Wickersham Boulevard, had connections in our city. I didn't wait to get home to call Dave. I stopped at a phone booth a couple of blocks from Concetta's apartment.

"Dave, this is Becky Usry," I said to his answering machine. "Please call me right away."

"I'm here, Becky," Colchis said, as he turned off the machine. "How are you?"

"I'm okay, Dave," I replied. "Listen, I hate to be rude but I'm so angry I can hardly think, and I want your help, or rather, your wife's help."

Dave had brought me several new clients during Melissa's absence, and I knew he didn't particularly want Missy to know that he'd been consorting with other streetwalkers. Also, Mrs. Colchis wasn't thrilled with her husband's behavior, but more than that, she didn't want it to become public knowledge. I had no intention of making the psychologist's sex life known to anyone, but, I thought, and rightly so, that he'd presume he was in no position to refuse me any favors.

"Sure," Dave responded. "What's up?"

I explained Paul's remarks about bribing a social worker and asked if Mrs. Colchis could investigate or at least give me advice. The psychologist promised to call me back as soon as he had discussed the matter with his wife. It was later that same evening that I heard from him. I was still angry and upset, and his answer did nothing to soothe me.

"Anyone who receives any county services, that is, welfare, food stamps, counseling, what have you, is listed on a county-wide computer system. Any clerk or social worker can retrieve an address from the system, so it's impossible to determine who gave Williams his wife's address," Dave Colchis related. "I'm sorry."

As I spoke with my husband about the events of the day, his wisdom made me feel a little better.

"You can't sacrifice the whole project to fight one pimp, especially when Concetta won't stand up to him," Lee admonished.

I knew he was right, but I didn't like it.

Six months passed and then we faced another altercation.

"There were six Speed Demons at the Mountainside Cafe tonight, Dad, and they mentioned Mom," David told Lee as he burst through the door at supper time one night.

A gang war had taken place between the Speed Demons and the Iron Eagles only a few years ago. The two motorcycle clubs controlled much of the street prostitution in our area, and they were bitter rivals. Any gang-owned applicant for our program had to be put into the underground railroad, because anyone who returned to her pimp would endanger all the others we'd hidden.

"Why did you stop there?" Lee asked.

"I wanted a cup of coffee," David replied. He held up a large Styrofoam cup with a plastic cover. "I'm going to work in the shed for a while. I'll skip dinner; my stomach hurts."

We ate and Lee settled down to watch television while Darroll and I went to the supermarket where he spent his quarters on video games as I shopped. David was still in the shed when we left.

About seven o'clock, David came into the house and told Lee, "I don't feel very well, Dad. I'm going to lie down."

When I got home fifteen minutes later, David began moaning. I shot Lee a "What's that?" look, dropped the grocery bags, and rushed into the room, where David writhed in pain on the bed.

"What's the matter, Son?" I asked nervously as I knelt beside him. Lee was in the room now, too.

"It hurts, Mom."

"What hurts? Where?"

"Stomach. Is that you, Mom?"

"Yes, David, it's me."

"Where are you?"

Lee and I traded frightened glances. He ran for the phone while I put my arms around our son, who was now delirious.

"Here," Lee shouted. "They want you to stay on the phone. I have to move the truck so the rescue chopper has room to land."

I took the phone and said, "Hello," but I couldn't see into the bedroom from there. As the 911 operator began to question me, I heard David fall off the bed. "I can't talk to you now. I have to take care of my son," I hurriedly told the person on the other end of the line.

In moments, Lee was back, and Darroll called 911 again. "Here, Mom, they want to talk to you."

I took back the phone while my husband stayed with David. I communicated his deteriorating condition.

"Can he tell you what happened?" the operator asked.

When I relayed the question to Lee, he replied, "David keeps repeating, 'The coffee, the coffee.'"

After what seemed an eternity, the helicopter arrived and the paramedics administered medications to stabilize David's condition. Placing him on a gurney, they carried him to the helicopter. I phoned my mother and Tom, then got in the truck with Lee and Darroll. As we waited for the chopper to take off, a paramedic asked Lee if he knew anything about some coffee. David had continued to ramble on about "the coffee," and his symptoms seemed to point to poisoning.

"I'll go look in the shed. I think he was drinking coffee in there," Lee said as he opened the door of the truck.

The truck was parked with its nose pointing downward toward the shed. As my husband walked inside the little building to investigate, the clutch slipped and we began to roll forward. Darroll was seated in the middle, and I screamed at him to hit the brake. He had never driven, and he saw only three pedals on the floor.

"The middle one! The middle one!" I yelled.

Just as his foot pressed the brake, we heard a crunch. When we looked up, we saw that we were just inches from the shed, where Lee, white-faced, stood in the doorway. He squeezed past the fender and surveyed the damage. Our left front tire rested on the remains of the portable toilet which had been removed from the charred ruins of the camper. My husband smiled reassurance at Darroll, who was trembling with fright.

"You killed the toilet, Son," Lee joked.

As Darroll sobbed with the realization that he'd almost let the truck run over Lee, we hugged him and reassured him that it wasn't his fault. It took some time—or it seemed to—for the paramedics to scramble into the helicopter. At last, the chopper lifted slowly, the mighty wind rushing from its blades flattening the grasses. Lights from the volunteer firefighters' vehicles which had come to our aid lit the ground around us. On the seat beside us, twelve-year-old Darroll sniffled from stress and fear. I remembered then that Lee had gone into the shed to investigate the coffee.

"What did you find?" I asked.

"The cup was empty," he told me as he backed the truck down the driveway. "I think the chopper's wind blew it over."

At the hospital they pumped David's stomach and found traces of rat poison. When he was stable enough to talk, Lee questioned him.

"I ordered coffee, then used the washroom, and when I came back, the waitress had left the coffee on the counter. It was next to where the Speed Demons were sitting," David told us. "I started feeling bad while I was driving home, but when my stomach was cramping so much, I thought maybe the coffee had something to do with me being sick, because it tasted bitter."

"You were right," we told him.

The warnings to us had grown more dire.

"The someone who was trying to kill us almost got two for the price of one tonight," Lee said, summarizing our evening.

Over the winter, Evie still did not tell anyone else about her rape. She was not pregnant but she was depressed, which made me worry, though I was thrilled to learn that Jerry had become a Christian under her husband's tutelage.

When the grant money arrived at the end of March, we held a meeting at the Evanses' home to form a Board of Directors which would guide Project New Life from now on.

"It's been years since I started the project and we need to run it on a more formal basis if we're to help more women and men," I said, a little sad to see some of the personal touch I thought so important being lost.

The newly-elected Board decided that the tasks involved in opening the House should be divided among committees. I was on every one of those committees. It wasn't so much that I liked to run things my way as that I wanted to be certain something got accomplished.

During this period, Darroll was unhappy in school. He preferred home schooling, but Lee and I made the decision that our son should have more social interaction, and we wanted the expanded curriculum that public school offered. Even though his first report card showed mostly D's and one F, we didn't allow him to withdraw from his classes and attend home school again as he suggested. Instead, we made an appointment to talk with his teachers.

We visited three instructors on the afternoon of March 15. It was a beautiful spring day, windy but sunny, when we met Darroll on the steps of Woodlawn High. David was at work, and Misty was visiting Claire for a few days. We spent an hour in conferences, then had a conciliatory ice cream at Carnival Sundaes.

We returned home to a new disaster. Opening the door, we saw papers strewn on the floor, drawers emptied, and the entire house a mess. Surprisingly, as we searched the debris, nothing seemed to be missing. Either we had arrived before the burglars had finished their work, or the purpose of their visit was harassment.

After that, we left a tape recorder hidden in a kitchen cabinet, and we told Misty, "Guard the house," whenever we were gone. On March 18, we returned from church to discover the dog locked in the bathroom and the house ransacked once again. When we played the tape, four voices, two male, one female, and one canine, could be heard.

"Woof! Woof! Woof!"

"What's that?"

"It's a dog, stupid. Here, puppy. Nice doggy."

"Shut it in the bathroom, over there."

"Got it. Chatto, you take the living room. Karen, you take the kitchen. I'll search the bedrooms."

After that, the sounds were too muffled to hear, so we took the tape to Lindsey whose ultramodern equipment filtered out the extraneous noise, but further conversation wasn't clear enough to discern. Greg Landers, his assistant, whose expertise had clarified our tape, suggested we think about another line of work.

"Trespassers who don't take things are there for another, more ominous, purpose," Greg told us. "Are you sure it's worth your lives to help hookers?"

17

RUNNING THE GAMUT
OF
EMOTIONS

While I was mired in the paperwork for our reorganiza-
tion, Lee worked on getting the House ready to open.
Since Lee's employer was getting ready to close the
last few stores in the chain, my husband had more and more free
time, which was difficult for us personally, but a boon for Project
New Life.

He placed ads for a fund-raiser, a grant writer, and a
housemother. He conducted interviews, set up files, looked for
a suitable house to rent, and, when he found it, filled it with
furnishings which he got at bargain prices.

On April 12, we were having Sunday brunch at home after
church when, suddenly, Misty growled, pawing at the door. I
couldn't see anyone when I peered through the kitchen window,
so I cautiously opened the door. A giant rattle snake was poised
on the step, hissing.

"Lee! Get a gun!" I shouted. "It's a rattler!"

"But it's sixty degrees," he called. "It's not rattler weather."

"Get the gun!" I screamed. I stood, transfixed, until my

husband arrived seconds later with a double-barreled shotgun. Shoving me aside, he peered at the step, and fired. Once, twice. The five-foot-long body rose in the air and then fell dead, shot through with holes. I bent over it. Around its neck was tied a black ribbon from which hung a printed card inscribed, "With sympathy."

"Don't touch it," Lee yelled. I obeyed, since the rattler's poison was as lethal in death as it had been during the snake's life.

David carefully carried the reptile to his car and placed it on the roof, out of reach of the dog. "I'll take it to the dumpster in town tomorrow," he said.

Coincidental? Hardly. Attempt on our lives? Probably. Of course, we couldn't be sure but we were nervous, highly nervous.

It was only one of many suspicious events which had happened since I had become involved in helping the sisterhood of the night.

It was still cold at night in the mountains in April, so when it was time to light the fire, David went outside for wood.

"Aaaagh!" he screamed from the driveway in the dark.

We ran to the door, only to find David grinning sheepishly.

"I saw the snake on the roof of the car, and I forgot for a moment I'd put it there. I thought it was alive!" he confessed.

Later, Lee started down the driveway to the shed where our son was working on wire sculptures.

"Yikes!" he screamed.

This time, I giggled as I ran to the door. My husband stood in the driveway looking at David's car, his hand over his heart.

"Dead snake," he announced as calmly as he could, and walked away.

The Shawn Tate Show's producers phoned me on April 13 to ask that I bring some former streetwalkers to sit in the audience. Their Tuesday guests were a call girl and two escort service prostitutes, and the producers wanted to air streetwalkers' views of the life, too. I had promised myself not to do any more talk shows, but the possibility of revealing a different side of prostitution appealed to me, so I agreed to appear on their show with my clients.

I thought perhaps it would do both Samantha Rice and Melissa Voorhees good to make a public break with the life by announcing on television that they were *former* streetwalkers, so I asked them if they would like to go. Sam always told me she'd do anything for me, and she agreed readily, asking only that they would shadow her face so her sister wouldn't be embarrassed. I assumed that Shawn Tate would be considerate enough to honor her request.

On the day of the taping, I picked up Missy first, then Sam, who was a knockout in a white dress with a smart red belt and matching high heels. A new stylish hairdo and professional makeup must have cost her forty dollars or more. All in all, she could have passed as a businesswoman or a wealthy housewife.

"Wow!" I exclaimed, "you look terrific!"

"Well, the television news crews always show streetwalkers dressed in miniskirts or jeans. I want the audience to know we're respectable people, just like the expensive whores," she explained proudly.

On the air, the two escort service prostitutes and the call girl extolled the benefits of their profession during the first segment. I heard Sam sniffle and glanced at her. She and Missy, with angry looks on their faces, were dabbing at their eyes.

"What's the matter?" I whispered, taken aback.

"It just makes me so mad when those women tell people how wonderful prostitution is," Sam declared tearfully. "They get to date nice well-groomed men in clean hotel rooms, and they get paid hundreds of dollars. The guys I dated were dirty and smelly, and sometimes they were drunk. I only got paid twenty dollars. It was degrading to me to have to do that."

Melissa added indignantly, "And we had to give head in a little front seat, or in some dirty motel room."

"Tell Shawn that," I suggested. "People need to hear what you're saying."

We rushed up front during the first commercial to make the request to shadow Sam's face.

"It's too much trouble," Tate's aide declared. "We only do that for the guests Shawn interviews on stage, if they need anonymity."

Fuming, we made our exit.

"C'mon. It's time you two learn how I deal with stress," I announced, tongue-in-cheek, as we calmed down and got into the car.

I took my friends to Carnival Sundaes and bought three hot fudge sundaes. Shawn Tate didn't know what he was missing.

It was April 15 when we got the House opened. I consulted with Martin Carson frequently, because, despite our differences, I knew he could give me realistic advice about shelter management.

Our neighbor's mother, forty-eight-year-old LaDonna Peterson, was to be our housemother. She'd had no experience with streetwalkers, but she was kindhearted, and I thought she'd do a good job.

Ginger Pettit was our first client in the House. The last time I'd seen her, she had been a nursemaid to her boyfriend Tim, the cancer patient who regularly injected drugs into his stomach feeding tube. I'd heard about Ginger during the past four or five years, of her "loads" addiction, of her hospitalizations, of her incarcerations, and I always wished she'd ask us for help.

When Ginger moved into our shelter, I learned she had a twelve-year-old son who lived with her grandparents. She wrote them regularly, but she hadn't seen any of them for ten years.

Ginger made rapid progress on her program. She got a job, started school, got much-needed dental care, and got her first ID in twenty years. There was a sparkle in her eyes and a spring in her step that I'd never seen before.

"I feel like I'm sixteen again and have my whole life before me," Ginger enthused to anyone who would listen. It was wonderful to hear.

One morning I checked everyone's room because we were expecting reporters from a local television news show. I experienced deja vu when I saw Ginger's mess. It was the same kind my children were so fond of leaving. Since my client had already left for work, I wrote her a note:

Dear Ginger,

I can tell you feel like you're sixteen by the way your room looks. Clean it up!

Love, Becky

She did.

I began checking Ginger's room every day after that so I could praise her for her good housekeeping. One morning, I saw my Bible, which I'd misplaced several days before.

"Oh, Ginger, you found my Bible," I told her later. "Thank you."

"I'm sorry, Becky," she replied. "I thought it was a donation, so I took it."

Pleased, I made it a point to give Ginger a Bible of her own.

David's birthday was on April 18. Lee barbecued hamburgers and I baked a cake. Afterward, Darroll and I drove to town to take David's gifts to my mother's house where we were having the family party the next day. At seven that night, the family was to meet Darroll and me at Cinema Six, where the birthday boy had picked out a double feature.

By seven fifteen the show had started, and, tired of toe-tapping, I bought tickets and took a seat near the entrance of the theater where we could see Lee and David when they arrived. After the first movie ended, I marched to the public phone and called the house, but no one answered. Finally, Darroll and I bought some popcorn and went back to watch the second show. When the movie let out, we waited while the theater emptied, in case we'd missed our men, but we didn't see them. We drove through the parking lot, but we couldn't find the truck anywhere. It was twenty miles, mostly up winding mountain roads, to our house, and darkness had fallen hours before. I drove the narrow lanes carefully, and it was after eleven o'clock when we got home.

As it turned out, when I'd left our home earlier that evening, Lee watched my station wagon disappear down the driveway and then turned to David.

"We've got an hour. Let's get out Darroll's Pacman!" he challenged.

For the next sixty minutes, they concentrated mightily on beating each other's score. At six thirty, David looked at his watch.

"Mom's gonna be mad if we're late. Let's go," he said.

David headed for the truck, which was lighter without the camper, while Lee locked the house. David hopped into the driver's seat, inserted the key without starting the engine, and shifted into first gear as he put his foot on the brake. His foot continued to the floor, but as he grabbed the steering wheel to control the truck, he realized it was still locked, because he hadn't yet started the engine.

Lee locked the front door and stepped outside. He saw the panic on our son's face as the truck began to roll. He knew David didn't have control of the vehicle, because of the angle at which it was traveling, so he dropped the house keys and ran toward the truck, which at that moment disappeared over the embankment.

The crash echoed through the mountains, and Lee, nearly paralyzed with fear, forced himself to look over the edge of the road. David could be seen through the cracked windshield. Blood dripped down his face from gashes on his forehead and nose. For once in his life, he couldn't manage his impish grin. Lee slid down the embankment and pulled the door open.

"I'm all right, Dad. I just banged my head on the steering wheel," David panted. "The brakes were gone."

My husband tugged our son from the vehicle and made certain that his injuries were minor. Then he took a flashlight from the glove box and examined the undercarriage. The brake lines had been cut.

They tried to use David's car to pull the truck to the driveway, but the car didn't have enough power. They'd have to wait until morning to call for a tow.

When Darroll and I rounded the curve in our driveway, our headlights lit the disabled truck about twenty feet down the side of the mountain, its tailgate wrapped neatly around a tree. I could see it was empty. Quickly I pulled up to the house and raced to the front door, where Lee greeted us.

"What happened, honey? Are you guys all right?" I cried.

"Someone cut our brake lines, but we're okay. The truck's in very bad shape, though."

"I tried to call . . ." My voice trailed off when I saw David's face and nose.

David related his version of the crash when we went inside.

"My heart was in my throat. I could see the embankment drop off behind me, then the truck began rolling down. I couldn't get out of my seat belt. I didn't have time to start the engine, the steering wheel wouldn't turn, I thought I was a dead man! When I saw that tree coming up in front of me, I started praying. Fortunately, the truck wasn't rolling too fast yet, or I might have been hurt worse when I hit the tree. If the truck had been just a couple of feet to either side, I would've been killed."

I phoned Lindsey the next morning.

"Becky, you have to move," the detective urged emphatically when I'd finished, "I know Lou will feel the same way. I want you to get an apartment with lots of neighbors. You need to be in the presence of potential witnesses at all times, because now we *know* someone's trying to kill you."

He was right. Much as we hated to leave our house in the country, Lee and I agreed it would be safer to move.

At least the move was easier this time, without twelve years accumulation to pack. We were able to rent an apartment by early May, in the heart of one of the little towns on the edge of the city.

Our new home had two large bedrooms and a bathroom upstairs, with a tiny kitchen, dining room, and living room below. We worried that Misty would miss the freedom she'd enjoyed in the country, but she quickly discovered that she could spy cats in many of the neighbors' yards from our bedroom, and she begged charmingly for me to lift her up to the window so she could scan the area whenever we went upstairs.

About that time, the police phoned to ask me if we had room in our program for Jill Cline, a young hooker whom they had taken to an emergency room after a knife-wielding john had cut her forearm. Jill was a sweet girl of nineteen who had a one-year-old baby. LaDonna got the pair settled, and I met them briefly. I should have realized immediately that there was one glaring discrepancy in her story, and not have accepted her into the program so quickly, but, worried about her child, I listened to my "mother's heart," instead of thinking things through.

Never had I been so busy. Fund-raising! There was constant publicity, television cameras, and newspaper reporters. I had to keep the hype going if we were going to generate enough income from the media blitz to remain in business. When another prostitute was found murdered in May, I decided to use the incident to help other streetwalkers.

I phoned a minister whose church was on Wickersham

Boulevard. Students at his church school had been harassed by pimps; members of his congregation had been propositioned; sex and drug paraphernalia frequently littered the church grounds. Together, we held a public forum to discuss the problem of prostitution in the area and what could be done about it.

Martin Carson waged a continuing battle to keep his project financed, and he'd brought together a strong team to sit on his Board of Directors. He and his family had made great personal sacrifices to keep Good Start running during its early years.

Our Board meeting for May was rapidly approaching.

I phoned Carson and explained my problems raising money.

"That sure sounds familiar, Becky," he sympathized. "I know firsthand what you're going through. The best advice I can give you is to keep the House in the news as much as possible. People will donate to keep it going and you'll attract more Board members."

This was very encouraging. I planned to mention his words at the next Board meeting, which was scheduled for Wednesday. After all, none of us had any previous experience in this sort of thing, and Martin was by now an old hand at it.

Lee had planned a barbecue for the May gathering. We thought a relaxed atmosphere and Lee's good cooking might help dissolve the money tension. The night went well and so did the meeting, except when Evie said, "I'd like to propose we postpone admitting any new clients until such time as Becky procures a greater funding base."

"Since none of us have had any practice in these matters heretofore," Lee objected, "I'd like to propose instead that we follow the advice of Martin Carson, the founder and Executive Director of the Good Start project. He suggests that an active clientele at our House will attract prospective donors. And may I remind the Board that some of you have spoken with other heads of similar projects who have also advised filling the House as soon as possible. I strongly recommend that we defer to the voices of experience."

"The fact remains," I said, "that I have clients already living at the House, and several more who are ready to enter as soon as they complete jail terms. And what about those who come to us off the street?"

"Has the funding committee come up with any resources?" Lee asked.

Heads shook and shoulders shrugged.

"Becky has held a media event and she's been calling in old promises of support," Jerry said supportively.

It was settled then.

My station wagon had seen a lot of use in its seven years. Not only had it transported hundreds of clients, but it had car pooled students and carried Lee and David to work, too. I had averaged five or more hours of heavy driving each day for most of the little car's life, and it was only my husband's and son's mechanical expertise that kept it on the road.

The car made growling, grinding sounds when it started up, and oil dripped on the engine, which made gray smoke rise from beneath the hood. The truck was damaged from the attempt on David's life, so with two such vehicles to keep running the men of the family spent a great deal of time in the parking lot of our apartment complex with their tool box and various vehicle fluids.

Our new neighborhood was an area of apartment houses, with as many as three hundred families living on a single block. Most of the buildings were attractive and well-kept, and children played safely within the walls of their complexes. Across the street, however, lodgings had been let soon after we moved in to some disreputable looking men who entertained leather-jacketed women and tattooed strangers. The rumor was they belonged to the Street Demons gang.

Late one afternoon, as Lee and David carried their toolbox to the truck to begin work, one of these men, clad in fashionably ragged jeans and no shirt, waved. He was working on a motorcycle with two other fellows on the lawn of the dubious complex. David immediately crossed the street to meet our neighbors, so Lee followed to keep him out of trouble. My husband and son conversed knowledgeably about motors, tools, and transmissions and struck up a tenuous friendship. "How's Becky doing with Project New Life?" said a man with knife wounds scarring his face who introduced himself as Bear Cub, the son of Grizzly Bear, the leader of the Speed Demons motorcycle club in our city.

Lee didn't like the remark one bit but replied, "Fine." Soon after, he and David left.

18

OPEN HOUSE / OPEN SEASON

The three women who, with me, comprised the umbrella organization of Project New Life had no experience in the day-to-day administration of the program. Thus, the House remained entirely "my baby."

Despite the dearth of assistance, I ran the House as best I could. Our clients didn't have even the most basic knowledge of cooking, so I planned lessons as a part of the program. LaDonna began by trying to teach Ginger Pettit how to make chocolate chip cookies. When the housemother took a phone call in the middle of the lesson, she left Ginger to finish adding flour to a batch of cookie dough.

"Turn off the beaters now and mix it by hand," she said as she left the room.

When she returned, Ginger was up to her elbows in batter, kneading it like bread dough.

"What are you doing?" LaDonna asked in surprise.

"I'm mixing it by hand, like you said," Ginger explained.

Incidents like this made me realize how much the project needed the people who knew and loved the prostitutes to run things, but I was involved by necessity in publicity and fund-raising. I was so harried now that I didn't even have time to properly train our volunteers.

Lee and I decided that Melissa wouldn't be among the residents of Project New Life House because she was doing so well that we hated to move her as long as Maxine was happy to have her. The one dark spot on her horizon was Dave Colchis, who might buy drugs for her. Dave, however, was Missy's idea of perfection: educated, intellectual, charming, and attentive. She adored him, and she assured me that she wouldn't touch narcotics if only she could continue to see him.

When Colchis was invited to speak at a public forum on prostitution in June, Melissa invited me to attend. I found myself in a ludicrous situation where I hoped no one recognized me. Missy and I sat in the audience, she in raptured awe of her handsome psychologist and I in disgust. Both of us were well aware that he was a street trick. I was galled at the positive impact he made on the reporters in the crowd.

"Prostitutes are entrepreneurs," Dave stated. "They are businesswomen, and their business should be decriminalized, or at the very least, legalized. There are many men who are ugly or disabled who cannot express their normal human sexuality in any other way than with a prostitute. Why should we as a society arrest women who are performing a valuable service?"

As he carefully made his points, the media people wrote furiously, and I shook my head in dismay. Because I was a guest, I couldn't even present an opposing argument. As so often happened, the meeting ended with opinions differing widely between people who live in prostitution areas, people who frequented prostitutes, and people who theorized about prostitution.

"I have to expose this racket, honey," I told Lee later. "I have to make people understand what prostitution is really about."

However, such plans had to wait. I was immersed in the duties of organizing the House for my streetwalkers. My work day now spanned eighteen hours.

Martin Carson had been right that people would want to help when we got the House open. Our phones never stopped ringing. Wonderful volunteers donated clothing, befriended the residents, taught health and craft classes, held drug and alcohol recovery meetings, and helped with transportation. Our only problem was ongoing funding. I checked the mailbox daily, and donations were coming in, but they were small, less than one hundred dollars a week. Definitely this was not enough to run the project.

I'd managed to bring in $18,000 in pledges, but none of this money would be forthcoming for more than six months. We hoped that the publicity generated by an open house would bring in immediate donations, because the cost per resident was almost a thousand dollars a month.

Inviting as many people as we could to the open house, we concentrated on our presentation. My husband made hors d'oeuvres, and we all pitched in to clean the House "like a hospital," as one of the residents complained. We had the beginning of the fund we desperately needed.

A few days later, I realized that my period was late. Lee rushed out to the drugstore immediately and bought an at-home pregnancy test. We rose early the next morning, I to supply the main ingredient and Lee to play chemist. Finally it was time to dip the little spatula in the vial where, in five minutes, a blue color change would indicate a blessed event in the offing, or no color change would mean disappointment once again. I went downstairs to await the final results, while my spouse eyed the test tube like a small boy watching the clock for recess. Before two minutes had passed, he let out a whoop and I ran up the stairs. He was holding the tiny bright blue wand as he danced around the room.

"We're going to have a baby!" he shouted.

The knowledge that I was pregnant made me more determined than ever to get the project on firm financial ground as soon as possible.

While I called in old promises of support, Lee and David worked on my station wagon. One cool and cloudy afternoon, our gang member neighbor Bear Cub waved to them to come visit. My husband and son weren't about to antagonize him, so they walked across the street.

"C'mon in and have a beer," Beer Cub offered.

Inside, Bear Cub switched on the television, and they watched the evening news while the men drank a beer and David had a Coke.

"The body of Deborah Basich was found on Lower River Road this morning. She was believed to have been a prostitute," the newscaster announced.

"They're gonna find another hooker dead on Mt. Pleasant this week, too," Bear Cub muttered.

"How do you know?" Lee asked, surprised.

"'Cause Debbie Basich was one of my hoes. The Iron Eagles took her out. They're the ones who leave bodies on Lower River Road. Now I owe them one," he stated matter-of-factly.

As quickly as they could, Lee and David excused themselves and returned home, pale and shaken.

"What are we going to do?" my husband groaned as he finished his tale.

I sat debating. The murders of streetwalkers had continued unabated for four years. Thirty-three women were dead by now. The bodies of one or two women had been found in various areas of the county almost every month, some near Lower River Road, others on Mt. Pleasant, some near the freeways, some in motels. The pieces of the puzzle fell into place for me. I was sure the murders were a continuation of the bloody battle between the Iron Eagles and the Speed Demons. So many people were gunned down in cold blood during the early days of the feud that the FBI had launched an investigation. The murders had come to an abrupt halt. It was shortly after this seeming calm had fallen that the murders of the streetwalkers began. The biker brotherhoods had discovered a way to hurt each other financially with little chance of a backlash from the establishment: no one cared if hookers died.

What indeed were we going to do? We had landed in the middle of a tangled web. If we went to the police, the bikers would know who had turned them in. If we didn't report the matter to the authorities, we became parties to murder. We made an appointment to talk with Louis Silverman and Lindsey Baxter when Lindsey returned from an out-of-town assignment on July 27.

Missy's children had all been adopted while she was in prison, and she grieved for them, but she was doing her best to adjust to life. Dave Colchis, in his Harold the Helper guise, needed Melissa to be dependent upon him. Her newfound strength, however tenuous it might be, was a threat to their relationship. Her return to drug addiction, therefore, would be to the psychologist's advantage.

It was her twenty-ninth birthday, the evening of July 18, when Dave phoned.

"Missy's dead," he sobbed.

Dead? Our Melissa? I couldn't believe what I was hearing. It was the worst blow yet about one of our clients.

Heartsick, I managed to ask, "What happened, Dave?"

"She shot herself after taking heroin," the psychologist sobbed.

"Where did she get the drugs?" I demanded, furious.

"Her brother put out word that no one was to sell to her."

"Well, I bought her some because it was her birthday," he admitted, his voice shaking.

"And where did she get the gun?" I said wearily.

"I gave it to her for protection."

"After you bought her the heroin?" I asked.

"Why yes. How did you know?"

"Good thinking for a shrink, Dave. Really good."

With a wife at home and all the whores on the Boulevard at his disposal, Colchis had to have our little lamb. Of course, Missy was responsible, too, but that didn't lessen my pain.

"You'll call Cajun Devil, won't you? I'm too upset to tell him," I lied. The truth was I wanted Dave to take responsibility for Missy's death even if the law couldn't get him. As for handling Cajun's wrath, if a contract should go out on Dave Colchis I wanted no knowledge of it.

I had passing thoughts of speaking with the police about Missy, but I knew that, to them, she was just another hooker, and except for Lou Silverman, the police didn't seem particularly concerned with the deaths of whores.

We heard on the Sunday evening news that the body of another prostitute was found on Mt. Pleasant, as Bear Cub had predicted. My family and I stared at one another thinking of the gang member's words. Darroll broke the silence.

"Mom, do you think . . ." he began.

"I don't know," I interrupted. "We'll talk to Lindsey and Lou."

Heidi Freeman lived only two miles from our apartment, and I made it a point to visit her a couple of times a week. Darroll often accompanied me, because he wanted to encourage little Tyler, who was having a difficult adjustment to school and to life without his brother Phil. I was proud of Darroll because he loved to help people, not only my prostitutes and their children, but also the elderly residents of a nursing home in our neighborhood. My son rode his bike a mile and a half to do volunteer work with the elderly patients twice a week.

On July 23, we awoke to find Darroll's bike missing from our enclosed patio. "Probably stolen by one of the drug addicts who live on the streets of our town," I said to Heidi that afternoon.

Tyler, who had been listening, said, "He can have mine! I got a new bike!"

The little boy's cherubic face lit up with that glow that children have when they do a good deed. I was delighted at his thoughtfulness but, of course, I refused.

"That's nice of you, honey," I told him, "but your old bike isn't working. That's why Grandma Evelyn bought you a new one. Darroll needs a bike that works."

When Darroll and I visited Heidi again two days later, Tyler excitedly took my son's hand and led him to the back porch. There was a battered red bicycle. It was old and too small, but it was in perfect riding condition. The seven-year-old boy had repaired his old bike to give to his friend Darroll. I felt tears well up in my eyes.

Ethan Freeman, I thought exultantly, you lose!

When I got to the House early the next morning, Jill Cline's sponsor was on the phone, and I didn't like what she had to say.

"Becky, I'm very concerned," the volunteer fretted. "Yesterday I dropped Jill off at the welfare office so she could pick up her check. I knew it would take several hours, because she had to wait in line with the paperwork they'd requested before they'd release her money, so I promised to meet her back there at four o'clock and take her to my house for dinner.

"When I returned a little early, I saw her getting out of a silver Rolls Royce. It even had a chauffeur. I asked her what she was doing, and she said, 'I was just talking to a friend.'"

"Thank you," I told her. "You were right to call. I'll talk to Jill."

When the other residents left for work, I confronted Ms. Cline.

"Jill, the rules here are: no drugs, no johns, no pimps. You were with a pimp yesterday," I stated flatly.

"I owed him five hundred dollars, so when I got my welfare check, I had to give him some of it," she said, embarrassed.

"You're talking about Thanh Duc Nguyen, aren't you?"

"How'd you know?" she asked, surprised.

"I recognized his car," I told her without further explanation. "How long have you worked for him, Jill?"

"Just a couple of weeks," she said innocently.

This was an old game with Nguyen. As chieftain of the Asian gangs in our area, he had to save face; he couldn't afford to give up the women he personally recruited as prostitutes. I knew he had plans for Jill, and if I interfered, he'd come after me.

"Now suppose you tell me the truth about how you got that cut on your arm," I demanded.

"I, uh, I told you, a john cut me," she hedged.

"No, it wasn't a john. Johns go for the belly or the throat. They want to kill, or sometimes they maim sex organs, but they don't cut whores' arms. Pimps hurt their women where it won't make any difference to the customers," I insisted.

She gulped audibly and admitted, "I told Nguyen that I didn't want to work the street after I paid him back. I promised to give him a hundred dollars a month out of my welfare check, but he said he wanted his money when it was due, and that I had agreed to pay him a hundred dollars a week. He let his bodyguards take me away and they cut my arm."

"How much does he want you to pay every week, now?" I asked.

Jill stared at me like I had a crystal ball in my hand.

"Two hundred dollars."

"Jill, you can never pay him back. Even if you managed to come up with every penny you owe him today, he'd kidnap your baby and force you to work for him. Now he knows where you are, and you've put every one of us in danger," I persisted.

Tears came to her eyes as she said, "I didn't tell him where I was living, Becky."

"You didn't have to." I knew he would have had her followed. I had to get her out of here, but even that wouldn't guarantee safety for the rest of us.

Thanh Duc Nguyen ran most of the Oriental massage parlors in the state and a lot of the escort services. His favorite recruiting device was to lend money to young women who were desperate, as Jill was. She had lost her job, and welfare made her wait until she could order her birth certificate from Philadelphia and get the baby's certificate from Chicago, so she was broke. Someone had told her Nguyen would lend her money, but not that it was his scam. He made the girls pay him back by selling their bodies on the street, then if they were attractive, he would train them and put them to work in his private brothels or massage parlors. No one escaped. I'd always avoided a confrontation with him because I knew I'd lose.

"You have two choices, Jill," I told her. "You can either go back to work for Nguyen or you can leave town, change your name, and never contact your friends again," I told her.

Jill chose the underground railroad. That night, Ginger Pettit and I drove her, dressed in her street garb, to the bus station. I held the baby and guarded her bags while Jill went to the counter to buy her ticket. As she stood in line, a pimp approached her, offering one of the usual lines about her great beauty and how he'd like to make her a star.

I grabbed the pimp by the arm.

"You find someone else," I warned. "She's with us."

The man backed off, a conciliatory smile on his face.

"Okay, okay," he said. "I thought she was alone."

The next day I went to the post office to pick up the mail and buy stamps. At the counter, the clerk, whom I had known for several years, told me that a man had been in yesterday.

"He said he wanted the Project New Life mail transferred to a box which he would rent here, Becky," my friend said incredulously. "This guy was all covered with tattoos and he spoke like he'd been in prison!"

"What did you do?" I asked, astonished.

"The postmistress came out and told him we couldn't do it," she replied. "Can you believe that?"

"The way things have been going lately," I muttered, I'd probably believe you if you told me Martians had landed."

We were glad when the twenty-seventh came and Lindsey Baxter returned to town. We joined him and police detective Silverman at his office.

Lindsey and Lou listened patiently as we recounted the events which had happened. When we finished, Lindsey looked at the floor a few minutes, then put his fingertips together and leaned back in his chair.

"There have been attempts on your lives, fires, a snake on your doorstep. We didn't know who was doing it until David was poisoned. Finally, we had suspects: the Speed Demons gang. You've helped some of their whores get out of the business, and they're obviously upset about it. At the moment they're only playing with you, like a cat with its future meal. I don't believe for one moment that members of the gang just 'happened' to move in across the street from your new apartment. They're getting serious now."

"Look how they've gone out of their way to appear friendly and yet tell you they know what you do," Lou broke in. "Then in front of Lee and David they casually discuss plans to commit a crime. That's a common recruiting device that gangs use. It's a twist on the adage, 'If you can't beat 'em, join 'em.' Even though they failed to scare you away from your work when you lived on the mountain, now that you have knowledge of a murder, you're in their power. Don't kid yourself. They are dangerous."

Lindsey leaned toward us and spoke quietly. "Lou's right. I think you'd be wise to relocate your family and get entirely out of this area while the going's good," our friend advised.

"I agree," said Lou. "We're in the midst of investigating one of the prostitute murders for which we have a strong lead. One that could put you in more danger. You better leave town; we'll keep you informed."

He paused and then went on hesitantly.

"Becky, there's something more close to home that I need to tell you," he said slowly.

"Go on," I said.

"We're after one of the guys who hangs around with your neighbor across the street."

"For?" I asked softly, almost not wanting to hear.

"You know what I'm going to say: the murder of the prostitute we found just out of town on Mt. Pleasant."

"I thought you weren't going to tell her," Lindsey protested.

"I had to," Lou said wearily. "I felt I had to."

Lee looked at me as I fought back tears.

"Becky, we don't have to listen to them. We'll stay and face this together. It's not fair after all the work you've done for them to ask us to run for our lives."

Now my tears flowed freely. I said, "No, honey, I love you for offering but Lindsey and Lou are right. We can't fight this alone any longer. We need to get out for the time being, regroup, and gather more support. I've been pondering all this for quite a while but haven't felt ready to talk about it. I think we need to mount our fight in a larger arena—the political one."

During the next few days we made hasty preparations for leaving town. The last afternoon we checked our mailbox one final time. We were surprised and happy to find a wedding invitation. Jerry Hudson was getting married to Audrey in three weeks. We wished we could stay for the ceremony, but both Lindsey and Lou kept repeating that we should leave immediately.

On a Saturday morning an hour before dawn, we and the children left our Southern California home and set out on our journey to safety. As we drove through the darkened streets toward the freeway, I turned to Lee. "Could you pass Wickersham Boulevard so I can take one more look at my prostitutes," I asked.

He nodded and made the next right turn. Streetwalkers dotted the sidewalk offering themselves to early risers and to those who wended their way home at this hour. I could only mouth a silent prayer that those in my organization remaining behind would help them while I was gone.

The first night on the road, I lay down on a strange motel bed and opened my old Bible. There inside the cover in Ginger's handwriting was an inscription:

To Ginger Pettit

    With Love from Becky Usry

Project New Life

If I had read it earlier, I would have inscribed the Bible I did give her. But I think she knew how I felt even if I didn't write it. My fighting spirit resurged. "We're going to win, Ginger," I promised. "No matter how hard it is or how long it takes."

THE FACTS

The following facts deal with the dynamics of prostitution. The statistics have been carefully collected, assembled, and collated.

In America, one person in a thousand is a prostitute. In other countries, such as Thailand, these numbers can be much higher—or lower. Of these, half are under the age of eighteen. The profession is rather evenly divided between males and females, that is, there is one male prostitute for every female prostitute. Transsexuals (partial or complete) may comprise as many as 5 percent of the prostitute population.

The average starting age for girls is thirteen; the average for boys is eleven. Ninety percent of runaway juveniles will be forced to turn to prostitution to survive within six weeks of living on the street. Sixty percent of all prostitutes are streetwalkers. This figure encompasses males and females, juveniles and adults; thus, only 15 percent of all prostitutes are adult female streetwalkers, which is the group most often targeted for prosecution.

Streetwalkers, truck stop prostitutes, massage parlor prostitutes, escort service and outcall massage prostitutes, bath house prostitutes, bar and hotel prostitutes, nude dance hall prostitutes, private strippers, brothel prostitutes, call girls, and gigolos comprise the vast majority of this population. There are other kinds of prostitutes, including dominatrices and sadomasochistic prostitutes, party games prostitutes (such as those who sell underwear, sex lotions and notions, and sexually promiscuous clothing), traveling prostitution rings which service men who work in rural groups, such as fruit pickers and loggers, and prostitutes who work in public bathrooms. Transsexual prostitutes (both those who have completed surgery and those who haven't) tend most often to choose streetwalking, stripping, or nude dancing (especially after surgery). I've never seen nor heard of female-to-male transsexual prostitution, but there's a first time for everything.

There is a significant difference in education level, income, and attitude among these groups. The average level of education for streetwalkers is sixth grade; for nude dancers/prostitutes, the mean completed grade is the ninth; for lower income bar and hotel workers, it's the tenth; many masseuses have completed high school; escort service prostitutes and private party strippers tend to have some college; and call girls and gigolos often are college graduates.

Adult female streetwalkers (including not-so-obvious transvestites and transsexuals) earn from twenty to forty dollars a trick. Young people earn a little more than their older colleagues. People who work the street can expect their eight to ten tricks per day or night to bring in one hundred fifty to four hundred dollars per work period, depending on their age, the areas where they solicit, and their specialties. Street prostitutes work seven days a week, 365 days a year. Masseuses earn from two hundred fifty to three hundred dollars in prostitution money, plus the hourly wages from the five to six massages they give each of the four or five days a week that they work. Escort service prostitutes earn one hundred to two hundred dollars an hour, and may have one or two customers two to four hours an evening, three to seven evenings per week. Call girls and gigolos also usually have one customer nightly four or five evenings a week, and earn five hundred to a thousand dollars and up each time, depending on the wealth of their clients and their reputation as prostitutes. Transsexual upper income prostitution is extremely rare, because it requires a tremendous amount of self assurance often lacking in people who feel they were born in the "wrong body."

People in the life are mostly victim, criminal, desperate choice, or adult choice prostitutes. Victim prostitutes enter the life because of need caused by the failure of their families or society to provide for them. Many were sexually abused (especially by stepfathers) as children, and ran away from home to escape incest. Some young parents turn to prostitution to provide for their families. Most eventually use drugs to help them cope with their lifestyle. Criminal prostitutes are those who use prostitution only to get drugs. They use any means at their disposal to obtain their dope, including a wide range of criminal activities, hence the nomenclature. To them, prostitution is only incidental. Desperate choice prostitutes are people in desperate need of money that they can't obtain elsewhere. Some have families to support. Some have relatives with serious illnesses. Adult choice prostitutes are people who have made a decision to enter the life, usually based upon financial (but not desperate) reasons, though sometimes for other reasons.

The attitudes of prostitutes toward their jobs and toward society vary from group to group, and also among males and females, juvenile and adults. Adult female prostitutes tend to be concerned about the role of women in society. Streetwalkers often believe that they are preventing rape and incest, yet statistics do not bear out this hypothesis. All forms of street crime diminish when streetwalkers leave an area: armed robbery, rape, strong-arm robbery, burglary, drug dealing, grand theft auto, and even murders drop dramatically, according to information from police departments in San Diego, Portland, and Seattle. Male street prostitutes, especially juveniles, often do not consider themselves to be homosexual, but think of their work as doing what they have to, to survive.

Women who work in groups, such as brothels and massage parlors, worry that by leaving prostitution, they are deserting the cause of women's liberation. Males seldom work in groups, except in the case of juvenile street prostitutes or brothel workers, who cater to orgies. These males usually detest their work and their johns, but even those who leave the life will return, albeit temporarily, in a financial pinch. Transsexuals in both lower and middle income groups have a fascination with the female sexual role and tend to relate to men in a sexual way more than either heterosexuals or homosexuals.

Call girls and other top money earners feel that they are helping the women's movement by out-earning men. Males who work in upper income prostitution tend to have female johns (maybe we should call them "joans?") more often than their brothers and sisters in the other income groups. The number of women as johns is in an inverse ratio to the size of the prostitution income group: that is, there are far more lower income prostitutes and, consequently, johns than there are middle and upper income prostitutes and johns, yet the number of female johns is greatest at the upper income levels. Male upper income prostitutes are less likely to have spouses and children than are females in the same income bracket, so their earnings are more likely to be saved for, and ultimately spent on, expensive nonessentials like cruises, luxury cars, and trips. They don't experience the social stigma of prostitution that females do, but find their friends and acquaintances eager to participate (especially in male-female prostitution) and envious that they not only get to have sex with multiple partners, but get paid for it, too.

Female juvenile prostitutes feel that they have control over their own sexuality. Many were forced to participate in sex with male family members when they lived at home, but as street-walkers, they can decide what they will do, with whom they will do it, when they will have sex, *and* they get paid for it. Girls often resist any attempt to "reform" them, because it would mean a return to submission to an authority figure. Both boys and girls require specially trained foster parents if they are to leave the life. Girls believe they are "in love" with their pimps, and juvenile prostitutes of both sexes may act in sexually seductive ways with adults.

Two of every three female prostitutes are also mothers. Three out of four of them do not have custody of their children. Approximately 25 to 30 percent have had abortions.

Despite popular myth, most female prostitutes are heterosexual. Only about the same number as in the general population are homosexual or bisexual when they are not working. Nearly all female prostitutes, especially in the lower and middle income groups, have male johns only.

Some male juvenile prostitutes are homosexual youths who use the life to express their sexuality, but many are runaway or throwaway kids who use prostitution to survive the street. Performing homosexual acts during the formative years often leaves these youngsters confused about their sexual identities, and many who profess that they are heterosexual during their youth adopt a gay identity as adults. This may or may not be due to the *acceptance* (I do not say or mean *encouragement*) of the homosexual community of gay prostitution versus the utter abhorrence of it by heterosexuals.

Adult male prostitutes do not display the camaraderie of their female counterparts, but relate more to non-prostitute homosexual males. Notably, there is no dedication to a "movement" so common among female prostitutes.

Pimps are a varied group. The most obvious, but actually smallest group, are the ostentatious street pimps who personally run stables of girls, and usually travel from city to city in search of new "hunting grounds." Organized crime figures account for the majority of pimps, but this does not necessarily mean Mafia. Other criminal brotherhoods include bike, street, ethnic, territorial gangs, and even "bad cops." Many pimps own various types of stables, such as escort services and strings of massage parlors. Although the dictionary definition of a pimp includes only those who actually pander, or get customers for prostitutes, I have applied this dubious distinction to anyone, except children, who profits from a prostitute's earnings. I prefer to think of men who profit from a prostitute's earnings, but who don't pander, as "Franks."

Johns range from factory workers to ambassadors. There are approximately ten to fifteen johns for every prostitute. It must be remembered that only one of every four prostitutes is a woman: the other three are a boy, a girl, and a man. In the United States the population is approximately 265,000,000. That means there are about 265,000 prostitutes, and at least 2,650,000 to perhaps 3,975,000 johns. Remember, half the prostitute population is under the age of eighteen.

"Joans" are becoming increasingly common, though they still are greatly in the minority. Some are the sexual partners of male johns, and are either willing or coerced parties to ménage à trois prostitution contacts. More often, they are women who pay male strippers, either at clubs or at private parties, to have sex. There are a few stereotypical older women who keep "toy boys" or gigolos.

Because I am not a medical expert, I will mention AIDS and STD's only briefly. There are prostitutes who are not only HIV positive, but ill with AIDS, having the characteristic darkened skin, low body weight, and sunken cheeks associated with the disease, who still work the street. I know some of these people. Who would hire someone who looks so bad, who is so obviously ill? There are men who believe they should be punished for having sex and actually seek them out.

Before 1960, *The Great Lie* was that rape was a sexual act. We now know it to be an act of violence, and society demands jail or prison sentences for rapists. The great lie which is still believed as we approach the end of the century is that prostitution is about sex: it is not. For the prostitute, money is the motivator and the ultimate equalizer: for the john, sex with a prostitute means power over another person—that is, he assuages his feelings of inadequacy by assuming control of his companion. Prostitution could be considered a less violent form of rape.

Prostitution, which damages the prostitute emotionally and physically in the vast majority of cases, is not a private matter between consenting adults. It is a matter of power wherein those that are strong use those who are weak. It is also a matter of money and of profit, often great, much of it raked off by organized crime. Half of all sex acts for hire include a juvenile, and pimps engage in the sale and trade of these human beings, most of whom are juveniles, thereby destroying their futures.

Police, in response to complaints from the public, arrest streetwalkers daily. The cost of incarceration varies greatly, but jails average about sixty dollars per day and prisons range from ninety to one hundred fifty dollars per day. The cost of rehabilitation for streetwalkers is only about eight hundred to a thousand dollars per month for six to twelve months, yet we continue to arrest prostitutes who are least affected by incarceration, and ignore the others.

During the past twenty-five years, shelters for battered women have become prevalent in every major city. I hope and pray that during the next twenty-five years shelters and self-help programs for prostitutes will abound, that we will handle all prostitution as the serious crime that it is, and that prostitutes will be treated with compassion since so many are victims, including children growing up too fast on violent streets.

PROPOSAL TO CONGRESS TO ADDRESS THE PROBLEM
OF PROSTITUTION NATIONWIDE

The problem of prostitution is not the absolute domain of communities for several reasons.

First, its proceeds finance organized crime, that is bike, ethnic, and street gangs, among others, as well as the Mafia. This money buys drugs, influence, and "protection" (from prosecution).

Second, espionage, both international and industrial, is common among upper-income (escort service workers and call girls) prostitutes. The threat to national security as well as business is very real.

Third, pimps often engage in the interstate transportation and *sale* of prostitutes, half of whom are under the age of eighteen.

The Federal government, on the other hand, cannot assume complete responsibility for the eradication of prostitution because acts of prostitution violate state and local laws, and must therefore be addressed by state and local law enforcement agencies. The role of Federal government, then, must be to enable local authorities to deal with the crime of prostitution effectively; encourage new programs to offer alternatives to people who want to leave that profession; and to educate the public.

INCARCERATION, REHABILITATION, EDUCATION

Law enforcement must change its revolving-door policy of incarcerating street prostitutes as its only means of dealing with prostitution. For years, this policy has placated communities, but has done little to stop prostitution. Because of the (heretofore unrecognized) seriousness of the crime, anyone involved in prostitution, including the prostitute, his or her customer, and the pimp, should *count on* jail time if they are apprehended.

Even as mid- and upper-level drug dealers are prime targets for arrest, so pimps should be. These people recruit young teenagers not only at bus stations where runaways congregate, but even at junior high schools. The most "successful" pimps sell their aging (eighteen years and over) hookers to other pimps. Human flesh is bought and sold with no fear of punishment every day on the streets of America. There are currently no Federal laws against pandering, even if the prostitute is under the age of eighteen. I suggest that anyone convicted of pandering (whether s/he actually offers the services of prostitute to a prospective john or simply profits from a prostitute's income, with the exception of family members who were unaware of the prostitution or unable to stop it) serve a minimum sentence of ten to fifteen years, and anyone convicted of pandering for a juvenile serve fifteen to twenty years.

Johns, or the customers of prostitutes, must be held accountable for their contribution to American crime. For every street prostitute, there are *at least* ten johns. The 159,000 street prostitutes have eight to ten sexual encounters daily, and the estimated number of encounters per john is one per week—a staggering number of men (95-98% of prostitutes' customers are male). Prostitution is *not* "a private matter between two consenting adults," because one of every two acts of sex-for-hire involves a juvenile prostitute. Neither is the male sexual urge so strong a biological drive that it must be satisfied, if not in marriage or other long-term relationship, then by a prostitute, *because prostitution is, like rape, not about sex, but about power.*

Prostitutes, too, must face incarceration. Streetwalkers are most often targeted for arrest, because they are the most obvious, and therefore, the group the public finds most objectionable. For streetwalkers, occasional jail time is a way of life, and it is ineffective. Incarceration would impact upper-income prostitutes greatly, however, because they move freely within their communities with a facade of respectability.

Legalization or decriminalization of prostitution *would not* merely free men and women to follow their chosen avocation: legal prostitution attracts illegal prostitution. The streets and casinos of Las Vegas and Reno are replete with unlicensed and unregistered prostitutes. Prostitution itself is a shill for other crimes: rape, robbery, auto theft, larceny, and even murder.

The interest, then, of the Federal government in eradicating prostitution should be such that a national program must be instituted to encourage and implement incarceration, rehabilitation, and public education projects nationwide. Local implementation of such a major policy shift requires the planning and management of federal government. This unique union would be most cost effective if performed in the following manner.

Five or more populous cities with large prostitute populations (perhaps Atlanta, Boston, Chicago, Philadelphia, and Seattle) would be selected to receive the first offers of Federal assistance to establish multi-phase anti-prostitution, prostitute-rehabilitation, and public education projects.

Two persons would begin the initial effort. First, a federal law-enforcement specialist would contact local police agencies and co-ordinate efforts to plan area-wide arrests of prostitution participants not usually impacted by "crackdowns." A time frame of several months would be required to gather and share intelligence, pinpoint prime targets, arrange initial raids, and engineer a bulwark against future prostitution encroachment.

(The preliminary effort should concentrate on those prostitution rings which can be linked with a high degree of certainty to organized crime, and whose cessation of operations would most damage criminal organizations.)

At the same time, a six-member team would effectively establish a three-phase community-sponsored rehabilitation program within six to twelve months. The first rehabilitation team member would be the second person in the initial contact team and at the same time that the federal law-enforcement specialist is engaged in preliminary planning, would speak with public officials and civic groups to propose and outline a plan which would provide (group) housing, job training, and psycho-social therapy for people who have been engaged in prostitution.

In the next phase, groups in the target cities which want to institute a rehabilitation program will communicate with a second rehabilitation-team member who will offer directions on early organization. The reason for such detailed assistance is that small-group members such as the one I started bring whatever talents they possess into their organization, which, unfortunately, often leaves the group at a disadvantage in many areas, such as business management, agenda-planning, and/or fund-raising. Many groups simply cannot meet the demands of intricate organization without outside help.

When the group's efforts reach a predetermined point of readiness, phase three will be instituted. In the third phase, three additional rehabilitation-team members will visit the infant organization in each city to teach members how to establish a solid foundation of support. A business/financial manager will help the project set up ongoing financial support in the form of gifts and grants. A medical-psychosocial adjunct will develop professional contacts within the community, and educate professionals about working with prostitutes in the psychosocial, educational, and medical fields. A fifth team member will train volunteers and staff. A start-up Federal grant of $5,000 to $10,000 at this point would be appropriate.

The needs of juveniles who work as prostitutes cannot be addressed in this type of program. Specialized foster homes must be trained to accommodate their unique needs. More on this issue upon your request.

The third part of the proposed Federal anti-prostitution program must be the education of the nation about why people work as prostitutes, their ages, and where their income goes. The news media has a fascination with prostitution, and, if asked to do so, would surely co-operate in efforts to enlighten the public.

During the second year, more target cities would be added, and a compilation of significant data begun.

The cost to the Federal government would be less than $500,000 per year, even with the added project in the second year, because the price includes the salaries of only seven persons, plus their expenses (the seventh team member is a statistician, added in the second year).

The success of America's anti-crime effort would be greatly enhanced by the establishment of this proposed project, with professional direction (both by federal law enforcement specialists and the rehabilitation-member team with its three-phase program). Important, too, is media involvement in the public education aspect of this proposed project, because as long as prostitution is mysterious and a taboo subject, it will have the public's unwitting stamp of approval.

If established as suggested, this proposal would serve to decrease crime through a Federally-encouraged grassroots effort; law enforcement money could be used more effectively because jail would no longer be a revolving-door for streetwalkers; organized crime would suffer a permanent financial reversal; and the most damaged of those inculcated, the children would be safer because they would cease to be targets for unscrupulous opportunists who seek to enslave them.

It is necessary and crucial for the Federal government to address the problem of prostitution in America. Our anti-crime agenda must include a comprehensive treatment plan for prostitution if it is to be effective.